Champion Jump Horse
Racing Jockeys

To Peter Williams,

Happy racing
-
very best wishes,

Neil Clark

Newbury 10ᵗ February 2024

To my Dear Parents, Joan and Roy, and all those
(people and horses) who make racing the great sport
that it is.

Also by Neil Clark

Flying Ace: The Story of a Racing Legend (Fresh Ayr Books, 1992)

Great Racing Gambles & Frauds (co-author, Marlborough, 1992)

*Stranger than Fiction: The Life of Edgar Wallace, the man
who created King Kong* (The History Press, 2014)

The author and the publishers are grateful to Chepstow Racecourse for
their support sponsoring the book.

Champion Jump Horse Racing Jockeys
From 1945 to Present Day

Neil Clark

WHITE OWL
AN IMPRINT OF PEN & SWORD BOOKS LTD.
YORKSHIRE - PHILADELPHIA

First published in Great Britain in 2021 and republished in this format in 2022 by
Pen & Sword White Owl
An imprint of
Pen & Sword Books Ltd
Yorkshire - Philadelphia

ISBN 978 1 39901 672 8

Typeset in INDIA by IMPEC eSolutions
Printed in the UK by CPI Group (UK) Ltd, Croydon, CR0 4YY

Pen & Sword Books Ltd. incorporates the Imprints of Pen & Sword Archaeology,
Atlas, Aviation, Battleground, Discovery, Family History, History, Maritime,
Military, Naval, Politics, Railways, Select, Transport, True Crime, Fiction,
Frontline Books, Leo Cooper, Praetorian Press, Seaforth Publishing,
Wharncliffe and White Owl.

For a complete list of Pen & Sword titles please contact

PEN & SWORD BOOKS LIMITED
47 Church Street, Barnsley, South Yorkshire, S70 2AS, England
E-mail: enquiries@pen-and-sword.co.uk
Website: www.pen-and-sword.co.uk

or

PEN AND SWORD BOOKS
1950 Lawrence Rd, Havertown, PA 19083, USA
E-mail: uspen-and-sword@casematepublishers.com
Website: www.penandswordbooks.com

Contents

Acknowledgements   vii

Foreword   ix

Introduction   1

Chapter One   Fred Rimell   3

Chapter Two   Jack Dowdeswell   12

Chapter Three   Bryan Marshall   21

Chapter Four   Tim Molony   30

Chapter Five   Fred Winter   39

Chapter Six   Dick Francis   48

Chapter Seven   Tim Brookshaw   57

Chapter Eight   Stan Mellor   67

Chapter Nine   Josh Gifford   77

Chapter Ten   Terry Biddlecombe   88

Chapter Eleven   Bob Davies   103

Chapter Twelve   Graham Thorner   111

Chapter Thirteen   Ron Barry   122

Chapter Fourteen   Tommy Stack   133

Chapter Fifteen   John Francome   140

Chapter Sixteen   Jonjo O'Neill   151

Chapter Seventeen   Peter Scudamore   160

Chapter Eighteen   Richard Dunwoody   176

Chapter Nineteen   AP McCoy   191

Chapter Twenty   Richard Johnson   203

Chapter Twenty-One   Brian Hughes   214

Chapter Twenty-Two   Harry Skelton   220

Appendix: Champion Jump Jockeys 1945 to Present Day   225

Bibliography and Further Reading   228

Index   231

Acknowledgements

Thank you to Natasha Weale, for acting as my de facto agent for this book.

Thank you to Sir Rupert Mackeson, not just for all the advice and assistance he has given me with this book, but for all his help down the years.

The following champion jump jockeys very kindly spared me time to answer some questions and discuss their careers: Bob Davies, Graham Thorner, Ron Barry, John Francome MBE, Peter Scudamore MBE, Richard Dunwoody MBE, Sir Anthony McCoy OBE, Richard Johnson OBE and Brian Hughes. The trainers or former trainers David Gandolfo, Philip Hobbs, Martin Pipe CBE, Matt Sheppard and John Spearing also kindly shared their thoughts on the champions who rode for them and others that they knew. Family members of the champion jockeys have also been very helpful. Evelyn Bracey, the niece of Jack Dowdeswell, whom I met by chance in the village churchyard in Fawley, on the Lambourn Downs, pointed me in the right direction for information about her uncle. Mick Dowdeswell and Liz Beard not only shared recollections of their father Jack but also went to the trouble of scanning photographs, race statistics and other articles about him to send to me. Elain Mellor, who despite having to care for husband Stan who was gravely ill, and also battling illness herself, still found time to see me and went out of her way to be of assistance.

Thank you too to Will and Danny Molony for some great photographs and their recollections of their father Tim. Thanks to Ruth Gifford and the Gifford family for photographs of Josh. Thank you to Kate Ive for the loan of a fascinating scrapbook on Forbra's Grand National win and a collection of press cuttings on Fred Rimell. Thanks to Scarlett Knipe, daughter of Fred Rimell, for talking to me about her father, to Mrs Sarah Oliver, chief executive of the Amateur Jockeys Association, and to Graham Dench.

Thanks to Jane Owen, daughter of trainer George, who 'trained' three great champions, and to Clive Bettison, a mine of information on Jack Dowdeswell.

I am very grateful to Tim Cox for allowing me to visit and research my book in his wonderful racing library in Surrey. Thanks to Jim Beavis for his book on the history of Fontwell Racecourse and other assistance.

For photographs, I'd like to thank Chris Pitt for ones of Tim Brookshaw, and to Bernard Parkin for permission to use some of his excellent work, and also to Desmond King for use of photographs of his late friend David Hastings. Thank you too to Graham Thorner for the loan of photographs of his riding career, including ones of jumping the fearsome Becher's Brook on Well To Do in the 1972 Grand National, to Fiona Marner for permission to use her photograph of Graham Thorner and 'The Captain', and to Henrietta Knight for the photograph of her late husband, Terry Biddlecombe.

Thanks to Steve Davies for his photograph of AP McCoy winning the Grand National on Don't Push It, which adorns the cover.

A very special thank you to Felix Francis, son of Dick, the 1953/54 champion, for very kindly agreeing to write the foreword.

Thanks to everyone at White Owl/Pen & Sword concerned with the production of this book, and in particular, editorial assistant Aileen Pringle, Heather Williams, and Linne Matthews for her great editing.

Finally, thank you to my parents, Joan and Roy, for their support and help with the proofreading, and to my wife Zsuzsanna.

Foreword

By Felix Francis

Are jump jockeys a breed apart?

All horse riders confront danger on a daily basis with the animal beneath them many times more massive than they are, and with a mind of its own to boot. Saddles with effective seat belts have yet to be invented and it is a long way down, as all of us who have ever ridden have found to our cost with bruises at best, and quite possibly far worse.

But for jump jockeys the peril is so great they can almost taste it, or at least they could if they were normal, rational human beings – but they are not.

The opening titles to the classic BBC television comedy *Porridge* does not feature theme music but is a voice-over by a judge (also played by Ronnie Barker) sentencing Norman Stanley Fletcher: 'You are a habitual criminal who accepts arrest as an occupational hazard and presumably accepts imprisonment in the same casual manner.' Jump jockeys are habitual too, riding repeatedly over huge fences at high speed and, on the face of it, they should accept racing falls as an occupational hazard and presumably accept injuries in the same casual manner.

But neither of these things is true.

In the same way that habitual criminals, contrary to their previous experiences, never think they will be caught next time, jump jockeys thumb their noses at the grim statistics and fervently maintain that, on every occasion they weigh out, they will get round safely, and maybe even win.

It is not that jump jockeys are stupid – far from it; it is simply that they live in the 'here and now', not believing that a history of falls and injuries is an indication of inevitable future similar disasters, and the associated agony.

Once they do, it is time to hang up their racing boots and retire.

Fences these days are more forgiving than they once were and hence a horse falling is somewhat rarer. Whereas, in my father's era, a steeplechase jockey could expect to hit the ground once every twelve or so rides, it is now nearer once in twenty. But top jockeys can ride five or more times a day, six days a week. Do the maths. Even if they don't break anything, they live continually with bruises, often hoof-shaped. My father broke so many bones he stopped counting: collarbones (six times on each side), skull (twice), nose (too often to remember), vertebrae, wrists, ankles, fingers, toes – he didn't even regard snapped ribs as proper breaks. He just strapped himself up and climbed back into the saddle, not wanting to lose a ride to someone else.

So I rest my case – jump jockeys are indeed a breed apart from the norm. But there is more.

To be the champion, a jockey must stare danger in the face and consciously dismiss it. Without doing so, he or she will never be the best.

Ruby Walsh, while never being number one in Great Britain and hence not featured in this book, was champion jockey in Ireland on no fewer than twelve occasions, a feat all the more remarkable because he rode for half of each year on this side of the Irish Sea. In addition, he remains the most successful jockey ever at the Cheltenham Festival with fifty-nine wins, almost twice as many as the great AP McCoy.

But there is another record that Ruby holds, one that is not so prestigious. Research shows that the horses he rode fell twice as frequently at the last fence than those under any other jockey.

This is not an aberration or just bad luck – the two are linked.

In steeplechases, horses are statistically more likely to fall at the last fence than at any other, as here they are at their most tired and are also being driven out hard towards the finish line. For Ruby, as with all of the champion jockeys discussed in this volume, it was always infinitely more acceptable to go crashing to the turf while attempting to win than to take a safety-first pull and finish second – and to hell with the injuries.

So enjoy reading about these remarkable men. In my eyes they all deserve to be awarded the Victoria Cross – For Valour.

Introduction

What makes a champion jump jockey? To help me answer this question I asked David Gandolfo, the former trainer, who engaged no fewer than eleven champions in his fifty-year long career, from July 1960 to 2009. 'All of them had super toughness and durability,' the man known affectionately in the racing world as 'Gandy' says. 'But I believe personality too is also important. I think all the champions would have excelled in whatever vocation they had chosen, even if they hadn't been riding horses.' He continues: 'As regards to race riding, Graham Thorner [champion in 1970/71] talks about "It" jockeys. What is "It"? It's about being in the right place at the right time. All the champions were not only great horsemen; they had it between the ears too. "Tick tock."'

Martin Pipe's winners helped propel Peter Scudamore, Richard Dunwoody and AP McCoy to numerous titles. When I ask the former Master of Pond House what made those riders stand out, he answers: 'Scu, Dunwoody and AP were all great jockeys and champions, exceptional in their field. They were very dedicated to the horses and the sport.' Dedicated. A key word. As the late Roy Castle told us all those years ago on his television programme *Record Breakers*: 'If you wanna be the best, and you wanna beat the rest, Dedication's what you need.' But it's not all you need. To add another musical line, this time from *My Fair Lady*, you also need 'a little bit of luck'. Luck to avoid season-destroying serious injuries and long lay-offs. We shouldn't forget that there have been a number of great jockeys since 1945 – the likes of Arthur Thompson, Michael Scudamore, Dave Dick, David Mould, Willie Robinson, Johnny Haine, Jeff King, Adrian Maguire and Mark Dwyer – who never became champion, but who were easily good enough to deserve that mantle.

This book tells the story of the twenty-two champion jump jockeys from 1945 to the present day.

In telling their personal stories we also trace the changes that we have seen, not just in National Hunt racing, but in society at large. When we begin, in a Britain that had only recently celebrated VE Day, 'health and safety' was minimal, if it even existed at all. Riders wore cork helmets without chinstraps. The fences were much stiffer (just look at the old pictures of Becher's Brook in the Grand National!), and the chances of a serious injury to both jockeys and horses was much greater. By the time the book ends, we're in a prolonged national lockdown for Coronavirus and much of the population is walking around in face masks. What would the jockeys of 1945, who took far greater risks every time they went out on the racecourse, have made of that? It really was a very different era.

Becoming a champion in the 1940s was certainly no path to riches. Jack Dowdeswell, who won the title in 1946/47, was so poorly rewarded he spent the summer working as a stunt man in films for £25 a day. In contrast, by the late 1990s the three-time champion Richard Dunwoody was earning around £200k a year (minus tax and expenses). Even that was surpassed by AP McCoy, who signed a lucrative retainer with billionaire owner JP McManus. While risks remain, the health and safety aspect has improved greatly, but arguably something has also been lost amid all the 'progress'. There is still great camaraderie in the weighing room but the sport – like much of life itself – has become more serious. The days of Terry Biddlecombe and Josh Gifford, two great 'cavalier' champions of the 1960s, riding winners in the afternoon at Kempton Park and then heading to a West End nightclub to party the night away before wasting away in the morning in the Savoy Turkish Baths in Jermyn Street (but keeping refreshed with a glass of champagne or two), and then catching a train to Folkestone or Wye to ride that afternoon, have long gone.

Yet despite the changes, becoming champion jump jockey remains just about the toughest challenge in sport. Consider this: to win the title you'll probably have to ride in about 800–900 races from April to April, run on all kinds of ground, in all kinds of weather and in temperatures ranging from near freezing to 30°C. You'll need to cover the best part of 2,000 miles on horseback and 100,000 miles by road, and get stuck in quite a few motorway traffic jams. And each time you ride there's always a risk of coming off and being carted away in an ambulance and ending up in a hospital ward with your leg (or another part of your body) in plaster. Or even worse. The tragic death of Lorna Brooke, who lost her life following a fall at Taunton in April 2021, showed that while the sport has become a lot safer, the dangers still remain. All of our champions got to the top of the mountain. How they did it, we're about to find out.

Neil Clark, August 2021

Chapter One

Fred Rimell

Champion 1945/46 (also 1938/39, 1939/40, 1944/45 (tied))

Fearless Fred

'I believe that, but for the war, I might now be writing of Fred Rimell rather than Fred Winter as the greatest of the greats.'
Tim Fitzgeorge-Parker, *Steeplechase Jockeys: The Great Ones*

Mention the name Fred Rimell and it's likely that racing fans now in their fifties and sixties will recall an avuncular man in a trilby who as a trainer had a habit of winning Grand Nationals and whose horses regularly featured on *Grandstand* and *World of Sport* on those cosy winter Saturday afternoons back in the 1970s. You may well link the names to equine stars such as Comedy of Errors (the Champion Hurdler of 1973 and 1975), Royal Frolic (Gold Cup winner in 1976) and that ultra-reliable Aintree specialist The Pilgarlic, who posted top five finishes in four consecutive Grand Nationals from 1977 to 1980. You'd have to be much older, probably deep into your eighties though, to remember when Rimell wasn't unsaddling horses or giving instructions to jockeys, but was in the saddle himself – when he was the finest jump jockey in the land, riding fearlessly and stylishly, over obstacles far stiffer than those of today, in pursuit of glory. The shadows of the Second World War hung over the country when Fred Rimell the jockey was in his prime, but his brilliance shone through in sharp contrast to the dire international situation.

Thomas Frederick Rimell was born at the Kremlin. Not the Kremlin in Moscow, 'that building with the huge onions', as he later joked in his autobiography, but at Kremlin House stables, Newmarket, on 24 June 1913. His father Tom, later a successful trainer, was head man to Joe Butters, who thirty or so years earlier had ridden for Matt Dawson when Fred Archer, aka 'The Tin Man', was the stable apprentice at Heath House. Although Butters was a good boss, described by Fred as a 'cheery, kind-hearted man who liked to do a good turn to everyone', Rimell's father subsequently moved across town to be head man to Bob Colling at Bedford Lodge. At the age of 9, young Fred was already riding fast work[1] for the yard. When he was 11, there was another move, as his father 'answered the call' of his home and returned to his native Worcestershire to set up as a trainer in his own right at Kinnersley, in Severn Stoke, on the Earl of Coventry's Croome estate. It was to be young Fred's base for the rest of his life, as a jockey and then as a trainer, where he would surpass even his father's success.

Like so many of the champion jump jockeys featured in this book, Fred's riding skills were honed in the hunting field. At the age of 12 he was whipping-in to the Croome Foxhounds. His career as a jockey began on the Flat. He rode his first winner, a horse called Rowlie, owned by his grandfather, in a 1½-mile apprentice race at Chepstow in 1926, when he was still only 12. 'Although my father was obviously very proud as I pulled up and came back to unsaddle, he was never one to show excessive enthusiasm,' Rimell later recalled. 'He just smiled and said: "Well done, son!"' His grandfather though was 'over the moon'. 'He kept repeating: "I owns him, me son trains him, and me grandson rode him!"'

Altogether Rimell rode thirty-four winners on the level, in competition with some of the all-time greats of the game – men such as six-time Derby winner Steve Donoghue, whom he described as 'kind and generous', 'Head Waiter' Harry Wragg, who was a family friend, and, of course, the twenty-six-time champion Gordon Richards.

In 1930, finding his weight a problem, Rimell took out a jumping licence. 'I was ready for my real job in life,' he later wrote. He never regretted his Flat racing years though, saying they taught him much that was to be vitally useful in later life, both as a jockey and as a trainer.

In November 1933, Fred's career – and indeed his life – could have ended prematurely when the car he was driving home from Worcester races skidded and overturned near Kinnersley. Rather miraculously, he was only bruised and was soon back riding winners.

In his later training career, Fred won the Grand National four times, a feat only equalled by Ginger McCain in 2004. Rimell remains the only trainer to win the world's greatest steeplechase with four different horses: E.S.B. (a fortunate beneficiary of Devon Loch's mysterious run-in tumble in 1956), the grey Nicolaus Silver in 1961, Gay Trip in 1970, and Rag Trade in 1976. Yet as a rider, Rimell had the most terrible misfortune in the race – another common

---

[1] Riding fast work is exercising a horse at speed on the gallops.

theme amongst many of our post-war champions. Perhaps we should call it the Aintree champion jockeys' jinx.

Rimell might have ridden the Grand National winner of 1932, but he was too inexperienced to partner the 50-1 shot Forbra, who was trained by his father. He had twenty-eight winners in his first jumps season in 1931/32, but at that point still hadn't ridden professionally over fences. Instead, the ride went to Tim Hamey after a lucky chance meeting with Rimell snr in a pub on the way back from Newbury races. Sadly, the only time Fred rode Forbra, who also posted top six finishes in the 1933 and 1934 Grand Nationals, was at Newbury when his father's stable star broke a pastern and was put down. The first time Rimell rode in the National itself, in 1936, there was a similarly wretched ending. He was on board the red-hot 100-30 favourite Avenger, who was also trained by his father Tom, but tragedy struck as the 7-year-old fell heavily at the seventeenth fence and broke his neck.

Rimell fell again in the race in 1937 when riding Delachance. In 1938 he did complete, in twelfth place on Provocative, but that tells only half the story. At the Canal Turn, he committed a great act of sportsmanship when he stretched out and pulled Bruce Hobbs, who was riding the 40-1 shot Battleship, back into the saddle as horse and rider were about to part company having pecked badly on landing at Becher's second time around. 'Where do you think you're going, matey?' he shouted out. ('Hey matey!' was Rimell's usual friendly greeting.) Hobbs, aged 17, was the youngest jockey in the race and was riding the smallest horse to take part in the National since the nineteenth century (Battleship was just 15.2 hands). Rimell's rescue act proved crucial as Hobbs and his mount went on to win the race, beating Workman in a photo finish.

A year later, riding 100-9 shot Teme Willow, he fell again, and it was the same story in 1940, when it was a case of Black Hawk down. By then he was already champion jockey. His Liverpool record may have been dreadful (not only did he never win a National, he also never rode a winner of any kind at the Merseyside venue), but elsewhere it was a very different story. In the 1938/39 season he had fought a ding-dong battle with his brother-in-law and close pal Gerry Wilson, the rider of Golden Miller, who had held the jump jockeys' championship for the past six years. Rimell won the title on the last day of action at Newport, beating Wilson 61-59. 'So I was champion jockey for the first time and I had taken the title from the man I liked and admired most,' he later wrote.

The war clouds were looming, though, and early in the following season, Neville Chamberlain made his famous radio announcement that Britain was at war with Germany. Rimell enlisted, but his army career didn't last long.

'They found I was medical category E and slung me out,' he recalled. He was then taken on as an RAF driver for the maintenance units in Worcestershire.

Racing continued during the 'Phoney War' 1939/40 season but only on a restricted zonal four-meetings-a-week basis. Fred was free to race on Saturdays and managed to retain his title. This time, twenty-four winners sufficed. In the 1940 Cheltenham Gold Cup, postponed for six days because of snowfall on the Wednesday night, he finished second on 20-1 shot Black Hawk.

We can only speculate on how many more titles he might have won if war hadn't intervened. Jump racing was suspended altogether from 1942 to 1944. But when it did resume, in January 1945, albeit on a restricted Saturdays-only basis, Fred showed his prowess had not waned when he and Frenchie Nicholson, father of David 'The Duke', tied for the championship on fifteen winners each. The highlight of that season for Rimell – and, indeed, he later said, of his entire riding career – was winning the 1945 Champion Hurdle on the 7-4 shot Brains Trust. The reason? The horse was trained by brother-in-law Gerry Wilson. 'Gerry must have been one of the easiest trainers to ride for. He would give you fewer instructions than anybody that I ever knew. He'd come up to the paddock and say: "This horse is very well. I think he'll win." That's all,' Rimell recalled. It was a good day, as he rode three more winners that afternoon at Cheltenham, the last day of the season.

Those who saw the 1945/46 champion in the saddle regarded Rimell as one of the all-time greats. Writing in 1971, former steeplechase rider, trainer and journalist Tim Fitzgeorge-Parker, said of him:

> Fred Rimell was the ideal combination – the natural horseman, born and bred to racing and hunting yet highly trained in the exacting school of the flat at a time when we had a vintage group of jockeys already led by Sir Gordon Richards. I remember Fred as a superb stylist, going with his horse over a fence as well as any of today's stars and just as tough as teak. On top of all this he could sit down and ride a finish with a power and a balance never before associated with steeplechase riders.

In December 1939, Gerry Wilson paid Rimell a generous tribute: 'In my opinion he is the best jockey since Fred Rees [a four-time champion from 1920 to 1924] and that is saying a lot. He has got a great seat, excellent judgement, plenty of dash and is as keen as mustard. Moreover, he is a strong finisher.'

Fred could also be highly resourceful too, and think quickly when in a spot of trouble. A classic example was when he was riding the strongly fancied

Poor Flame, trained by his father, in the National Hunt Handicap Chase at Cheltenham. The horse was jumping badly to its right, on the left-handed course. Fred tried to rectify things with his whip, which he then lost. He saw jockey Nicky Pinch on Black Hawk, who looked to have no chance. 'You don't want that, do you?' he asked, and before Pinch had the chance to reply, Fred had pinched Pinch's whip! 'Then I proceeded to ride a tremendous finish, with my "borrowed" whip. I don't think I have ever driven harder up that hill and I got the verdict by a head. I had to give Nicky a fiver. We had a lot of fun in the weighing room in those days,' he recalled years later.

The 1945/46 season was to prove Rimell's swansong, but what an annus mirabilis it was. With the war finally over, the public flocked to the racetracks and other sporting venues as never before. Capacity crowds turned up to watch a three-match Test cricket series between an England XI and Australia. In October, 90,000 attended Ibrox to watch Glasgow Rangers draw 2-2 with Dynamo Moscow.

The racing landscape was now quite different to that of 1938/39, the last full season before the war. No fewer than eighteen venues where race meetings had taken place before the war, many of which Fred had ridden winners at, never again hosted racing under Rules after 1945. Among the more famous tracks lost – all commemorated in Chris Pitt's excellent book *A Long Time Gone* – were Derby, which hosted its last jumps meetings on 21 and 22 February 1939 (at which Fred was among the winners), and Gatwick, the course where three substitute Grand Nationals were run during the First World War and which became transformed into a major international airport. A number of other tracks weren't closed permanently, but didn't reopen again for some time afterwards. At Uttoxeter, for instance, racing did not resume until April 1952.

Fred became champion jockey that first season after the war, with fifty-four winners. The highlights included four winners at Windsor on 8 December, one of which, as Jim Beavis relates in his history of Windsor Racecourse, was a 15-year-old called Rightun who was in the midst of chalking up a four-timer himself. As Beavis points out, a number of older horses were brought back into action in 1945/46, as the supply of younger animals had been interrupted by the war. Rightun, for instance, had eight years earlier won the Scottish Grand National as a 7-year-old; he was back to race in the Cheltenham Gold Cup of 1945, aged 15.

At the two-day Worcester meeting held a week before Christmas 1945, Fred rode five winners, bringing his season's total up to twenty-six, nine more than his nearest pursuer, Frenchie Nicholson. On Boxing Day he rode a treble at Windsor, which included an 8-length success on odds-on shot Poor Flame.

On 7 January 1946 it was reported that Fred and his father had come to an arrangement to help him become champion jockey. From now on, Fred would be free to choose his mounts in any race, and not be obliged to ride his father's if he felt he had a better chance on something else. 'My son is very anxious not to miss any chance offered to him of riding a winner,' Tom Rimell explained. At that point Fred was on the thirty-three-winner mark, with his lead over Nicholson extended to fourteen.

The New Year meeting at Cheltenham in 1946 had been lost to frost, likewise the two-day meeting at Worcester on 4 and 5 January, but when racing did resume, at Fontwell on 10 January, Fred was there to ride a double. On Saturday, 12 January at Windsor, he piloted Comique to a 5-length success in the Long Walk Hurdle. In the second half of January there was another cold spell and yet more meetings were lost to frost.

As he chased another title, Fred was already planning for the future. In February 1946 he received a licence to train under National Hunt Rules. 'If you start training while you're in demand as a jockey people send you horses just so they can be ridden by you,' he later explained. He was also finding it an increasing struggle to keep his weight down and admitted to having to waste very hard to do 10st 6lb, when his weight rose in the summer to 12 stone.

At Cheltenham, on 2 February, Rimell won what was described as a 'magnificent race' when Poor Flame, carrying all of 12st 9lb, beat Suzerain II by a short head in the Stroud Handicap Chase. He chalked up his fiftieth winner of the campaign at Taunton on 8 March. Special cheers greeted him as he made his way into the winners' enclosure on Birthlaw. Four days later, in the 1946 Champion Hurdle, he lined up on multiple winner Carnival Boy, attempting to win the race for the second year running for brother-in-law Gerry Wilson. This time, however, he could only finish second, beaten 4 lengths behind the odds-on Dorothy Paget-owned favourite Distel, who became the first (of many) Irish-trained winners of the event. In the Gold Cup he also finished second, on Poor Flame, 5 lengths behind Prince Regent, the best chaser of the 1940s, although he did enjoy 1946 Festival success on the Fulke Walwyn-trained Boccaccio in the Severn Springs Handicap Chase.

Just one week after Cheltenham, on Wednesday, 20 March, Rimell's season was cut short. He broke his neck following a fall from Poet Prince, the winner of the 1941 Gold Cup, at Wincanton. It meant a lengthy lay-off but fortunately he still had enough winners on board to take the jockey's title. He had to wear a plaster cast over his head and down to his waist for three months, which his wife Mercy later said made him look like some monster from a television horror programme.

Fred started training first in the bottom yard at Kinnersley, but when his father transported his now predominantly Flat string to Lambourn, he moved into Kinnersley proper.

The 1946/47 season was badly hit by the worst winter in living memory. The first icy blasts came on 23 January when snow fell heavily over the South and South West of England. The big freeze, which was compounded by post-war shortages of fuel and food, lasted until March. In many parts of Britain snow fell on twenty-six of the twenty-eight days of February. Sports schedules were badly disrupted. The football season in 1946/47 finally ended on 14 June, making it the longest of all time. There was no racing from 21 January to 15 March, and even then the meeting at Taunton was threatened by a fresh snowfall.

Because of the weather, the Cheltenham Festival in 1947 was postponed until April and it was then that Fred's riding career came to an abrupt end. He broke his neck (for the second time within a year) in a crashing fall on Coloured Schoolboy, whom he also trained, in the Gold Cup, and by doing so, missed out on a winning ride on National Spirit in the Champion Hurdle. That night, there was due to be a dinner at Prestbury Park in honour of the reigning champion jockey, but instead he lay in bed in Cheltenham General Hospital. Nevertheless, the dinner went ahead in his absence. 'It is a real tragedy,' said Lord Mildmay, proposing the toast, 'and I feel that what we are doing now is rather like having a wedding in the absence of the bridegroom.'

Despite breaking his neck twice in twelve months, and his ankle once, Fred had actually been quite lucky with falls, riding during a 'pre-health and safety' era when fatalities, though still rare, were more common than today. Lest we forget, this was a time when there were no back or body protectors and jockeys wore cork helmets with no chinstraps, which could easily come off in a fall or split upon impact.

The prospect of another eight months in plaster meant it was time for Fred to call it a day. You could say that the first great decision he made in his life was to become a jump jockey, and the third was retiring in one piece. The second was marrying Mercy Cockburn, in June 1937. Fred and Mercy were a formidable team. With Fred out of action, Mercy ran the stable, and played a key role in its subsequent success. She did all the paperwork and decided where the horses would run. Fred did the training. Or, as their stable jockey Terry Biddlecome later put it: 'She [Mercy] loaded the bullets and Fred fired them.'

'It is the most satisfactory combination possible,' Fred wrote in 1977, and few in racing who knew the Rimells and how they operated would disagree – though woe betide anyone who got on the wrong side of Mercy! By that point

Fred had been at or near the top of the training tree for almost thirty years. He landed his first trainers' championship in 1951, and won it again on a further four occasions, in three different decades – the 1950s, the 1960s and the 1970s. In 1979 he became the first trainer to earn £1m in prize money for his owners. In addition to the four Grand Nationals (good karma for helping Bruce Hobbs in 1938?) there were also two Gold Cups, two Champion Hurdles, two Welsh Nationals, a Scottish National, a Whitbread and four Mackesons in a row from 1969 to 1972.

In 1976, Fred became the first trainer for twenty-three years to win the Gold Cup and the Grand National in the same season – a feat only matched in 2021 by Henry de Bromhead. And no one, apart from the two fantastic Freds – Rimell and Winter (who features in Chapter Five) – have been both champion jump jockey and champion trainer. 'He was very kind and considerate and dedicated to his horses,' Rimell's daughter Scarlett says. She also says her father was something of a training pioneer. 'They say Martin Pipe was the first to introduce interval training but my father was doing it earlier.'

An article by Brian Spoors in the *Evening News* on 6 June 1981 scotched rumours that Rimell was about to retire. Just a month earlier, Gaye Chance had won the valuable Royal Doulton Handicap Hurdle at Haydock under Sam Morshead. The Rimell string amassed fifty-one wins in the 1980/81 season, and finished fifth in the prize money table. A drawing of Fred appeared in the paper, with the caption: 'FRED RIMELL – looking forward to more success.'

Sadly though for Fred it was the end of the road. On Thursday, 9 July he fractured his pelvis in a freak accident while pursuing escaped cattle on his farm. He died in the early hours of the following Sunday morning after suffering a blood clot. He was 68. Racing was in shock at the loss of such a great personality. 'He was a tremendously alive man,' said his long-time stable jockey Terry Biddlecombe. 'Always jovial, always quick to offer anyone a cigarette, or a quick "livener", and appreciative of a pretty woman. His humour and warmth are greatly missed; he was a vital cog in the racing machine.'

'Everyone missed him; the smiling rock was no longer there,' said Sam Morshead.

Fred had passed on, but the Rimell story continued.

Mercy took over the licence and two years later, Gaye Brief, a brother of Gaye Chance, won the Champion Hurdle. Matt Sheppard, later a trainer himself, worked for Mercy in the 1980s. 'Mrs Rimell was a formidable woman,' he remembers. 'One of her favourite sayings was, "If they don't like it, they know what they can do! They can fxxx off!"'

Mercy retired in 1989, having trained over 200 winners, but in 2007 there were dreams of another Grand National win for Kinnersley, thirty-one years after Rag Trade had delivered the last, when the Mercy-owned and John Spearing-trained home-bred gelding Simon, out of a half-sister to Gaye Brief, lined up at Aintree. The impressive winner of that season's Racing Post Chase was travelling well in a prominent position having negotiated second Becher's, but alas, he came down at second Valentine's in a softish fall. A year later, it was an almost identical story, when he unseated at the same fence.

I remember Mercy at John Spearing's owners' days when she would sit there smoking, and still immaculately dressed, deep into her nineties. She died aged 98 in 2017, bringing to an end a remarkable chapter in National Hunt history, one that will probably never be equalled.

Big race wins (as a jockey)
Champion Hurdle 1945 (Brains Trust)

Chapter Two

Jack Dowdeswell

Champion 1946/47

'Jumping Jack', National Hunt's Mr Indestructible

'I can truthfully say I have never known a braver man than Jack.'
Tim Fitzgeorge-Parker, *Steeplechase Jockeys: The Great Ones*

The utterly irrepressible and much-loved Lambourn legend Jack Dowdeswell broke practically every bone in his body as a jockey (and some several times over), yet was still riding and schooling horses well into his seventies and lived to the ripe old age of 94. His story is an inspirational one as it shows us what can be achieved if you live without fear and maintain a cheerful disposition, whatever calamities are going on around you.

Like Fred Rimell, Jack's career straddled the Second World War. Born in Purley, Surrey, on 27 May 1917, he was one of three sons of Arthur Dowdeswell, a huntsman with the Craven. Like his brothers 'Son' and Tom, Jack was on the back of a horse at an early age. 'I'd sit on the pommel of his saddle when he'd come back from hunting, I was two or three at the time,' he recalled of his father in the book *Tales of Old Horsemen*.

He left school at 14 and began an extremely tough apprenticeship with trainer Ted Gwilt at Saxon House Stables, Upper Lambourn. Racing historian David Boyd noted, 'Gwilt entered racing in Edwardian England and continued for the remainder of his training life as though that era had never ended.'

'It was slave labour,' Dowdeswell recalled. 'I worked fourteen hours a day and was never taught a thing. All for two shillings a week. I could not have gone to a worse stable. He never gave apprentices a chance. He never "made" a jockey.' Despite that rather unhappy start, Dowdeswell kept at it.

Like Rimell, he started off on the Flat. His first ride in public was on a horse of Gwilt's called Who's He, in a 5-furlong seller at Newbury on 8 June 1932. He finished eighth. Among the famous riders up against him that day were Gordon Richards, Harry Wragg and Freddie Fox. Dowdeswell's first winner at Newbury came just one day later, when he rode Bob, owned and trained by Gwilt, to victory in a 1-mile apprentices' race. But so few were the opportunities, he had to wait over two years for his next winner.

When Gwilt offered him a position as a paid lad at the end of his apprenticeship, Dowdeswell didn't have to think too long about refusing it. But he did gain one very rich dividend from being Gwilt's skivvy. At the end of each long day, he had to walk a mile and half each way to the local shop to collect the evening paper for his guv'nor. It was there, when he was 15, that he happened to meet a pretty local girl called Betty. There was a strong racing connection: Betty's father, Archie Austen, was a jockey, as was her great-uncle, Frank Dainty, who won a Scottish National. Jack and Betty fell in love, and married in 1940; they celebrated their seventieth wedding anniversary in 2010. They were actually together for the best part of eighty years. They had a son, Michael, a daughter, Liz, and several grandchildren and great-grandchildren. So you could say Jack's long walk to get the paper each evening was well worth it.

While meeting and marrying Betty was the best thing Jack ever did personally, professionally, his best decision was moving to the yard of Captain John Beresford 'Bay' Powell at Aldbourne. Although in Wiltshire, Hightown Stables was still only 6 miles from Lambourn, so Jack could keep in close contact with Betty.

Captain (later Major) Powell is all but forgotten today but was an important figure in horse racing in the mid-twentieth century. A former jockey, he had rebuilt Hightown Stables, which had burnt down in 1921, into a modern training complex. The winners soon followed and the yard became one of the most powerful in the country. After less than a year at Hightown, Dowdeswell was riding winners for his new boss. His first over jumps was Lady Rowley in a 3-mile chase at Kempton on 4 December 1937.

By the time war broke out Powell had trained over 400 National Hunt winners, many of them ridden by Dowdeswell. In his book *The Riding Career of Jack Dowdeswell*, Clive Bettison tells how Bay Powell, as a reservist, was immediately called up, leaving Jack to assist Mrs Powell in running the yard. Jack joined the Royal Horse Artillery in May 1940, having married Betty in January that year.

For two years, Jack served at home, while still riding in what was a very restricted race programme. In the 1939/40 season he rode ten winners and then two more in 1941/42. But his racecourse activities got him into trouble with the army. 'I was asked to ride this chaser in a valuable race at Cheltenham and took what was known as "French leave",' he told the *Racing Post*'s Rodney

Masters in 2001. 'I would have got away with it too, but the horse won and my name was across the sports pages. I was called before my commanding officer and he took a stripe off me.' A few weeks later, on 7 January 1942, Dowdeswell did the same thing again – and the horse, Irish Duke, won at Cheltenham. After that his CO couldn't wait to get him posted.

Dowdeswell saw action in both North Africa and Italy. Meanwhile, Hightown was requisitioned for military use. In 1943, the American 506th Parachute Infantry Regiment, 101st Airborne Division, the 'Screaming Eagles', moved into Aldbourne, with 'E' Division – later to be commemorated in the book and Steven Spielberg film as the *Band of Brothers* – occupying the stables.

When the war ended Jack had to stay on for an extra year in Italy waiting to be demobbed. But it was an enjoyable time. His regiment had been allocated half a dozen horses that the Germans had used to pull their guns. Soon Jack was back riding in races at makeshift venues. His first winner in Italy was at a former aerodrome called Aiello. Major Powell, however, was keen to get his stable jockey back. His secretary sent Jack a letter to say that the major wanted him to return to ride in the 1946 Grand National. Dowdeswell told this to his colonel – and he was on his way home within twenty-four hours. Ironically, his mount in the National was a non-runner, but three days later, on 8 April 1945, he rode his first post-war winner, Alger, at Wye. Between then and 19 June, he rode nineteen winners, a portent of what was to come in his first full season after his return.

Dowdeswell got the 1946/47 season off to a great start, winning the very first race at Newton Abbot on the 13-year-old hurdler Mospey on 3 August and had two more winners at the two-day meeting. By 4 September, he'd already reached double figures, chalking up repeat victories on a small number of horses. For instance, he won a novices' hurdle at Buckfastleigh on Phantom Brig, then was first past the post on the same horse five days later at Devon and Exeter and then again at Newton Abbot on 4 September, where his mount carried 12st 7lb to victory.

On a bright sunny day at Cheltenham on 13 November, he recorded his thirty-second winner of the season, piloting Montcalm to his sixth consecutive win in the 2-mile handicap chase. By 22 November he had ridden thirty-five winners, eighteen more than Fred Rimell, his nearest pursuer, who was resuming after breaking his neck. Major Powell had provided over 50 per cent of Jack's winning rides, including the triumphs on Montcalm.

A coughing epidemic hit racing that winter meaning that fields for many steeplechases were relatively small. But as soon as the epidemic began to subside, there was another problem for the sport. As previously mentioned, the

1946/47 season was badly affected by the wintry weather, with no racing at all in Britain from 21 January to 15 March. Just before the snow intervened, Jack rode a double at Birmingham. The second of these was somewhat fortunate, after the Rimells' Coloured Schoolboy, who was 10 lengths clear, fell at the last in the 2½-mile steeplechase. Vat 69 'had to be snatched up' to avoid the fallen horse, allowing Dowdeswell on the appropriately named Lucky Time (trained by who other than Major Powell) to storm home.

Half an hour earlier, Jack had ridden Powell's Montcalm to a 6-length win, his seventh consecutive win of the season, at odds of 4-6. He was warmly applauded by the racegoers as it was his first winning ride since being out of action following a fall at Windsor ten days earlier in which he had dislocated his shoulder and splintered a bone. 'What sort of fellow is this Dowdeswell?' asked The Scout in the *Daily Express* after his Birmingham success. 'Well, he's 29, has a voice charming enough for the BBC (though he's reluctant to use it about himself), looks taller than his 5ft 3in, and appears heavier than his handy weight of 9st 10lb.'

Although there was no racing for two months, the military-minded Major Powell didn't let the weather interrupt his training schedule. 'With prudent foresight Bay Powell removed his Aldbourne string to the south coast, enabling the horses to take advantage of the coastal sands for their exercise. The horses were transported daily by horse-box from their Goodwood base to the Wittering beaches near Bognor,' writes Clive Bettison.

When the competition resumed, and helped by the fitness of the Powell horses, Jack simply carried on where he left off. At a snowy Taunton on Saturday, 15 March, he won four of the seven races. Unfortunately, no doubt because of the weather and fears that the meeting would be yet another abandonment, it was reported that 'there was only a small attendance' to see the champion jockey elect in such blistering form. Everything was going so well for Jack, but on the last day of March there was some sad news when Montcalm, who had contributed so much to his success that season, was put down after breaking a leg in a freak gallops accident while being prepared for the Gold Cup. Who knows what heights Powell's brilliant novice chaser might have scaled with Jack in the saddle. 'He was a fast front-runner and quick and fluent jumper, really enthusiastic, always looking for the next fence. A lovely horse and a great loss – probably the best I ever rode,' he later said.

The death of Montcalm took some of the gloss off Dowdeswell's championship, and for what had been an excellent season for Powell too, who trained fifty-two winners and finished runner-up behind Fulke Walwyn in the trainers' championship.

Dowdeswell won his title with fifty-eight winners; an impressive total given that so much of the season was lost to the weather. His strike rate was an excellent 25 per cent. 'Had it not been for the terrible winter then Jack, barring injury, may well have approached a century of wins,' says Clive Bettison. Jack was eleven clear in the final championship table from Bryan Marshall, with Ron Smyth in third place, the leading amateur Lord Mildmay in fourth, and Fred Rimell in fifth.

Jack's accomplishments were honoured at the special champion jump jockey's dinner at Cheltenham on 21 November 1947, attended by eighty-five guests. A sign of the times was that one of the speakers, Lord Willoughby de Broke, said that racegoers could overcome the problem of petrol restrictions by banding together to organise bus parties to take them to race meetings. Lord Mildmay congratulated Dowdeswell, humorously noting how he had ridden winners on the Flat before transferring to 'the superior branch of racing'. In his reply it was reported that Dowdeswell thanked the owners and trainers for whom he had ridden, 'with particular reference to Major Powell', who had given him his chance.

Dowdeswell was at the top of his profession but in 1947 that didn't mean riches. 'Even as champion jockey, he was so inadequately rewarded that he used to work as a stunt man in the film studios sometime in the summer, earning £25 a day for some of those horrible falls that thrill the movie fans, even though he had broken every bone in his body,' records Fitzgeorge-Parker. That shrewd judge thought that Dowdeswell came back from the war too heavy for the Flat, but really too light for jumping. 'He was the wrong shape too, with his great leonine head, powerful broad shoulders and short little legs – like a big Gordon Richards.'

Yet despite these physical disadvantages, this extremely gutsy jockey had reached the top. Fitzgeorge-Parker thought that Jack's Flat training meant that he rode a finish much better than most of his contemporaries. If he was still in contention after the last, everyone else had reason to fear him. His great mental attitude was also a huge bonus. Dowdeswell was always cheerful, whatever the circumstances. He would go anywhere, not just to ride, but also to school horses. He was totally in love with the game. 'I never refused a ride as I could always do 10 stone quite easily,' he said in an interview with the *Newbury Weekly News* in 2007. 'I ended up riding a lot of bad animals as well as good ones. I got a great thrill getting bad jumpers round, and a bit of a headache when I didn't!'

Injuries played their part in preventing Jack from adding to his 1946/47 jockey title. While he continued to be friends with and ride regularly for

Powell, the trainer's shift in focus to the Flat meant Jack lost his retainer. The highlight of the 1947/48 season was winning the Grand Sefton on Good Date in November, his first victory over the famous Aintree fences. The race was run in thick mist with one report saying it 'ruined' the chase as a spectacle; one doubts that Jack was too concerned.

He had ridden twenty-one winners by the time he was taken to hospital after a fall on Glengyle at Kempton in December. He then fell and injured his shoulder at Leicester in January, when in pursuit of Bryan Marshall, and at Ludlow on 11 March 1948 he broke a leg, which ended his hopes of retaining his title. After an eight-month lay-off he was back in action in December 1948 but broke the same leg again just one month later when he collided with the rails at Sandown after a fall. This meant him missing a winning ride on Cadamstown in the Topham Trophy. He returned to action again on the first day of the 1949/50 season at Newton Abbot in August and rode a winner, Cairo III. Racegoers were delighted to see the ex-champion back in the winners' enclosure. 'I've never in my life had a reception like it – the crowds went crazy, they knew – hats were going into the air, the girls in the tea room were throwing cups in the air and catching them, it was wonderful!', Dowdeswell remembered. He rode Cairo III to two further victories that month on the West Country circuit. He ended the 1940s by riding the Major Powell-trained novice chaser Gold Branch to victory at Manchester on New Year's Eve 1949. He could look back during that evening's celebrations on what had personally been a very fulfilling decade.

At Cheltenham, in January 1950, he was kicked in the face when coming down on Cadamstown at the last fence, but still rode four winners that month. Later that year he might have won the King George at Kempton. He was booked by Vincent O'Brien to ride Knock Hard, but fell three out when still going well. In 1953, the same horse won the Cheltenham Gold Cup.

A story from the newspapers in 1952 exemplifies the sort of indestructible character Jack was. On 25 January he was taken to hospital following a fall from Gibus in the Weybridge Chase at Kempton. About half an hour later, according to the *Yorkshire Post*, he was on the telephone to his wife to tell her he'd be home late that evening. 'Don't worry, it's nothing,' he told her. His wife commented: 'He would say that if he fractured his skull.' In *Tales of Old Horsemen*, Jack told of another occasion when he had a 'terrible fall':

My horse fell on the flat round a bend and my arm broke off, pulled out and stuck in my ribs, it looked a hell of a mess. I was picked up and was supposed to be unconscious; they gave me morphine and things. In the ambulance room some jockeys came in and one said 'How's Jack?' and the doctor, who thought I'd passed out, said quietly 'He'll never race again'; but I croaked, 'I bloody well will'!

He kept riding deep into the 1950s. In 1951 came his first Cheltenham Festival winner, Town Crier in the Gratwicke Blagrave Cup. Two more Festival wins followed in 1953 and 1954, while in 1956 he finished runner-up in four races. In the summer of 1953 he even made a return to the Flat, riding two winners, and came fifth in the Goodwood Cup. In March 1954, he rode 20-1 shot The Pills to victory in the Imperial Cup, an important hurdle race.

In October 1954, when he was 37, the *Birmingham Post* opined that Dowdeswell was riding 'better this season than at any time since he was champion jockey'. He was then leading the jockeys' championship with thirteen winners. He finished the season with what proved to be his biggest success, in the Queen Elizabeth Chase at Hurst Park. A valuable end-of-season staying handicap chase (worth £3,460 in 1955), which had been inaugurated in 1949, the race was the forerunner of Sandown's Whitbread Gold Cup. Jack rode 9-1 shot Limb of the Law, trained by Tom Yates at Letcombe Bassett, to victory, taking up the lead two out.

Jack rode in the Grand National eight times but never once got round. That had little to do with his horsemanship, but a lot to do with the fact that he was nearly always on rank outsiders. Six of his mounts started at 66-1 or longer, and his first four rides were 100-1 shots. In 1951 he was one of eleven jockeys who came down at the first. In 1955, Aintree historian Reg Green records how he was 'buried in a flurry of hooves' after being brought down on the 66-1 shot Roman Fire. A year later, he was on Fulke Walwyn's Armorial III, which went off at 20-1. The pair led for much of the way, but came down five from home. Jack thought he would have won and if so, what a wonderful climax to his career that would have been. In the end, Devon Loch went clear only to dramatically capsize very near to the winning post, gifting the race to E.S.B.

Dowdeswell finally called it a day on doctor's orders after injuring his spine in a bad fall at Buckfastleigh on 19 May 1956, just a week before his thirty-ninth birthday. Towards the end of his career, having had both collarbones removed, he wore, in the words of Tim Fitzgeorge-Parker, 'a sort of cricket pad, with a hole for his head, over his shoulders'. The doctors told Dowdeswell that if he fell again it would be 'curtains', so he did the sensible thing. In a career stretching all the way back to 1932, he had ridden a total of 352 winners under National Hunt Rules, and four on the Flat. One hundred and fifty of his wins over jumps had been on horses trained by Bay Powell.

A year before he retired, his old patron saw his career come to an abrupt end. In 1952, a horse trained by Powell, and ridden by Lester Piggott, tested positively for dope. Powell was exonerated. But three years later, it happened again, and this time the major lost his licence, even though there was no evidence of him being guilty of any wrongdoing. Unfortunately for Powell, the rules of strict liability then applied.

Three years after he retired Jack was in the news again. In May 1959 he revealed in a BBC television programme called *Jockey Club*, hosted by Woodrow Wyatt, that he had once been offered a bribe of 'as much as £1,000' before racing. When asked if he thought bribery still occurred in the sport, he declared: 'I think so – undoubtedly.' Veteran Flat jockey Charlie Smirke said, 'It hasn't happened to me, although a lot of people think so.'

Having worked as an assistant to Commander Bisgood, and also having spent time poultry farming at Lambourn, 'Jack of All Trades' Dowdeswell took up training in his own right in 1960. He saddled his first winner – after an objection – at Plumpton in January 1961. But he enjoyed only moderate success as a trainer and in 1970 he relinquished his licence. Not that it bothered him unduly. He stayed in racing, working for David Nugent and then for a number of other trainers in the Lambourn area. 'I started as a stable lad and I'm still a stable lad,' he remarked with characteristic humility. He was still riding out and schooling well into his seventies, alongside another Lambourn legend and champion jump jockey, John Francome, and only gave up after he had a hip operation. In 2007, Newbury Racecourse presented him and Betty with a special print to mark the seventy-fifth anniversary of him riding his very first winner.

In 2009, at the age of 92, Jack attended the official opening of Oaksey House, the Injured Jockey's Fund residential and rehabilitation centre in Lambourn.

The man who risked life and limb in a career in the saddle that lasted almost a quarter of a century, died at the ripe old age of 94, in July 2011, following a fall at home. His beloved Betty, aka 'The Queen of Lambourn', passed away on Christmas Day 2015, aged 95.

Tributes from the racing community spoke volumes about the affection in which Jack was held. 'I've known Jack since 1947 and I used to play with his kids when he was champion jockey. Jack was a wonderful man and never had a bad word to say about anyone,' said the former Flat trainer Barry Hills.

'Jack was a wonderful man and a very good rider. When I started he was very good to me and I remember whenever he couldn't ride after a fall, he would say "Michael will ride it,"' said former weighing room colleague Michael Scudamore.

Let's finish with a lovely anecdote from BBC Radio Berkshire listener Tony Buckle:

> When I was about eleven years old (1947) Jack Dowdeswell, the then leading NH jockey, broke his leg and spent some time in the Radcliffe hospital in Oxford. I wrote him a letter, wishing him a speedy recovery and asking him several questions about his career. I thought nothing of it, until some weeks later he had taken the trouble to reply in length, answering all my questions and thanking me for my good wishes. His hand writing was immaculate and it made a young lad very happy!

They don't make them like Jack Dowdeswell any more. More's the pity.

Big race wins (as a jockey)
Grand Sefton Chase 1947 (Good Date)
Imperial Cup 1954 (The Pills)
Queen Elizabeth Chase 1955 (Limb of the Law)

Chapter Three

Bryan Marshall

Champion 1947/48

Inside Job

'One of the truly great National Hunt jockeys – as brave as a lion as a soldier in World War Two and absolutely fearless on the racetrack.'
Sir Rupert Mackeson, who spent time with Marshall in the 1950s

On Wednesday, 29 December 1948, the third champion jockey of the post-war era was honoured at the special annual dinner given by the directors of the Cheltenham Steeplechase Company at the Queen's Hotel. Presenting the new champion with a gold engraved cigarette case (this was a time when top sports performers were expected, like everyone else, to be smokers), Lord Willoughby de Broke said there were two reasons why Bryan Marshall had turned out to be such a good rider. First, he was born in Ireland. Second, there was his breeding. His mother Caroline, aka Binty, was a first-class horsewoman, in the hunting field, in show-jumping and in the show ring.

The man from Cloughjordan in County Tipperary won the jockey's title only once, but his glittering CV included back-to-back wins in the Grand National and two King Georges.

Bryan Marshall was born on 29 February 1916, and as a 'leap day' birth it was perhaps appropriate that it was a horse called Leap Man that, three decades later, propelled him on the way to glory.

He was riding (and falling off) horses at the ridiculously early age of 3 – and going out hunting before he was 5. 'So when most children of his age were just starting school, Bryan was jumping at shows and hunting, hunting, hunting – equipping himself mentally and physically for the career which lay ahead,' says Fitzgeorge-Parker. By the time he became champion in 1948, the dark-haired Irishman had already been riding horses for almost thirty years. No wonder he was described as the most polished rider of his generation.

He was sent to England for the school holidays, beginning his apprenticeship with the legendary Atty Persse at Chattis Hill in Hampshire. Persse, a brilliant former amateur rider, went from training jumpers to specialising on the Flat, with his most famous horse, The Tetrarch, widely considered to be the best British-trained 2-year-old of the twentieth century. In 1930, Bryan's third year with him, Persse became champion trainer. Persse gave Marshall his first ride in public at the age of 11. He rode his first winner, Cheviotdale, at the age of 13 at Kempton Park.

Like Rimell and Dowdeswell before him, Marshall switched to the jumps when he was getting too heavy for the Flat. He spent time in the US working for Gerald Balding (father of Ian and Toby), and then for the Irish trainer Hubert Hartigan, in Cumberland. Hartigan was a tough character, as illustrated by this anecdote from his assistant, Noel Murless (later an extremely successful Flat trainer): 'One day a horse choked badly on a carrot. Hubert never hesitated. He took a penknife from his pocket, there and then cut a hole in its throat, removed the carrot and saved the horse's life. Can you imagine any modern trainer doing that? Hubert was a real man – a hell of a man.'

When Murless left Hartigan in the mid-1930s to set up on his own in Yorkshire, Marshall joined him. He rode his first winner over jumps, a horse called Intelligent Outlook, for Murless in a hurdle race at Carlisle in December 1935. His progress before the war was gradual rather than spectacular. He rode seven winners in the 1937/38 season and eleven in 1938/39.

In early 1940 he joined the cavalry, and a year later was commissioned in the 5th Inniskilling Dragoon Guards. He took part in the Normandy D-Day landings in June 1944 but was almost killed on the first day, when he survived a sniper's bullet in his neck.

He was demobbed as a captain in 1946, and with leave, was able to ride twenty-two winners in the 1945/46 season. The most significant of these was on the aforementioned Leap Man in the Cathcart Challenge Cup at the Cheltenham Festival. Marshall was booked for the ride by Fulke Walwyn, the coming force in the training ranks. Walwyn was clearly impressed and engaged Marshall as his first-choice jockey at his Saxon House Stables in Lambourn in the summer of 1946. It was this association with a very powerful yard that helped him win the title. In 1946/47 Marshall was runner-up behind Jack Dowdeswell but the following year everything went right for him.

It was to be a vintage season for fans of jump racing. 'After the crippling effects of an exceptionally hard winter upon its predecessor, it was appropriate that the 1947/48 season should have an almost unbroken run, and the open winter, good racing, large attendances and high stakes combined to produce as brilliant a period of National Hunt racing as that sport has ever enjoyed,' enthused John Hislop in his review of the season in *The Horseman's Year.*

On 27 August 1947, the *Gloucestershire Echo* set the scene, predicting that due to the reigning champion (Dowdeswell) still suffering from injuries, the retirement of Fred Rimell and Frenchie Nicholson riding only seldom, there was likely to be a new champion to celebrate. The prediction came true, but Dowdeswell, as one might expect, didn't go down without a fight. Marshall got off to a good start but, on 25 November, Dowdeswell rode his seventeenth winner of the season at Birmingham by a neck to cut the lead to nine. Marshall rode two third places on the card. The competition continued at Sandown on 28 November when Dowdeswell rode a double. Marshall bounced back in the third, winning on Fulke Walwyn's 6-1 shot Mill Boy.

That Christmas, Marshall won the first-ever King George VI Chase to be run on Boxing Day. Today, the race is as integral a part of the Yuletide festivities as the Queen's Speech and Christmas pudding, but it's worth remembering that when it was first run, in 1937, as a tribute to the new monarch, it was scheduled for February. After Kempton reopened for racing in 1947 it was switched to a different time in the racing calendar to allow more of a gap between it, the Gold Cup and the Grand National. But would the public buy it?

Marshall rode Fulke Walwyn's 8-year-old Rowland Roy, the 1947 Scottish Grand National winner, to victory in 'perfect sharp winter weather'. 'The punters came too,' wrote John Tyrell, 'and soon an afternoon in the brisk fresh air to blow away the cobwebs of festive excess became as traditional a Londoner's day out as Derby Day had been for generations.'

In the new year, buoyed by his Kempton success, Marshall kicked on again. At Leicester on Monday, 12 January, he rode four winners, but one of his mounts, Coventry, was disqualified following an objection after finishing first. The treble consisted of wins on the well-backed Jack Tatters and Tredilion, both trained by Walwyn and owned by The Hon. Dorothy Paget, and Milord II, who beat twenty-eight rivals in the finale.

That was Marshall's forty-second winner of the season, and put him nineteen ahead of Jack Dowdeswell. 'Marshall ... combines artistry with strength – he seldom rides below 11st,' noted 'Flashlight' in the *Nottingham Journal* on Tuesday, 13 January 1948 in a report entitled 'Marshall forging ahead in riders' championship'. That day, at Leicester, Marshall rode no winners, but Dowdeswell fell and injured his shoulder when Top Heavy fell in the selling handicap chase and missed a winning ride when Major Powell's 8-1 shot Cadamstown took the Breedon Handicap Chase by 10 lengths.

At the Cheltenham Festival in March, Marshall maintained his 100 per cent record in the Cathcart Challenge Cup. He'd won the race in 1942 on Roi D'Egypte and in 1946 on Leap Man, and in 1948 he partnered Jack Tatters to victory.[1]

A week later, on 11 March, Jack Dowdeswell's title challenge ended when he broke his right leg following a fall on Double Bridge in a chase at Ludlow, and was taken to hospital in Oxford. Nine days later, Marshall piloted his King George winner Rowland Roy to sixth place in the Grand National won by Sheila's Cottage.

Marshall landed his title with sixty-six winners from 239 rides, but sportingly acknowledged at his award dinner that but for Jack Dowdeswell breaking his leg, he would not have been in the place of honour. Although he never again won the jump jockeys' championship, in the next few years he enjoyed plenty of big race successes – and was involved in his fair share of controversy too.

On 29 September 1948, he rode the first five winners at Folkestone, who were all owned by the eccentric The Hon. Dorothy Paget, owner of Golden Miller. But 'Miss P', who was notoriously hard to please, reportedly expressed her displeasure when Marshall was beaten into second place on her sixth runner, Loyal Monarch, in the last race. That was nothing, though, compared to what happened in November 1951 when Marshall eased down Paget's Lanveoc Poulmic on the run-in at Sandown, when well clear in a novices' hurdle race, and was caught on the line. Paget had gambled heavily on her horse, and understandably was furious. The story has it that she went to hit Marshall with her shooting stick but missed and hit the horse.

Suffice to say, Marshall never rode for her again, which meant him missing out on riding Paget's 1952 Gold Cup winner, Mont Tremblant, a half-brother to Lanveoc Poulmic. The ride went to Bryan's closest friend and playmate Dave Dick, of whom we'll hear more later. On the subject of Paget, Marshall told an amusing story to Sir Rupert Mackeson. One evening in the restaurant of Liverpool's Adelphi Hotel, which was then one of the smartest hotels in the world backed up by the transatlantic ocean liner trade, Paget came down to dinner alone and ordered two prawn cocktails and two fillet steaks with all the trimmings. Half an hour went by and no food had arrived so she beckoned the maitre d' over. 'Where's my food?' she asked. The maitre d' replied, 'Will you start without your guest?' To which The Hon. 'Miss P' replied, 'Who

---

[1] He won the race again on a further two occasions, in 1951 and 1952.

said anything about a guest?' Maitre d': 'Sorry madam, the prawn cocktails will be with you soonest.'

On Boxing Day 1950, Marshall won a second King George on the then Queen's (later the Queen Mother) Manicou, trained by Peter Cazalet. 'Always in a handy position, Manicou jumped perfectly in the hands of that superb steeplechase rider Bryan Marshall, and when Silver Fame drew up to him approaching the last fence, he sprinted away to win convincingly, to the enthusiastic applause of the huge crowd assembled to see the race,' was how John Hislop described the race in *The Horseman's Year.*

Marshall rode other winners for Her Majesty, including one Devon Loch. But just three months after his second King George win he had a very stressful family tragedy to contend with when his mother died in mysterious circumstances in Ireland. Her body, dressed in full hunting costume, was found floating in the Suir River, 12 miles from Waterford. The jury at the inquest returned a verdict that the deceased had been found drowned, but there was no evidence of how she got into the water.

'Binty' Marshall sadly never lived to see her son (who was going very well on top-weight Freebooter when falling at the Canal Turn in the 1952 Grand National) win back-to-back Nationals in 1953 and 1954 on the Vincent O'Brien-trained, Joe Griffin-owned pair Early Mist and Royal Tan. No jockey had won the race two years running since Ted Wilson on Roquefort in 1885 and the feat was not matched until Brian Fletcher on Red Rum twenty years later.

Marshall's National wins were quite contrasting and demonstrated different aspects of his skills in the saddle. On Early Mist he took the lead after the fourth fence of the second circuit when Ordnance fell, and was always going better than his nearest challenger, the Gold Cup winner Mont Tremblant, who had 12st 5lb to carry. He steered his charge, who was carrying 11st 2lb, to a facile 20-length victory in a race in which only five finished.

But that only tells half the story. Early Mist, a 20-1 shot, had fallen at the first fence in the previous year's Grand National when owned by J.V. Rank, and there were obvious doubts about him completing. Vincent O'Brien later said of the horse:

> He was not a natural jumper, and relied largely on getting his rider to make his mind up for him. I decided Bryan Marshall would be the ideal partner. He only sat on him once before the race, on the 17th March, when they jumped two fences. On dismounting, Bryan remarked, 'He's a hesitant sort. I agree with you – I'll have to do his thinking for him.' Bryan did exactly this with him at Liverpool

and the horse responded to his mastership. Valentine's was the only fence where he stood a bit far back, and brushed the fence hard. On the other hand, if Bryan had not asked him to take off when he did, he would probably have got too close, and fallen.

It is said that O'Brien told owner Griffin to 'have a good bet' on his horse and that he won around £100,000.

A year later, on Royal Tan, Marshall prevailed in the closest finish to the race since Battleship had beaten Royal Danieli by a head in 1938. It was a well-deserved victory as the horse had seen his chances disappear at the last fence in both 1951, when he recovered to finish second, and 1952, when he fell.

It seemed he might be denied again in 1954 as Tudor Line rallied strongly on the run-in and looked like he would catch him, but Marshall used all his strength to get his mount over the line to win by a neck. Considering Royal Tan was conceding exactly a stone to his rival, and was carrying top weight of 11st 7lb, it was some effort.

Again, there was an interesting backstory that made the jockey's exploits in the race even more impressive. Owner Joe Griffin was a classic wartime/ post-war wide boy spiv – rather like a Dublin version of the *Dad's Army* character Private Walker (who was also called Joe) – who always knew how to make money from the black market. Griffin's nickname was 'Mincemeat Joe' as he had found a loophole in the regulations regarding the use of sugar in the preparation of food in the late 1940s and made a fortune out of the sweet mincemeat that goes into Christmas mince pies. Another very paying venture he was involved in was the importation of shoes from Italy. He sent all the right-foot shoes to himself in Dublin by sea and on arrival refused to accept delivery and pay the import duty, so they were sold at a Customs and Excise auction, where he bought them for under one penny each. He had all the left-foot shoes shipped to Cork in a friend's name, and the refusal and then buying at auction scam was repeated. Marshall was to find out what a slippery character Mincemeat Joe was at the 1954 Grand National meeting as he was still owed £500 (around £20,000 in 2020's money) for his win on Early Mist. He told Griffin that unless he got the money he would not ride Royal Tan the next day. Somehow Joe got his hand on £450 in cash on the day before the National and gave it to Bryan, who was staying at the Adelphi. Marshall was still adamant that he would not ride Royal Tan unless he got the outstanding £50 and it was not till around 4.00 am on the Saturday morning that matters were settled, when Vincent O'Brien's brother Dermot managed to borrow the £50 and shove it under Bryan's bedroom door.

After all this drama, less than twelve hours later, Marshall had not only ridden another Grand National winner for Mr Griffin, but also provided Mincemeat Joe with a third big race winner of the meeting as he piloted Galatian to victory at odds of 6-1 in the Liverpool Hurdle.

Has there ever been such professionalism shown by a top jockey? Unfortunately Bryan was not so lucky in getting paid after Royal Tan's National win as soon afterwards Mincemeat Joe went bankrupt, and his two Grand National winning horses were sold. Marshall pursued Griffin through the courts, but in February 1955, the judge dismissed his claim of £2,781 that he said was due to him. This was in spite of Griffin admitting that he had bought diamond earrings and a pendant for his wife for £625 in December 1953 (after Early Mist's National win) and a diamante double-clasp brooch for £565. He had also given his wife fur coats (including a mink coat) and stoles. But it seemed he couldn't pay his jockey.

Marshall, though badly short-changed, wasn't destitute. After his first National win he had got married for the second time, to the very rich international showjumper Mary Whitehead.[2]

In December 1953, Marshall showed his prowess at Liverpool again when he rode the first three winners on the card, including two for the steward of the meeting, Lord Sefton. Two of the wins were over the new Mildmay steeplechase course. Aside from Liverpool, if there's one track Marshall rode particularly well it was Sandown, notwithstanding the Lanveoc Poulmic episode. In 1952, he had won the inaugural running of the Mildmay Memorial (named after the late amateur jockey Lord Mildmay, who had died from drowning in 1950) on the peer's own favourite horse, Cromwell, trained by his great friend Peter Cazalet. Marshall chalked up his fortieth career win at Sandown in November 1955. By the time he retired in 1957, he had ridden over 500 winners. He had already taken out a trainer's licence in 1954 (with his first success as a trainer-rider coming appropriately enough at Sandown in November 1954) and then turned to training full time at Berkeley House in Lambourn.

Sir Rupert Mackeson, an accomplished amateur rider in the 1960s, spent two summer holidays when still at Harrow riding out for the ex-champion jockey in Lambourn. He says:

---

[2] Mary's cousin, Sue Whitehead, was also an international showjumper and married trainer Roddy Armytage. Their son, Marcus Armytage, won the 1990 Grand National on Mr Frisk.

He was an interesting character. He was almost certainly the natural son of Atty Persse, who probably paid his Downside public school fees for a short period. He was a wonderful horseman. He rode show-jumping in the US and went well to hounds. As an ex-showjumper he was inclined to bully his horses and tell them where to take off. He was great out in the country, but his apprenticeship on the Flat meant he was more than useful at the finish.

Like all our other champions, Marshall was extremely brave. George Whiting's sports column in the *Londonderry Sentinel* on 18 November 1952 listed the injuries Marshall had by then suffered: 'Left arm broken in four places, two broken legs, one broken thigh, three broken collarbones, more broken ribs than he can remember, spells of concussion, black eyes, lacerations from top to toe.'

Whiting noted that at Fontwell the preceding month, Marshall had injured his left eye in a fall. Eight days later, he rode at Cheltenham wearing an eye patch, had another fall and then ended the day 'collecting face and chest injuries' when brought down by a loose horse. Marshall's response was:

> Think nothing of it. I should hate to have to count how many bones I've broken in my time, but it is all part of the business. You've got to take a few chances if you are going to be good at this or any other job. The too-careful fellows never get anywhere. In any case there's always plenty of bones.

The only gripe Marshall had was the relatively poor financial returns for jump jockeys. 'We fellows do not mind taking risks, but we are not paid half enough for taking them – especially with income tax at whatever it is percent.'

Whiting described Marshall as 'a champion rider of supreme artistry' and few, if any, who saw him would have disagreed with that assessment. Fitzgeorge-Parker went so far as to call him 'one of the greatest horsemen the world has ever seen'. Marshall had an almost uncanny instinct to understand what the horses he rode required, as his piloting of Early Mist in the 1953 Grand National demonstrated. Vincent O'Brien said of him, 'he always wanted to master any horse he sat on.' If a horse was in two minds about what to do – no problem, Marshall would help it make the right decision.

As to tactics, his preference for going on the inside was well known, so much so that he received the nickname 'Inside Maniac'. 'It was like an obsession with him, a kind of phobia,' says Graham Thorner, the 1970/71 champion jump jockey, who rode for Marshall when he was training.

When you were schooling for him he was very easy going but in races you HAD to go on the inside. I remember speaking to Fred Winter about it and he said that he saw Bryan get beat more than once when he was riding because he had been trapped on the inside. But he would always say that the inside was not only the shortest way round, it also meant you only had interference from one side. Yes, it was rather an obsession with him but I had the greatest respect for him and am actually very grateful for his advice, which helped me come a close-up fourth in my first ride in the Grand National [in 1971] and then win it in 1972 on Well To Do when I kept to the extreme inner throughout.

Thorner remembers Marshall as being an 'extraordinary man' who was remarkably tough.

His motto was 'Mind over Matter'. There was one story that he was in hospital with a broken leg but he told the nurse 'I want to walk'. So he got out of bed and walked to the window. He must have been in unbelievable pain but he did it. Everything was 'Mind over Matter' he'd say. … He was also the most immaculate of men. He'd always wear gloves to open stable and horsebox doors, he was always clean shaven, with his hair gelled down. He was always very smart.

Marshall gave up training in 1973 to run a horse transport business. He died aged 75, in hospital in Reading on 9 October 1991, having suffered a heart attack while recovering from a minor operation.

Dick Francis, who features later in this book, paid him a generous tribute: 'He was one of the all-time greats and never lost his courage and sense of humour through life's ups and downs.'

Big race wins
King George VI Chase 1947 & 1950 (Rowland Roy, Manicou)
Grand National 1953 & 1954 (Early Mist, Royal Tan).
Stayers' Hurdle 1953 (Jack Leal)

Chapter Four

Tim Molony

Champion 1948/49, 1949/50, 1950/51, 1951/52, 1954/55

'The Rubber Man'

'I've never believed in getting off too soon. I always reckoned to drive my horse into the ground – to the point of no return – before ever letting myself fall. You don't have so far to fall.'

Tim Molony, *The Book of Racing Quotations*

The first three champions featured in this book each won the title once in the post-war era. We now come to our first multiple winner. By winning the title five times from 1948/9 to 1954/5, the brilliant Tim Molony became, with the leading inter-war jockeys Fred 'Dick' Rees and Billy Stott, the joint third most successful champion since the title was first awarded in 1900. He only finished behind the six-time winner (Frank 'Titch' Mason 1901, 1902, 1904–07) and seven-time winner Gerry Wilson (1932/33 to 1937/38 and 1940/41).

Molony's sons Danny and Will pay tribute to their remarkable father. 'He was physically incredibly strong,' says Danny. 'He was as hard as nails – he rode in races, as jockeys did in those days – with injuries they regarded as minor but which nowadays would be judged as too serious to allow a rider back in the saddle.' 'These fellows were tough and hungry,' says Will. 'I can remember Tim saying that he used to ride for £1 a mile, a £3 fee for a 3-mile chase!'

In addition to his all-round toughness what helped Molony achieve the success he did was that he generally avoided very bad falls. 'His motto was "always get off at the bottom",' Danny recalls. His fellow jockeys called him 'The Rubber Man': Molony always bounced back. He combined strength in the saddle with remarkable finesse. Fred Winter, who was to succeed him as champion, described Molony as 'a most beautiful horseman'. 'Horses never appeared to pull with him. He always said, well you know if you pull against them, they pull against you. Give them a long rein and don't fight against them and they won't fight against you, which most of the time is perfectly true.'

Yet for all his success, and all the plaudits he received, Molony always insisted that his younger brother Martin, who was runner-up to him in 1949/50, but who had to retire at the age of 26 due to serious injury, was a better rider.

Tim Molony was born in Rathmore, County Limerick, Ireland, on 14 September 1919. He was educated at the Jesuit-run Mungret College, where he sat at the next desk to Dermot O'Brien, the brother of legendary trainer Vincent, for whom Molony later rode a Champion Hurdle and Gold Cup winner.

Like the champions who came before him he learnt his riding skills in the hunting field, and in particular, racing over banks in the west of Ireland. He became champion amateur in his home country in 1936, learning, he later admitted, 'style and finishing' from riding in bumpers (National Hunt Flat races). Danny Molony says his father was told to go professional by the Irish Jockey Club as they thought he was so good as an amateur (he won the title four years running) that he was 'taking the bread and butter out of the mouths' of other jockeys. Molony didn't think he could make a living riding in Ireland, where there were only meetings at weekends, so he came over to England in 1940. At the outbreak of the war Tim was 20 so it's fair to say that some of his best years as a jockey were sidelined by the hostilities and the restrictions on racing. It's worth noting that AP McCoy, the twenty-time champion, won his first title at the age of 21.

Tim, though, was not deterred by the hiatus and it didn't take long for him to make an impact after the war had finished. In March 1947 he was involved in a dramatic race over the Grand National fences at Aintree, which illustrates the extraordinary hardiness of the jump jockeys of the post-war era as well as the greater demands exacted from both horse and rider before the 'health and safety' era. In the Stanley Steeplechase every one of the sixteen runners fell. Two horses were killed. Molony won the race, having remounted Billykin. The *Dundee Courier* reported that the winning jockey 'received an ovation when he returned to the winners' enclosure, blood streaming from his face'. The second horse, called September Air, which was also remounted, passed the post a full ten minutes later.

Molony rode first for Sonny Hall at Russley Park, on the border of Berkshire and Wiltshire, then moved to Clifford Nicholson, and after that became stable jockey to the powerful Willie Stephenson yard at Royston in Hertfordshire. That set him up for his title bid in 1948/49.

On Boxing Day 1948, severe frost caused the cancellation of the King George card at Kempton and Wincanton, but Wetherby escaped and Molony was able to make up ground in the title race. He rode a four-timer on Brighter

Sandy, Freebooter (a subsequent Grand National winner), Caviar and Carmody to take his seasonal tally up to twenty-one and move him up to fourth place in the jockeys' championship. He continued in terrific form in early 1949. On 4 March, he brought his seasonal tally up to forty winners when he piloted Hypernod to success in the Holy War Handicap Chase at Lingfield.

The champion jockey Grand National jinx, which we've mentioned earlier, certainly affected Molony even when everything else was going well. On the day before the 1949 National, he rode a big race Aintree double, piloting Carmody to success in the Stanley Chase and winning the Champion Chase on Freebooter, where he benefited from the last fence fall of the leader, Silver Fame.

He had ridden George Owen's Russian Hero in the Grand National trial (then run at Leicester) in February but in the big race itself on 26 March he was on board Bricett, his partner a year earlier, when they had fallen. He had bought the horse for just £9 with Willie O'Grady (father of trainer Eddie O'Grady) for his mother Kit, but it was sold before it ran in the National. This time he came ninth after remounting. The race was won by ... yes, you've guessed it ... Russian Hero, at odds of 66-1.

Molony won his first title with sixty wins, fourteen clear from the 'Cock of the North' Arthur Thompson, but the following season faced stiff competition from his own brother, Martin. Martin Molony's CV was quite amazing. He rode his first winner over jumps at the age of 14 and by the time he was off the mark in England, in December 1947, he had already won the Irish National twice. But it wasn't just over jumps that he excelled; he was a top jockey on the Flat too. He rode the winners of three of the Irish Classics and finished third in the 1951 Epsom Derby, the same year he won the Cheltenham Gold Cup.

Unsurprisingly, Martin Molony is regarded by many shrewd judges as the greatest all-rounder in the history of the sport. It's certainly what Tim thought.

'Tim and Martin were really close but with totally different personalities,' says Will Molony. 'They both stayed at the same house in London for meetings such as Sandown and Hurst Park. It was said that on Sunday mornings Martin and Tim would be seen out together, Martin on his way to church and Tim on his way back from a nightclub!'

Sir Rupert Mackeson points to another difference between the brothers, who both possessed enormous courage. 'It was said that Martin learnt to overcome his fear and was an utterly fearless rider, whereas Tim never knew fear and was incredibly brave whether he was riding in races or out hunting.'

In 1949/50, Martin put in a spirited challenge for his brother's title despite spending half of his week in Ireland. He would come over on the boat to race in England and return across the Irish Sea a few days later. It was certainly an eventful season.

On 28 November, Tim and Martin, plus fellow jockey Leo McMurrow, were involved in a car crash near Newark on their way to Leicester races. Their vehicle overturned, but it didn't stop the Molonys both walking away unscathed and then each riding a winner when they got to the racetrack. McMurrow rode Russian Hero, the horse on which he won the Grand National, but this time the Aintree winner turned a complete somersault at the first fence. McMurrow again walked away unhurt, so you could say the three jockeys had a guardian angel looking after them that day.

Two days later, on 30 November, Tim rode his twenty-sixth and twenty-seventh winners of the season with a double at Haydock. At Wetherby on Boxing Day 1949, he enjoyed a festive four-timer for the second year running, with all four of his winners trained by Willie Stephenson. But then followed a losing run of twenty-seven rides, which was only broken when Molony won a chase on Queen of the Dandies at Leicester on 9 January 1950. The *Nottingham Evening Post* praised the 'great finish' Molony had ridden as he rallied his mount to pass 11-8 shot Cavaliero on the run-in. For good measure he doubled up on Archstone in the selling hurdle.

Molony had definitely got his mojo back. At Hurst Park on 18 January he got the better of his old rival Bryan Marshall in another thrilling finish to the January Chase. Riding the front-running Le Jacobin, he just held off the challenge from Marshall on Prince of Denmark to win by a neck. On 6 March, though, there was another setback: he was hurt in a car crash, his second of the season, about half a mile away from his home in Lincoln when he was driving to Worcester races in thick fog. That meant missing the Cheltenham Festival. It was a blow, but he more than made up for it in the years to come.

At the same time, brother Martin posted three winners at Southwell to close the gap. His tally in Britain was hugely impressive considering that in the season 1949/50 he rode ninety-four winners in Ireland, a record that stood until 1992 when broken by Charlie Swan. Tim rode his eightieth winner of the season at Ludlow on 26 April. He finished the campaign on ninety-five (from 438 rides), ahead of Martin, on sixty-two (from 219 rides), and Arthur Thompson, on sixty (from 232 rides).

In the 1950/51 season he faced another challenge from brother Martin and the likes of Bryan Marshall and Arthur Thompson, too. It was an abnormally wet winter, which meant many meetings had to be abandoned. On 23 November, it was reported that Tim had ridden a 'well-judged race' to win on the top-weight Kelek in a handicap chase at Doncaster. That was his twenty-fourth winner of the campaign. On 12 December, the *Sheffield Daily Telegraph* compared the rivalry of the Molony brothers with that of Fred and Billy Rees over twenty years earlier. The day before, at Birmingham, the brothers had ridden three winners between them: Martin had a double, while Tim had one. That put Martin on twenty-one winners, eight behind Tim, but on the day of 12 December itself, Arthur Thompson drew level with the reigning champion when he too rode a double at Birmingham. It was shaping into some title race.

The competition only inspired Molony to even greater efforts. The year 1951 was to prove a momentous one – in the course of it, he rode 112 winners. On 22 January he rode a double at Wolverhampton, on Spy Legend and Brown Jack III, bringing his total for the season up to forty-five. The first of those wins was classic Molony: trailing at the last, he got his mount up on the line to win by a neck.

That year at the Cheltenham Festival, Tim began a remarkable sequence when he piloted Hatton's Grace to victory (his third successive) in the Champion Hurdle on 6 March. He only got the ride because Aubrey Brabazon – who had ridden the horse to his first two Champion Hurdle successes – had been claimed to ride the favourite Average, and brother Martin, who was lined up as the replacement, was ill with a chill. It was a memorable renewal run in extremely testing conditions. Hatton's Grace was 11, but also in the race was National Spirit, the 1947 and 1948 winner, who was now 10. Molony timed his challenge to perfection. 'He delivered it as they jumped the last with such intensity that poor National Spirit was quite unnerved,' records Tim Fitzgeorge-Parker. 'Although he never touched a twig of that obstacle, he faltered on landing and fell heavily, leaving Hatton's Grace to gallop at the hill and beat the French pair (Pyrrhus III and Prince Hindou) by five lengths.' Molony was to win the race for a record four years in a row, the next three renewals on Willie Stephenson's Sir Ken, about whom we'll hear more later.

Flooding meant that the remaining two days of the 1951 Festival had to be postponed until the end of April. But when the Gold Cup was eventually run, Martin Molony won it on the 'grand old' 12-year-old Silver Fame, who beat Greenogue by a short head. The magnificent Molonys really were at the top of the racing world that spring.

Tim's momentum was only stopped (temporarily) when he broke his collarbone following a fall in a novices' steeplechase at Fontwell on 15 March. The doctor who treated him was quoted in the newspapers as saying it was doubtful that his patient would be able to make the Grand National, just three weeks away. However, make it he did, only to fall on the 6-year-old Arctic Gold.

Molony's third jockeys' title was achieved with eighty-three winners, putting him ahead of Bryan Marshall (58), Arthur Thompson (56) and brother Martin (45) in fourth place. Sadly, that was the last time that Martin was able to take part in the jump jockeys' championship. In September 1951, he suffered a crashing, career-ending and almost life-ending fall at Thurles in Ireland. Aged just 26, he was forced to retire from the sport in which he had excelled over the past twelve years. One can only imagine what further greatness he would subsequently have achieved.

In the 1951/52 season Tim Molony faced stiff competition from rising star Fred Winter, who had finished fifth in 1950/51. Winter broke his collarbone on the first day of the season and was out of action until early September, but then enjoyed a tremendous run. He still had the champion to catch, though. On 20 November, Tim earned the plaudits again for riding a 'brilliant finish' to win the Tamworth Hurdle at Birmingham. Red Trump led over the last but the champion forced his mount, D'Artagnan, up in the last 50 yards to win by half a length, at odds of 7-2. He got his half-century of winners for the season up in early December and went into 1952 with a clear lead in the jockeys' championship.

On 14 January, it was reported that Molony would be resting for a fortnight after an X-ray found he had a crack in his head, following a fall at Plumpton the previous week. A few weeks later saw the death of the ruling monarch, King George VI, and the accession of his daughter Elizabeth to the throne. A new 'Elizabethan Age' may have been dawning in Britain, but on the racecourse, it was business as usual for Molony.

At the Cheltenham Festival in early March he rode the first of his three wins on the brilliant French-bred hurdler Sir Ken in the Champion Hurdle. The 'big raking bay', as described by Tim Fitzgeorge-Parker, had won his previous eight starts over hurdles in England with ease. He was prominent throughout the race and forged clear after the last to win by 2 lengths. A year later, Tim took it up earlier than he would have wished, due to the lack of pace, but still won by 2 lengths from Galatian. The toughest win of all came in 1954, and required all of Molony's skill and determination to seal the deal. 'I started to ride hard on Sir Ken two out and realised Impney was a big danger. The old horse showed all his brilliance at the last jump and ran on to win after one of the hardest races I have ever had,' Molony said afterwards. Not surprisingly, he regarded Sir Ken as the greatest hurdler of all time, or at least the best he had ever known. '[He] was a terrific jumper. Fantastic! He stood off so far at his hurdles that you could feel your tummy going.' The gelding's record of sixteen straight victories stood for nearly sixty years until broken by the Paul Nicholls-trained staying hurdler Big Buck's in 2012, another horse who was so good he scared away the opposition, although admittedly in a less competitive division.

Back to 1952, on 10 March, despite his Cheltenham success, Molony was just eleven ahead of Fred Winter in the title race. A week later, he increased his lead by riding a double at Doncaster, while Fred was having a day's rest. On 22 March, Winter's challenge effectively ended when he suffered a cracked arm at Newbury when his mount dived through the wing. He returned to action in April, and although he had a late flurry, winning fifteen races in the last fortnight, Molony maintained his advantage.

On the final day of the season, at Huntingdon on 2 June, he rode the winner of the first race, but three second places in the four races open to him left him on ninety-nine, agonisingly just one short of his century. Molony had now won four titles and so it's a good time to analyse why he had been so successful. In addition to his brilliance in the saddle, and his avoidance of heavy falls, there was also what he did away from the racetrack to consider. 'He was known as Telephone Tim,' says son Danny. 'He was the first jockey to ring around for rides; he didn't have an agent. Tim was also one of the first jockeys to use a plane to get to the races.'

Being based in the North Midlands also meant he could get to tracks around the country more easily than a jockey based in either the North or South, an important factor in the era before motorways. Molony not only rode more winners than anyone else – he also had more rides ... sometimes a lot more. For instance, in his first four championship seasons his number of rides was 378, 437, 430 and 438. The number of rides for the runner-up in those seasons was, by contrast, 232, 219, 254 and 402. The story of the 1952/53 season, in which Fred Winter won his first title, is told in the next chapter.

Although he was dethroned as champion, Molony did have the satisfaction of winning his first (and only) Gold Cup on the Vincent O'Brien-trained Knock Hard, in the same year he completed the Champion Hurdle-Gold Cup double and also won the Arkle (then known as the Cotswold Chase). Knock Hard, who, like Hatton's Grace, was owned by Harry and Mary Keogh, had fallen at the second last in the 1952 Gold Cup when holding every chance and had a habit of clouting at least once fence. On the day of the big race he was an easy-to-back 11-2 chance. But on fast ground, and given a great ride by Tim, he never made a single mistake. Molony made his challenge approaching the last and went on to win by 5 lengths from Halloween, ridden by Fred Winter. In 1953/54, Winter was out injured for the whole campaign and the championship was won by Dick Francis, who is featured in Chapter Six.

But in 1954/55, the 'Rubber Man' bounced back to win his fifth title. Among the highlights was a four-timer at Liverpool in December 1954, which included a treble for Willie Stephenson. There was a tremendous tussle between Molony and Fred Winter for the championship that year, which proved to be the closest title race since the war. Winter drew level with and then overhauled Molony in the final fortnight but Molony 'equalised' with a win at Uttoxeter. The two men were on sixty-five winners apiece when it came to the last day of the season, Whit Monday. Fred had to go to Hurst Park to ride his old favourite Halloween (on whom he had won two King Georges) in the Queen Elizabeth Chase, the only jumps race on a mixed card. But Halloween was unplaced and Tim, who had a book of four rides at Towcester, won on two hot favourites.

It looked as if Molony would win his sixth title in 1955/56, as he led for most of the campaign, but this time Winter had the last laugh with a great late run to win 74-70. Winter got married two days later and Tim, who was one of the many guests, joked that the title was his wedding present. That year he did have the compensation of winning the Costwold Chase at the Cheltenham Festival on his old friend Sir Ken, who had now been sent chasing.

Molony's lack of serious injuries – helped by a sensible policy of avoiding steeplechasers confined to 4-year-olds in which falls were more common – meant that he was still riding at the top as he approached 40. His luck, however, finally ran out at Easter 1958 when one bone-crushing fall, which left him with a broken femur, seven broken ribs and a dislocated shoulder, ended his career. It was on Oxo in the Midlands National at Uttoxeter. One year later, the same horse, under Michael Scudamore, won the Grand National. The champion jockeys' Aintree jinx had struck again.

What makes the hoodoo all the more baffling in Molony's case is that he otherwise had a great record at Aintree. He won the Grand Sefton twice and, in addition to his earlier four-timer in 1954, also had a hat-trick at the Becher Chase meeting in December 1957, including a win on the 1956 National winner E.S.B. Yet in the National itself, Tim's record, like so many other great champions, was distinctly underwhelming. His mounts fell in eight of his first nine attempts, and the other horse, Dominick's Bar, whom his brother Martin had ridden to victory in the 1950 Irish National, dropped dead after the second fence. The best he managed was fifth places on Key Royal in 1956 and Goosander in 1958.

The Aintree Blue Riband aside, what Molony achieved in his career was quite outstanding. He remains the only man to win four Champion Hurdles in a row. He was the first National Hunt jockey to reach 700, 800 and then

900 winners. He rode fifty winners at Cheltenham, arguably the toughest National Hunt course on which to succeed as the racing is so competitive. And his post-war record of five titles stood for thirty years, until John Francome broke it in the 1980s.

After he had retired from the saddle, Tim began training near Melton Mowbray in Leicestershire in 1960, first with a mixed licence but from 1963 focusing on the Flat. That was so he and wife Stella, whom he married in 1951, could go hunting in the winter. Ironically, given his bad luck in the big race itself, he went on to buy the most successful Grand National horse of all time, the three-time winner Red Rum, for a 'giveaway' 400 guineas as a yearling, and trained him to dead-heat in his first race at Liverpool, a 5-furlong selling plate for 2-year-olds, in 1967. He bought Red Rum for Manchester businessman Maurice Kingsley, who owned Sir Ken.

Molony's son Will recalls:

> As a boy I loved accompanying Daddy to the races as even well after he had retired from race riding there were always strangers coming up to him to say hello and reminisce on some of his greatest triumphs. Without exception he shared his stories, was ever popular and a great man for parties!

Although he won some good races, Molony did not enjoy the same level of success as a trainer that he had grown used to as a jockey. 'He was a superb judge of a horse but too nice really to succeed in business; he would give you the last penny in his pocket,' says Danny Molony. Tim found chasing owners who wouldn't pay their bills more difficult than riding steeplechase winners.

He retired from training in 1981 and passed away in December 1989, aged 70. Molony told his son Danny that few would remember him in the years to come because, for all his success, he failed to win a Grand National. But how can we ever forget a jockey who won the title five times in a period when there were so many great jockeys riding – and who did it all with a smile on his face? Fittingly, statues of Tim and his brother Martin (who died in 2017 just before his ninety-second birthday) stand at Limerick Racecourse to greet the jockeys when they go out and remind them of the magnificent men who came before them.

Big race wins
Champion Hurdle 1951 (Hatton's Grace), 1952, 1953, 1954 (Sir Ken)
Grand Sefton Chase 1952 (Wot No Sun), 1956 (Key Royal)
Gold Cup 1953 (Knock Hard)

Chapter Five

Fred Winter

Champion 1952/53, 1955/56, 1956/57, 1957/58

More than a Winter's Tale

'He was a superb human being, if he'd never gone into racing Fred Winter would have gone to the top of whatever he chose.'
Richard Pitman, stable jockey to Winter in the 1970s

The date: 17 June 1962. The place: Auteuil, on the outskirts of Paris. The weather is hot and steamy. Fred Winter, four-time champion jockey, is riding Mandarin, dual winner of the King George and Hennessy Gold Cup and the gallant winner, at the age of 11, of that year's Cheltenham Gold Cup. What happens next is quite remarkable, even in the 'stranger than fiction' annals of jump racing. As he approaches the fourth of the thirty fences, Mandarin's rubber snaffle bit snaps. 'Suddenly Fred found himself with no control at all and twenty-one fences to jump,' wrote Tim Fitzgeorge-Parker, one of only two British journalists at the race. Fred later conceded that he didn't know what on earth to do. 'I couldn't pull him up and I was too windy to throw myself off.' Somehow, horse and rider managed to stay in the race. 'As they went away from the stands for the last time, Fred was badly squeezed for room and it seemed that the bay favourite could run out. By sheer power of his legs, his jockey kept him inside the ring,' Fitzgeorge-Parker reported.

Mandarin jumped the last fence in front but broke down 3 furlongs from home when being strongly challenged by the French horse Lumino. Yet the little steeplechaser with bottomless reserves of courage kept going. The horses passed the line together and a photo finish was announced. When the result was announced, and Mandarin and Winter declared the winners by a head, Fitzgeorge-Parker said he saw hardened English, French and American racegoers crying openly with tears streaming down their faces.

It's likely no horse or jockey at Auteuil has ever had the reception that Mandarin and Winter got as they were led into the winners' enclosure.

Everyone present knew they had witnessed something very special. But the story doesn't end there.

Winter, like his mount, was utterly exhausted, yet somehow he summoned up the energy to ride a driving finish to win the next race too, the 4-year-old Champion Hurdle, on Beaver II, for Captain Ryan Price. He had wasted in the Turkish baths to reduce his weight to 9st 10lb to ride the horse and the fact that he had arrived at the course in such a weak state to begin with puts his heroics on an even higher level. 'I have never seen a man in such depths,' fellow jockey Stan Mellor, who helped Winter to weigh in, remarked later. 'You would think he'd be too weak to ride again for days, let alone go out half an hour later.'

That epic day at Auteuil, almost sixty years ago, will be remembered so long as horse racing exists. It was the greatest moment in a glittering career that had many high points. Yet Winter's achievements would all have seemed far-fetched considering that he was an ex-Flat jockey who broke his back after just his third victory over jumps and came within a whisker of chucking it all in.

The National Hunt jockey, who Atty Persse judged to be 'the greatest of them all', was born in Andover, Hampshire, on 20 September 1926. His mother came from good Irish farming stock, and his father, also named Fred, was a successful Flat jockey who won the 1911 Oaks on Cherimoya when he was just 16. When Fred jnr was born his father was first jockey to trainer Frank Hartigan at Weyhill; the family later moved to Newmarket and then near to the Epsom Downs.

Given his background Fred was only ever going to work with horses. As a youngster he enjoyed showjumping and was very good at it: at the age of 13 he won joint first place at the Richmond Royal Horse Show. At the same age, he rode for the first time under Rules, finishing ninth for his father in a 6-furlong nursery at Newbury. The same horse, Tam o'Shanter, became his first winner at Salisbury in May 1940. Fred snr wanted his son to have more opportunities so arranged for him a move to Newmarket. But it was a hard time to make an impact. Racing was limited due to the war and Fred only rode two winners in 1941. Too young to join the RAF, he worked in a factory where damaged aircraft were repaired. Later on, he joined the Parachute Regiment, and then served in Palestine.

It was there that he made the decision that was to change his life. Winter was sitting in the officers' mess one day reading an illustrated magazine and saw photographs of horses in a steeplechase. His weight ruled him out of a return to Flat racing, so why not try his hand at National Hunt? He wrote to his father asking if he could ride some of his jumpers. On demobilisation leave in December 1947, Lieutenant Fred Winter rode his father's veteran chaser Carton over three fences in the paddock, and then approached a family friend for a ride at Kempton on Boxing Day.

What happened over the next few months classically illustrates the ups and downs of jump racing. Fred's inexperience was on show in his first ride as he set too fast a pace on Bambino II, who finished exhausted in fifth place in a 2-mile hurdle race.

But the very next day, at the same racetrack, he rode his first winner, partnering Carton to a 6-length success in a 2-mile chase. The *Sporting Chronicle* hailed 'a welcome addition to our ranks of NH riders', yet, just three rides later, Winter was on the deck following a fall from Carton's half-brother and was out of action for a month with a dislocated shoulder. He ended that first season with nine winners, and could have looked forward realistically to further progression in 1948/49. But on only his third ride that season he suffered a crashing fall at Wye in which he broke two of his vertebrae, putting him out of action for a year. It would have been quite understandable if, during that enforced year out, Winter had decided to call it a day and accept that jump racing was not for him. But as he later admitted, he had to prove to himself he had the guts to carry on. When he did return to action, he did so gingerly. After a safety-first ride on Carton he was told by a man in the paddock that he had never seen such a windy ride in his life. Had Fred lost his nerve? The turning point was a race at Hereford. 'There were nineteen runners … and the ground was not inviting for anyone contemplating a fall,' writes David Hedges, Winter's biographer. Fred was nervous, but when the 'bowler-hatted official' shouted 'Jockeys please', he saw that the first man to stand up and make his way to the paddock was Jack Moloney, who had finished second in the Grand National three times and who was still riding moderate horses around the country meetings at the age of 52. 'Honest to God,' thought Fred, 'if that man can get up and walk out like that with no nerves at all, what the hell is wrong with you, Winter?' Moloney won the race, but more importantly, Fred had got his courage back.

In 1949/50 he rode eighteen winners. In 1950/51, it was thirty-eight.

By now he had struck up a partnership with Findon trainer Captain Ryan Price that was to last sixteen years and lead to much glory for both men. In 1951/52, Winter more than doubled his previous tally by riding eighty-five winners from over 400 rides and but for two injury-enforced lay-offs he would probably have overhauled Tim Molony. He clearly was the coming man. 'He rides beautifully throughout a race and it is a pleasure to watch him gradually bringing his mount into a challenging position. He often wins his races between the last two fences and then rides a finish worthy of a flat race jockey,' enthused journalist Richard Baerlein.

That season, 1952/53, Winter not only broke Molony's run of championships, he also recorded the highest ever total of winners (121) and became the first jockey to get a century up since Fred Rees in 1924. His strike rate was a very impressive 25.6 per cent, meaning he won on more than one in four of his rides.

Two factors in particular helped him forge ahead of the opposition. First, Price's yard was on fire, setting a National Hunt record of seventy-six wins. Fourteen of Fred's first sixteen winners were for his main employer. Then, in November, his best pal Dave Dick suffered a freak injury and Winter took over on leading owner Dorothy Paget's horses. That led to five wins on the promising young chaser Lanveoc Poulmic, a half-brother to Paget's Gold Cup winner Mont Tremblant, who, as we've seen, was earlier the ride of Bryan Marshall. 'Fred Winter next Jump Champ?' asked Templegate of the *Daily Herald* on 26 November, and so it proved.

At Kempton on Boxing Day 1952, Winter won his biggest race to date, the King George VI Chase on the 7-4 favourite Halloween. In March 1953, he rode Halloween in the Cheltenham Gold Cup, but could only finish second. He had one win at the Cheltenham Festival that year but did win the Triumph Hurdle (then run at Hurst Park) on the Ryan Price-trained Clair Soleil. Winter passed his century at Sandown Park on Imperial Cup day and both the Queen and the Queen Mother came down to the paddock to congratulate him. 'If ever a man was riding on a cloud it was that day at Sandown Park, when the public flocked to cheer him,' wrote David Hedges. He rode his final winners of the season at Fontwell on 25 May and such was his dominance that year, he finished all of forty-eight winners clear of runner-up Dick Curran.

Winter had reached the top of his profession, but the very nature of jump racing means you're only ever one fence away from coming down to earth with an almighty bang. He thoroughly enjoyed his summer as champion, but at Newton Abbot on 1 August, at the very first fence of the first race of the 1953/54 season, Fred broke his left leg from a fall on Cent Francs in a 2-mile novices' chase. It was a compound fracture and a number of complications kept him out of action all season. Yet Fred later wrote philosophically about his dramatic reversal of fortune: 'I think this is the really wonderful aspect of this game. No matter how successful you are you can come to earth again very, very quickly. Any fellow who starts getting big-headed is only asking for trouble, because along comes something which slaps him down in very smart time.'

It was to be almost one year later, at Newton Abbot on 31 July 1954, that Fred returned to competitive action at the start of the new 1954/55 season.

Even then his leg was still hurting. He got beaten on his first ride but won on his second. It was only a selling hurdle, but how relieved he must have been to be back in the winners' enclosure.

That season he fought a terrific tussle with Tim Molony for the Jump Jockeys' title. He won his second King George on Halloween in December. Despite fighting the flu he also won a thrilling 2-mile hurdle race on the second day of the Christmas Kempton meeting. 'If Fred Winter continues in his present form he may be voted TV personality of the year,' said the *Daily Herald*.

On 9 March 1955, he won the Champion Hurdle on Clair Soleil for Ryan Price, defeating, among others in the twenty-one-strong field, Molony on Sir Ken, who was going for his fourth consecutive win. Fred's instructions had been to come late, but he found himself in front with a mile to go. He decided not to hold the horse back and to head for home. On the run-in, though, he was passed by Stroller. Fred riding with all his power got Clair Soleil to make one last effort and he landed the race by a head. He returned to the winners' enclosure to a rollocking from Ryan Price, who wasn't happy he had disobeyed orders. It was, he later admitted, one of only three rockets he received from Price in all the years of riding for him.

As we saw in the previous chapter, Winter lost out on the jockeys' championship on the final day of the season to Tim Molony, but a year later he was able to turn the tables on his old rival. He got the 1955/56 season off to the best possible start by winning the first race, at Newton Abbot, on Alfaraiso. Molony 'equalised' on the same card, and indeed led for most of the 1955/56 campaign, but Winter caught up in April. Molony then went ahead again, but the challenger pulled clear in May, winning 74-70.

It was a very happy time, for just two days after the season finished, Fred married Diana, whom he had first met and fallen in love with during his enforced year off.

In season 1956/57, Winter not only retained his title with eighty wins, finishing twenty-two clear of the runner-up Michael Scudamore, he also ended his own Aintree hoodoo. Prior to 1957 he had failed to get round in a number of attempts in the Grand National. His mount that season, the giant 17½-hands gelding Sundew, had fallen in the previous two Nationals, including under Fred in 1956, and had jumped abysmally in the 1956 Grand Sefton. The 11-year-old, who had gone off at 8-1 a year earlier, was now a 20-1 shot, with many punters, not unreasonably, believing his chance had gone. But Fred always believed in the horse.

The turning point in his Aintree fortunes was talking, ahead of the 1957 race, to ex-jockey Dudley Williams, who had won the 1933 National on

Kellsboro' Jack and had twice been placed. Winter asked him for his opinion of the best way around Aintree. Williams told him to jump about the middle of the left half of each fence the whole way round and that consequently became the route that Fred followed in all his subsequent races at the course. Winter and Sundew were in front from after the fourth fence onwards, but it was not plain sailing. Sundew ploughed through a few fences and pitched on landing at second Becher's. He looked to be running on empty after he cleared the last but Winter got his mount home, to record an 8-length success over the Scottish-trained Wyndburgh. He had finally won the most famous steeplechase in the world.

While the National was the icing on the cake, Fred was consistently among the winners all season. His longest losing run was seventeen rides. His title campaign was helped by avoiding serious injury, though he did lose the top of a finger following a fall in a hurdles race at Sandown in November.

David Hedges told an amusing story about Winter after he had ridden a double at Newbury on 27 December 1956. An American hunting enthusiast called Dudley Fort was staying with the Winters. 'On the way back from Newbury races they called at Oxford, where Diana was due to see the gynaecologist for a check-up. After he had examined her, the doctor informed Diana that she was going to have twins, which prompted the remark from Dudley Fort: 'Gee what a day. A double in the afternoon and a double in the evening. What a guy you are, Winter!'

His hot streak continued into the new year. He got 1957 off to a flyer with a win at Cheltenham's New Year meeting on Variety Club and doubled up with victory on Fare Time. A day later he won the Long Distance Handicap Hurdle on Marally.

'Rarely has the champion jockey, Fred Winter, ridden in better form than this season, and his consistency has certainly earned its reward. He has already ridden over 40 winners, and looks sure, barring accidents, to be champion yet again,' reported the *Shields Daily News* on 16 January 1957.

And so he was, ending the season on eighty winners.

Winter won his fourth and final title in 1957/58, in what some regarded as the master jockey's greatest season of them all. From riding the winner of the very first race of the campaign at Newton Abbot, Happy Mullet, for Ryan Price, Fred never looked back. He rode the 500th win of his jumping career on Taxidermist at Ludlow on 31 October and passed the fifty mark for the season with a double at Nottingham on 29 January. After he had ridden Pounding to victory in a long-distance hurdle at Sandown in January 1958, the *Sporting Life*'s Tom Nickalls enthused: 'I feel sorry for anyone who has to ride a finish against this inexorable and superlative performer, for it seems no matter what you do, Fred Winter's horse gets there just in front.'

Winter's fourth title was achieved with eighty-two winners (twenty-three clear of runner-up Tim Brookshaw), and a strike rate of 22.84 per cent. He would probably have landed his fifth title – and his fourth in a row in 1958/59 – had he not fractured his skull in a heavy fall at Leicester in early April. That allowed Tim Brookshaw, whose story is told in Chapter Seven, to beat him by nine. Just a month before his fall, Fred had ridden five winners at the Cheltenham Festival, including his second Champion Hurdle, on Fare Time for Ryan Price.

He continued to ride with his customary brilliance for five more seasons. He could, and should, have landed another title in 1959/60, as he was six wins ahead of Stan Mellor in early May. But with a lead of one, going into the last day of the season, Fred decided to join his family on holiday in Cornwall. Mellor went instead to Uttoxeter and rode two winners to pip him for the title.

That was to be Winter's last title challenge but not the end of the big race wins. In March 1961, at the Cheltenham Festival, he won his third Champion Hurdle, on Eborneezer, for Ryan Price, and then two days later, his first Gold Cup, on the Don Butchers-trained Saffron Tartan. He also won the Triumph Hurdle on Cantab for Price, at Hurst Park. In 1962, he won the Gold Cup again on Mandarin, and a second Grand National, on the Ryan Price-trained Kilmore, once again beating Wyndburgh into second place, as he had done five years earlier. A few months later came his epic win on Mandarin in the Grand Steeplechase de Paris.

During the calendar year of 1962, Winter not only won top races in France, but in Ireland (Carraroe in the Galway Plate) and the United States, where he rode Moonsun to victory in the Temple Gwathmey Chase, the most valuable race in the American jumping calendar. Fred contemplated retirement following a bad fall at Chepstow in April 1963, but decided to go on for one more season. That same year he became the first jump jockey to be honoured for services to the sport, when he received a CBE.

As the 1963/64 season progressed, racegoers knew they were witnessing the final circuit of a National Hunt legend. On 29 January and 1 February 1964, Winter rode five winners from six rides at Sandown and Windsor. At Newbury on 29 February he rode four winners from five rides.

There was a sting in the tail that final season as Ryan Price lost his licence to train following the return to form of the back-to-back Schweppes Gold Trophy Hurdle winner Rosyth. He later reapplied and got his licence back, but in the meantime his horses had to be dispersed. Syd Dale, formerly Price's head lad, took over the handling of Kilmore, and Fred rode the 14-year-old again in the 1964 Grand National. The pair fell at the twenty-first fence when still travelling well. Fred thought he would have won.

His last day in the saddle was at Cheltenham on 11 April 1964. It was some occasion. 'They came by the trainload (£3 return, Paddington to the racecourse station first class; £2 second class) to cheer him as a jockey for the last time,' wrote Peter O'Sullevan. Sadly, Fred didn't go out with a winner and came sixth in his last-ever ride in public. But what a record he could look back on! From a total of 4,284 rides in Britain since 1947, he had ridden 923 winners, 577 second places and 509 third places. He had fallen 319 times. His wins-to-rides ratio was almost one in four.

What made him so exceptional? Tim Fitzgeorge-Parker believed one of his most priceless assets was his ability to leave a horse entirely alone when necessary. 'Because he was so intelligent, Fred quickly learnt to leave his horses to their own devices. And because he was a genius, he instinctively differentiated, choosing the right horses and the right moment for individual treatment.'

Winter found the key to horses that other jockeys couldn't. Fitzgeorge-Parker cites the example of Halloween. On his six rides on the Bill Wightman-trained horse from 1951 to 1953, Winter won five times. But from eight starts the following season when Fred was out of action, and Halloween was ridden by four different jockeys, he only won once, and a minor race at that. When Winter returned on Halloween he won four of his seven starts, including another King George and a second place in the Cheltenham Gold Cup.

One can also cite Winter's determination to seek advice where necessary, as he did on the Grand National with Dudley Williams. The way he had to overcome his fear in becoming a jump jockey also helped. We have to mention Winter's faith, too. A church-going Catholic, he admitted, 'One was living with fear the whole time, particularly after I broke my leg. It helped me to be able to get down and pray for courage – which I did quite often.'

It was surely racing's shame that Winter was told there was no chance of him becoming a National Hunt starter following his retirement from the saddle. Yet that disappointing cloud had a rather large silver lining as it meant that he had no other option but to start training. He made an incredible start, winning the Grand National with two different horses (Jay Trump, 1965, and Anglo, 1966) in his first two seasons. By strange coincidence, a Scottish-trained horse (the gallant Freddie) once again finished second to Winter's two National winners as a trainer, as Wyndburgh had done when he was a jockey. Winter's yard at Uplands in Lambourn became established as the most powerful in the country. By February 1970 he had already passed the 200-winner mark and joked it was more than he had achieved in his first five years as a jockey. He won the jump trainers' championship title eight times from 1970 to 1985 and for five years in a row from 1970/71 to 1974/75. In 1973/74 he became the first jumps trainer to win prize money in excess of £100,000 in one season. Among the big races wins were four Champion Hurdles (with Bula in 1971 and 1972, Lanzarote in 1974, and Celtic Shot in 1988), two King Georges (with Pendil in 1972 and 1973), and the Gold Cup (with Midnight Court in 1978). That last success was particularly poignant given that Winter had lost two of his greatest equine stars, Bula and Lanzarote, following injuries at the National Hunt Festival a year earlier. Midnight Court's victory meant that Winter became the first person to win the 'Big Three' – the Grand National, the Champion Hurdle and the Gold Cup – as both a jockey and a trainer. No one has matched the feat since, or is probably ever likely to.

'His attention to detail was quite extraordinary,' says David Gandolfo. 'I remember he arrived at our yard early one morning to discuss me training for Sheikh Ali Abu Khamsin (a leading owner in the early to mid-1980s). He had gone back through every one of my runners in the last two years.'

Winter suffered a stroke in 1980 followed by a second in 1987, which was accompanied by a fall on the stairs. That left him with some loss of speech and physically disabled; he was to spend the rest of his days in a wheelchair. He died on 5 April 2004, aged 77, and the whole racing world mourned. Three days after Winter had retired from the saddle in 1964, a special 'tribute luncheon' was held for him at The Savoy. Fred had to make a speech in response to all the heartfelt tributes and what he said spoke volumes about the man. He thanked everyone who had made his success possible, including, of course, his family, his doctor, his physio and Ryan Price, before saying: 'But these aren't all. There are the gatemen at courses all over the country and all those newspaper sellers who can make your day with a grin and a cheery "good morning". These are the people, ALL of them, who have given me my career. Thank you.'

We thank you too, Fred, for all that you gave us.

Big race wins (as a jockey)
King George VI Chase 1952, 1954 (Halloween), 1960 (Saffron Tartan)
Champion Hurdle 1955 (Clair Soleil), 1959 (Fare Time), 1961 (Eborneezer)
Grand National 1957 (Sundew), 1962 (Kilmore)
Gold Cup 1961 (Saffron Tartan), 1962 (Mandarin)

Chapter Six

Dick Francis

Champion 1953/54

Stranger than Fiction

'I heard one man say to another, a little while ago, "Who did you say that was? Dick Francis? Oh, yes, he's the man who didn't win the National." What an epitaph!'

Dick Francis, *The Sport of Queens*

The 'Grand National champion jockeys' hoodoo' is a running theme throughout this book, but were any of our featured riders quite so unlucky as Dick Francis?

The 1953/54 champion was less than 50 yards from the winning post when riding the Queen Mother's Devon Loch in the 1956 National, but the horse famously did the splits and big race glory was snatched from horse and rider in the cruellest fashion. Francis later wrote:

The calamity which overtook us was sudden, terrible and completely without warning to either the horse or me. In one stride he was bounding smoothly along, a poem of controlled motion; in the next, his hind legs stiffened and refused to function. He fell flat on his belly, his limbs splayed out sideways and backwards in unusual angles, and when he stood up he could hardly move.

Various theories were put forward to explain Devon Loch's dramatic collapse, but according to Francis:

Heart failure, ghost jump, cramp, and a shock wave of sound may still not include the real cause of his fall, and in this tantalising mystery there is no Sherlock Holmes to unravel its elementariness on the last page. What happened to Devon Loch is Devon Loch's secret, and I doubt even he remembered it afterwards.

The most humorous theory for the capitulation came in 1991, from *The People* newspaper (as cited in *Racing's Great Characters* by Graham Sharpe), which reported that the horse had an over-tight girth. Reporter Brian Madley announced: 'Today I can reveal that Devon Loch's back legs almost certainly gave way because of the most natural reason in the world – it let rip with a good, old-fashioned fart.'

Whether or not he was literally 'gone with the wind', it wasn't the first time the gods had failed to shine on Francis at Aintree. In his book *Fearless: The Tim Brookshaw Story*, Chris Pitt records that in the Molyneux Chase, another race over the National fences in 1951, Francis had been leading on the run-in when his horse, Possible, suddenly faltered, swished his tail and pulled himself up. 'For Francis, the manner of Possible's defeat provided an unwelcome and prescient foretaste of what was to occur on the Queen Mother's Devon Loch,' Pitt writes. Then there was the Russian Hero story.

As an amateur rider attached to George Owen's yard in Cheshire in the late 1940s he had forged a successful partnership with a horse called Russian Hero. He helped save the horse's life in 1948 when it came down with colic, by keeping it walking all through the night. Earlier that year, Francis had taken on the position as second jockey to Lord Bicester, to be available while Martin Molony, brother of Tim, was away riding in Ireland. Lord Bicester had some of the best horses in the country, and of course Francis was excited at getting the job. He would combine riding for Owen and for Bicester's trainer George Beeby in Berkshire. That year, Francis was due to ride Parthenon (whom he had partnered to second place in the Grand Sefton) in the Grand National. Martin Molony was booked for Roimond, the main hope of Lord Bicester. But a few days before the 1949 National Molony was injured, so Francis, who had ridden Roimond to second place in the 1948 King George VI Chase, got the ride. The top weight ran a great race, and with a mile to go Francis thought he might win. In fact, Roimond finished second to a 66-1 outsider – an uncertain stayer and sometimes iffy jumper who would fall at the first fence in the following year's National. The name of the horse?

Russian Hero!

The horse Francis had previously partnered to victory and whose life he had helped to save had denied him National success. What made it worse for Francis was that George Owen had wanted to run Russian Hero in an easier race that week, but his owner, Fernie Nicholson, a tenant farmer of the Duke of Westminster, insisted he went for the National. Perhaps the fact that he had £10 on his horse at odds of 300-1 might have had something to do with it.

Francis so easily could have won two Grand Nationals, but ended up winning none. But at least his second great ambition, of becoming champion jump jockey, was achieved.

Richard Stanley Francis was born at his maternal grandparents' farm in Pembrokeshire on Halloween 1920. He learnt to ride when he was 5, on a donkey. Like other champion jockeys, he was certainly bred for the part. His grandfather, Willie Francis, and his half-brother, Robert Harries, were both top amateurs in South West Wales in the late nineteenth and early twentieth centuries. His father Vincent was a jockey too, whose career was truncated by the First World War. When Dick was born, Vincent was manager of a hunting stables near Maidenhead. 'I was extremely fortunate in the circumstances of my father's job, and few boys can ever have had more opportunity than I had of learning to ride every possible sort of pony,' he later wrote.

He graduated from gymkhanas to the show ring but his biggest passion was hunting. 'My dreams were filled with hedges rushing past me and foxes of super-vulpine speed and cunning streaking ahead of me, and my waking hours were divided between memories of the last hunt and plans for the next one,' he recalled.

He left school at 15 and set his heart on becoming an amateur jockey for a steeplechasing yard. He had already ridden out on the beach for Tenby trainer David Harrison and so had some experience. When he was 16 his father took him to his old friend Gwynne Evans, who was training for J.V. Rank at Druid's Lodge. Evans told Dick, 'You're a bit too young, come back when you're seventeen.' Dick could hardly wait but then a few months later came the awful news that Evans had been killed in a car crash.

Francis then helped his parents as they set up their own riding stables near Wokingham. He was going to ride point-to-pointers for Oliver Dixon in early 1939, but then, more bad luck, as Dixon died.

It did seem that Francis was fated never to get going as a jockey, especially when the Second World War broke out shortly afterwards. In 1940 Francis volunteered for the Cavalry, but they didn't want him. He ended up in the RAF. He worked first as an airframe fitter, but really wanted to be a pilot. Each time an interview for pilot training came up he tried to think of a hobby that would convince the board to take him on. But bird-watching, kite-flying and star-gazing did not move them. Finally he decided to tell the truth. A 'rather peppery' squadron leader asked him what his hobbies were. 'Huntin', shootin', fishin',' Francis replied.

'Get out of here at once,' the squadron leader bellowed. 'I'll have none of your bloody cheek!'

Eventually, after spending time in the Middle East and North Africa, Francis got what he wanted. He was given a transfer to Rhodesia (now Zimbabwe) to learn how to fly. He piloted Spitfires and then switched to Bomber Command, flying Wellingtons on diversionary attack missions, including on one occasion for the legendary Dam Busters.

On being demobbed he wrote to every trainer he had ever met, or who had ever met his parents, plus others, to ask if they wanted a 'totally inexperienced amateur jockey', but to no avail. His big break came when his brother Douglas said that trainer and farmer George Owen would take him on as his secretary. Francis was made to feel at home by Owen, his wife and daughters, and soon fitted in. He discovered, when trying to sort out his employer's mountain of paperwork, that Owen had not sent out a single bill in training fees for over six months. He also found that there were no vets' bills. Owen's vet, Bobby O'Neill, described by Francis as 'a happy-go-lucky Irishman', didn't send out bills to his friends either.

That's how business was done, it seems, in the far less money-orientated 1940s.

Francis had only been with Owen a week before he got his first ride, at the now defunct course of Woore in Shropshire. The horse had never run before and was owned by an old friend of the trainer's. His name? You've guessed it … Russian Hero, the future Grand National winner.

Francis finished fourth but his hopes of riding his first winner were put on hold on account of the Arctic conditions of the 1946/47 winter. Eventually, the unavailability of other riders meant he got his chance to ride Wrenbury Tiger in a hunter chase at Bangor-on-Dee on 2 May 1947. The Tiger roared to victory and Francis was finally off the mark. He rode his second winner, a novice chaser called Blitz Boy, on the same card. He ended the season with nine winners – not bad considering that he had only opened his account in May 1947.

Despite a slow start the following year, Francis continued his progress. As an amateur he reached the ten-winner mark in early March. He had ridden in more than a hundred races that season; only four professionals had had more mounts. Francis was happy to continue as an amateur but the stewards at Cheltenham gently pointed out to him that by taking so many rides he was potentially harming the livelihood of professional jockeys. They suggested he either restrict himself to amateur-only events or turn pro himself. He decided on the latter. However, his career as a professional didn't get off to the best of starts – he broke his collarbone at the 1947 Cheltenham Festival and had to spend three weeks on the sidelines. Francis rode six winners as a professional in the closing weeks of the 1946/47 season (starting with the appropriately named Resurgent at Ludlow on 14 April). He was relieved that George Owen's owners were using him almost as much as before.

In 1948 he began to ride the horses of Lord Bicester, and divide his time between Cheshire and Berkshire. Not long after the disappointment of finishing second in Russian Hero's Grand National, his career got another forward push when he was asked one morning by George Beeby to school a horse for Ken Cundell. The horse was called Fighting Line. Cundell told Francis that his usual jockey was in Ireland and asked if he could ride the horse at Cheltenham a few days later, in his debut over fences. Francis said yes and piloted Fighting Line to an impressive pillar-to-post victory. In those days the Welsh Grand National was run not over Christmas but at Easter, and Cundell booked Francis to ride his promising novice in the race. The pair won easily.[1]

There was further big race success in 1949 for Francis when he partnered Lord Bicester's Finnure – a horse that had been bought for just fifty guineas as a yearling – to victory in the King George VI Chase at Kempton on Boxing Day. It was the first time the race had been televised and those who watched either at home or after having managed to get to the course despite a rail strike saw a stirring finish. The favourite was the brilliant Vincent O'Brien-trained chaser Cottage Rake, two-time Gold Cup winner and winner of the King George the previous year. Ridden as usual by Aubrey Brabazon, Cottage Rake had never been beaten over fences in England but after a terrific duel from the last, Francis got his mount, who was in receipt of 11lb from the favourite, to prevail by half a length. 'The tremendous thrill and satisfaction of winning such a race produced a sort of choking feeling in the throat, so that between joy and exhaustion I could hardly speak when Lord Bicester greeted us in the winners' enclosure,' Francis later recalled. However, at Cheltenham in the spring, Cottage Rake and 'The Brab' got their revenge at level weights in the Gold Cup, beating Finnure (ridden by Martin Molony), by 10 lengths, to record a hat-trick of wins in the Blue Riband event.[2]

---

[1] It was the first time the race had been run at Chepstow.

[2] Just two horses since then have achieved a hat-trick of Gold Cups: Arkle (1964–66) and Best Mate (2002–04).

Three factors helped Francis go from a top rank jockey to champion. In 1952, he began to ride for Frank Cundell, cousin of Ken, who was expanding his jumps operation at Aston Tirrold. The Frank Cundell horse Francis became most associated with was Crudwell. Although short of the very highest class, this doughty performer won a Welsh National and no fewer than fifty races in a long career, which was a twentieth-century record.

The second, even more important break came in March 1953 when he was asked by leading trainer Peter Cazalet to deputise for his regular jockey Tony Grantham on Statecraft in the Gold Cup. According to one story, as told by Cazalet's son Edward (later a High Court judge), on the same day that Francis first went to Fairlawne, Cazalet's very grand country house in Kent, his father, who had the living rights for the local parish, was due to interview a new vicar.

> When Dick arrived for his interview, so the story goes, his charming manner was so much more like that of a parson than a jockey that my father spent a quarter of an hour discussing hymns and the length of sermons before Dick was able politely to point out the mistake.

Cazalet was the trainer for the Royal Family and introduced Francis to Her Majesty the Queen and the Queen Mother in the parade ring at Cheltenham. Francis's first-ever ride in the Gold Cup (he'd previously always missed it due to injury or horse withdrawals) ended unhappily (Statecraft pulled a tendon and was pulled up), but six weeks later, Cazalet asked Francis if he would ride for him regularly the following season. Francis was ecstatic, later writing:

> To ride for him meant riding the Royal horses: it meant as well that I had come the last few rungs of my personal ladder; and even Sir Edmund Hillary, who at that very instant was climbing his way to immortality, could not have felt more on top of the world.

The upshot of it all was that Francis began the 1953/54 season in a very strong position, riding for Cazalet, top owner Lord Bicester, and also for Frank Cundell, when neither Cazalet nor Bicester had call on his services.

His position became even stronger, in relation to the jockeys' title, when an injury to Fred Winter in the first race on the first day of the season put the reigning champion out of action for the entire campaign. Francis won the very next race at Newton Abbot on the Peter Cazalet-trained Diego Rubio and rode a double on the card. Francis recalled:

> Mr Cazalet had a number of young horses which won several novices each. Lord Bicester's horses as usual were running mostly in high-class 3-mile handicap chases so they clashed far less than might have been expected. The Cundell charges too seemed to fit nicely into the gaps, so that I rode a great many horses. And I won a great many races.

On 26 October 1953, Francis wore the blue and white buff stripes and black velvet cap Royal colours for the first time as he rode the Queen Mother's new horse M'as-Tu-Vu at Nottingham, where they finished second. On 27 November, Francis piloted the horse to victory at Kempton Park. The pair were last on the first circuit but began to improve rapidly in the final three quarters of a mile and eventually won by two lengths. 'He was favourite at evens and the success was very popular with the crowd,' the *Liverpool Echo* reported. Francis wrote of the 'tremendous roar' that greeted his victory. Just eight days later, the pair won again at Lingfield, with the Queen, Queen Mother and Princess Margaret all in attendance. The Queen Mother was reported to have said to Cazalet's head man Jim Fairgreave: 'That was an exciting race, wasn't it?' while the trainer went with his jockey into the weighing room.

By Christmas, Francis had surpassed his total in 1952/53 and, indeed, in other seasons. He continued his blistering form into 1954. At the Cheltenham New Year meeting he won on Lord Abergavenny's Legal Prince. On 15 January he landed a treble at Sandown Park to take his seasonal total to fifty-four. His first winner of the card was Deal Park, and on board the second horse, Stranger, was one Lester Piggott, then riding over jumps. Many years later, when Piggott first retired, he asked Francis to write his official biography, proving once again that truth is stranger than fiction.

Francis's treble at Sandown meant that he had won on eight of his last thirteen rides. And the winners kept on coming. On 19 March he piloted Lord Bicester's Marcianus to victory at Newbury. But there was to be no Cheltenham Gold Cup fairytale for him, as once again he missed the race. He was booked to ride Lord Bicester's strongly fancied Mariner's Log, on whom he had finished third in the King George in December, but dislocated his shoulder following a fall in a hurdle race earlier on Gold Cup day. As his wife Mary helped him through the door of Cheltenham Hospital, the casualty sister took one look at him and declared: 'Not you again!' For his own part, Francis joked that as he had seen her at least six times in the past three years he might as well subscribe for a bed so that it would always be ready for him.

On this occasion, Francis's shoulder was quickly put back into place and he was even in time to return to the racecourse in a taxi to see the end of the Gold Cup, in which his intended mount came second.

Francis was crowned champion at the end of May 1954 with seventy-six winners, eighteen ahead of Rene Emery. It was to be the only time he won the title but he still enjoyed plenty of success in subsequent seasons, before retiring after a bad fall at Newbury in early 1957 when in the lead in the jockey championship. In March 1956 came the heartbreaking agony of Devon Loch. That was obviously a huge disappointment but, as he later admitted, he gained more from the horse's dramatic collapse than he would have done from its victory. Francis's heroic near-miss made him the Captain Scott of National Hunt racing. The British love a winner, but they love a gallant loser even more, and the self-effacing Francis fitted the bill perfectly.

He was asked to write a number of articles for the *Sunday Express*, who then offered him a job as a racing correspondent. He was also approached to write his autobiography. *The Sport of Queens*, published in 1957, was a big success, which led Francis, assisted greatly by his wife Mary, on to writing fast-paced racing thrillers. These proved to be tremendously popular and established the ex-Royal jockey as the new Edgar Wallace. For forty years, Francis kept his reading public enthralled. His bestsellers (his books sold more than 60 million copies in thirty-five languages and were turned into a television series and a film) made him a very wealthy man. He moved with Mary, who had suffered from polio, to warmer climes for her health: first to Florida, and then the Cayman Islands, but always came back home each year for the Grand National meeting. In 2002, Francis arrived the day the Queen Mother died, and stayed on a couple of extra days for her funeral. During his last visit in 2006, he officially opened the new Aintree weighing room. He died in 2010 aged 89, but it was not the end of the Dick Francis story, or, more precisely, the Dick Francis stories. His son Felix, who had also helped his father with his literary work, took over the thriller writing franchise and has enjoyed considerable success too. The publisher and former amateur rider Sir Rupert Mackeson, who knew Dick extremely well, described him as 'one of the true greats of the post-war generation'. 'He was a great horseman rather than a pure jockey – he had wonderful hands and was quite fearless.'

Away from the racetrack Francis differed from many of his contemporaries in that he did not subscribe to what Tim Fitzgeorge-Parker described as the 'Eat, drink-and-be-merry-for-tomorrow-we-die-wine-women-and-horses philosophy' of jump jockeys.

We've already heard the story of how Peter Cazalet mistook Francis for a vicar. For his part, Dave Dick, the colourful, fun-loving jockey who enjoyed sports cars, waterskiing, drinking whisky and chasing women, nicknamed Dick 'Mother Francis'. Dave Dick, it is said, always reserved two rooms at Liverpool's Adelphi Hotel, in case he got lucky. On one occasion he even managed to charm a lady traffic warden into not giving him a parking ticket by inviting her to come to the Grand National party, which she did. You can't really imagine Dick Francis doing something quite as cheeky as that, or staying up carousing deep into the night. But he did have a great sense of humour. At the 1953/54 champion jockey's dinner at the Queen's Hotel in Cheltenham, Francis had to make a speech. But he hated giving speeches so simply recited his favourite rude poem, entitled 'The Great Farting Contest at Stilton-On-Tees'. The contest is won by a Mrs Bindle, 'who shyly appeared, And smiled at the clergy who lustily cheered, And though it was reckon'd her chances were small, She let rip a winner, and out-farted them all!' Francis was invited by Lord Vestey to repeat his recital at Cheltenham Racecourse during Tony McCoy's 2003/04 championship dinner to mark fifty years since he was the champion. It's fair to say it was a rip-roaring success once again.

Francis was a kind and considerate man, who never forgot to reward hard work, as this anecdote from Tim Fitzgeorge-Parker, who the 1953/54 champion rode out for, illustrates:

> How well he appreciated the value of stable-lads. Always friendly, seeking their advice on their particular horse, never in any way condescending, he kept a list, like Sir Gordon Richards, religiously recording the lad who 'did' each winner that he rode during the season. Every lad received a present at Christmas. 'But Dick, I'm sure you gave Leslie his present for that more than two months ago ...?' 'No, I didn't. He's not crossed off the list.'

Big race wins
Welsh Grand National 1949 (Fighting Line), 1956 (Crudwell)
King George VI Chase 1949 (Finnure)
Molyneux Chase 1950 (Possible)

Chapter Seven

Tim Brookshaw

Champion 1958/59

The Man who Laughed at Danger

'Another fall on the spine could kill him. But he just laughs and says he is happiest of all when he is riding.'

Brookshaw's stable lad, Arthur Bevan

Ludlow racecourse, Thursday, 27 February 2020. While parts of Shropshire still lie under water due to the floods, racing goes ahead, on a bright, cold day. There's a reasonable enough crowd, and among them are some familiar faces from the past. There are former jockeys Bob Davies, Ivor Markham and Ken White; Jane Owen, the daughter of trainer George Owen; and Steve Brookshaw, trainer of the 1997 Grand National winner Lord Gyllene. It's a day when in addition to enjoying some good National Hunt racing, friends and families of a former champion jump jockey are gathering to celebrate the launch of a new biography telling the story of Tim Brookshaw. The book, by Chris Pitt, who signs copies throughout the afternoon, is called *Fearless*. Even by the very high standards of champion jump jockeys, the story of Tim Brookshaw is quite extraordinary. It's about how a dairy farmer from Shropshire finished second in the Grand National without his stirrups, became champion jockey and then broke his back in a horror fall, before overcoming paralysis to walk again and even take part in equestrian competitions following his injury. 'They say you shouldn't meet your heroes because in the end they're just like you and me,' Sir Mark Prescott, the renowned Newmarket trainer, said of Brookshaw. 'But I met him and he wasn't like you and me. He was a hero. A proper man.'

Tim Brookshaw was born at Atcham, near Shrewsbury, on 25 March 1929. He came from a family of farmers, and grew up, with his two brothers Tony and Peter and sister Mabel, around horses. The first obstacle he had to overcome was suffering as a child from osteomyelitis, a rare disease affecting the bones in the arm and leg. 'The fungal infection grew on the bone and reached a point when it became life-threatening. He would bear the scars for the rest of his life, a huge cut mark that went deep to the bone,' writes Pitt.

Tim rode ponies, played rugger at school, and, in the words of his brother Tony, 'was an absolute daredevil'. He was out hunting regularly with his brother Peter in his late teens and then started riding in point-to-points. He rode his first winner under National Hunt Rules, a horse called Ike II, in a hunter chase at Woore on 13 May 1948. Just two weeks earlier he had cracked a facial bone in a fall in a point-to-point but he didn't let having to ride with a bandage round his jaw bother him.

In 1948/49 he began riding for the Tarporley stable of George Owen, who won that season's Grand National with Russian Hero. There was no question at this stage of Tim being anything other than a farmer who occasionally rode in races as an amateur. His canny father had bought both Tim and Peter their own farms. But after he had ridden twelve winners in the 1949/50 season, he got the usual friendly encouragement from the Jockey Club to turn professional, which he did on 1 October 1950. Still, though, the farming came first.

Tim would usually start the season late, after the harvest, putting him out of contention in the jockeys' title race. In the period from 1948 to 1956, the earliest he rode a winner over jumps was on 8 September, in 1956. He rode twenty-nine winners in his first season as a professional, and his tally was fairly consistent over the next six years: 24, 19, 25, 25, 16, 22. Whereas in the period up to and including 1953/54 most of his winners were for George Owen, from 1954/55 he began to ride more for other stables, including for Fred Rimell, Roy Whitson and Solly Parker.

Tim had made a name for himself as one of the best riders 'out in the country' and for his tactical prowess. No one would claim that he was a great stylist – as Chris Pitt says, 'that old fashioned, raised whip action at the last … looks ungainly by today's standards' but Brookshaw was not a man you'd want to see jumping the last just a length or so behind you, as he'd drive his mount in to the fence. Sometimes that meant a fall, other times it was the difference between defeat and victory.

As hard as nails on the racetrack, he was also one of the most extrovert characters of the weighing room. He was friendly and always cheerful but there was a mischievous streak too. Chris Pitt cites an anonymous northern jockey who remembered going down to the start with Brookshaw for a race at Perth. 'Suddenly a hand grabbed him by the balls with Tim shouting "How you doing, cocker!"'

Among Tim's most important wins in the first half of the 1950s were the Molyneux Chase over the Aintree Grand National fences on George Owen's

Royal Stuart in 1951 and the Golden Miller Handicap Chase at Cheltenham in April 1954 on Fred Rimell's Womage.

The season when Tim showed he could be a serious player in the jockeys' title race was 1957/58. That year his win tally more than doubled – from twenty-two to sixty – and he finished second in the championship. He began the campaign earlier than usual and recorded his first success at Newton Abbot on 5 September. He had eight winners on board by the end of the month, and kept the good run going through the autumn. The year 1958 began well, with doubles on both days at Manchester's New Year meeting. Tim had a good run in the Grand National in March on Pippykin, on whom he had won earlier in the month at Haydock. The pair were still going well when coming to grief at second Becher's. Fred Winter won the title (his fourth, with eighty-two winners), but the next season, the challenge from Shropshire was even stronger.

Brookshaw was in action for the first time on day one at Newton Abbot in early August and duly rode a double, the second leg of which was on the appropriately named Full Charge. There were seven further winners in August and fifteen in September. Instead of making hay while the sun shone, as he'd done in previous years, Farmer Tim was now making an all-out assault on the jockeys' title.

'Tim Brookshaw is riding well enough to become champion jockey this National Hunt season. He had only three rides at the Devon and Exeter meeting yesterday and he won on all of them,' reported the *Birmingham Daily Post* on 12 September. By the end of the month, Brookshaw was twenty-two clear of Fred Winter.

In November he won his second Molyneux Chase, run over the Grand National fences at Aintree, this time on the Fred Rimell-trained Oasis. It was quite an historic occasion as it was the first race from Aintree shown live on television. The BBC would maintain their coverage of the big races from Aintree until 2012, when the national broadcaster sadly withdrew from televising horseracing altogether.

By the end of November 1958, Brookshaw had ridden forty-five winners, twenty-four of them trained by Fred Rimell. In addition to mopping up on the West Country circuit he had ridden winners at courses as far apart as Folkestone in Kent and Wetherby in Yorkshire. The closer link in the 1950s with National Hunt racing, and the hunting world, can be seen by the fact that five of Brookshaw's wins in his title-winning season came on Jimuru, a horse owned and trained by Lord Leigh, Master of the North Warwickshire Hunt.

Brookshaw rode five winners from 22 to 28 November, but after a success at Aintree on 4 December, he went to Manchester and broke his collarbone following a fall. But the 'Iron Man' was back in action before the year's end, to ride a New Year's Eve double at Cheltenham to take his total to forty-nine. During the calendar year of 1958, he had ridden ninety-two winners.

There were three more in early January 1959, but then the weather intervened. Racing was badly hit by a deep frost, which lasted until early February. When the action resumed, Tim just carried on from where he had left off, riding doubles at Wolverhampton on 24 February and at Ludlow a day later.

A first Cheltenham Festival winner would have been a nice way to adorn his run of success, but it was not to be. Tim's best chance at the 1959 Festival was in the Champion Hurdle, where he rode the Fred Rimell-trained 9-4 favourite Tokoroa, who had finished second the year before. Alas, the horse almost came down three from home. Instead the race was won by Fred Winter, Tim's nearest rival in the jockey championship, on Fare Time. The reigning champion won four more races at the Festival, and took the lead in the title race, but Brookshaw struck back with a double at Hurst Park on 7 March and then posted a fabulous four-timer at Doncaster a couple of days later, which put him back in front by two.

A win at Worcester on 18 March on Sputnik One, named after the famous Soviet satellite that was launched into orbit in 1957, set him up nicely for the Grand National meeting starting a day later.

His ride in the big race was Wyndburgh. Trained in the Scottish Borders by Rhona and Ken Oliver, the 9-year-old ex-hunter chaser had some great Aintree form to his name. He had finished second and fourth in the last two Grand Nationals and had also won the Grand Sefton over the National fences in 1957. He was going into the 1959 National carrying nearly a stone less than in 1958, so all things considered, Tim had every reason to be confident. And after a circuit safely negotiated and his horse going well he must have thought he was in with an excellent chance of landing his first National win. Wyndburgh was up with the leader Oxo, ridden by Michael Scudamore, as the pair successfully cleared Becher's for the second time. But on landing, his jockey realised something had gone wrong. Brookshaw looked down and saw that his nearside stirrup iron had snapped off. He immediately took his foot out of the other iron to restore balance. He could have pulled his horse up, but Wyndburgh was jumping so well, he decided to embark on 'Mission Impossible' – to try to complete the race, and even win it, without irons. 'From Becher's onwards, Tim had to hold on to his horse's head by tugging at its mane,' writes Chris Pitt.

Wyndburgh pecked on landing at a number of fences as his jockey couldn't exercise full control without stirrups but he still kept up with Oxo – and continued light-hearted bantering with Michael Scudamore. As they came to last, Oxo had developed a clear lead and Brookshaw thought the race had gone. But Oxo didn't put in a good jump and was clearly tiring on the long run-in. The gutsy Wyndburgh, with his equally courageous jockey, were gaining with every stride. Could he get up? It would have been one of the most remarkable Grand National wins of all time, but Scudamore and Oxo managed to hold on, by a 1½ lengths. 'It would have taken only another few strides to catch Oxo, who was by then really spent,' Brookshaw recalled in 1979, in John Hughes's book *My Greatest Race*. Nevertheless, Brookshaw and Wyndburgh had, by their gallant efforts, established themselves in Grand National folklore. Stan Mellor, the future three-time champion jump jockey, and who rode The Crofter in the 1959 race, said that Brookshaw's ride was 'the most remarkable achievement' he ever saw. 'It wasn't just the fact that he did it, it was the wonderful spirit in which he did it. He was laughing all the way.'

The morning after his Aintree heroics, Brookshaw was up early milking the cows on his farm, his only comment being was that he felt a 'bit stiff'. There's no doubt that if his iron hadn't snapped, he would have won the Grand National, but he was from a stoical 'Mustn't grumble, mustn't complain' pre-Second World War generation that simply shrugged off disappointment and carried on the next day as if nothing had happened.

Four more winners followed before the month of March was out, and Brookshaw added another three to his tally at the two-day Bangor meeting in early April.

That same day, 4 April, he was effectively handed the title after his nearest pursuer, Fred Winter, who was just five wins behind him, suffered a crashing fall in a novices' chase at Leicester which left him with a fractured skull. Brookshaw rode his eighty-third winner of the season when he steered Chauffeur to victory in a selling hurdle at Taunton on 2 May, but just half an hour later, his season, like Winter's, came to an abrupt end when he broke his right leg in a fall in a handicap chase. It didn't matter; the title was already his. He had achieved his ambition. What an effort it had been. Leaving his farm early in August to head to Newton Abbot had been well worth it.

Almost inevitably, the 1959/60 season proved somewhat anticlimactic. Brookshaw's first winner came in a seller at Cheltenham in October, but he then made up for lost time by riding twelve winners in November. On 3 December, any hopes he might have had of trying to retain his title were dashed when he fell and fractured his right ankle at Aintree. Tim faced a race against time to get fit to ride Wyndburgh again in the Grand National but he was forced to miss the ride. Instead, his old pal Michael Scudamore, who had beaten him on Oxo, was on board. This time, Wyndburgh came down at first Becher's, the only time in six National appearances he failed to get round. Brookshaw was back in action on 30 March and rode eleven winners before the season was out, but on thirty for the season, he was well behind the new champion, Stan Mellor, who posted sixty-eight.

The 1960/61 season was a different story. Brookshaw actually rode seven more winners in this campaign (ninety) than he did when he was champion. The only trouble was that Stan Mellor managed to ride even more (118). Brookshaw drew level and actually went ahead of Mellor in November, but the reigning champ struck back.

In the Grand National of 1961, Brookshaw was reunited with Wyndburgh. It would have been a fairytale result had they won, but a combination of the extra weight (the horse had to carry 7lb more than in 1959) and the unsuitably fast going meant that this time the partnership could only manage sixth.

An article in the *Liverpool Echo* on Saturday, 25 November 1961 drew contrast between Flat jockeys and their jump racing counterparts:

> The flat rider is a dedicated man who seems to take himself and life most seriously, but their National Hunt colleagues are happy-go-lucky, and generally speaking, on the best of terms with their rivals. … perhaps the greatest character among the National Hunt riders is Tim Brookshaw. With his wave of the whip at every jump, just as if he was leading the Charge of the Light Brigade, it is easy to spot him at a distance. Tim always rides at the last fence as if it was not there, and with his round, red face, he looks more like a farmer than a jockey and in fact he does combine those callings.

Tim rode thirty-seven winners in the 1961/62 season, among them one Mill House, in a handicap chase at Cheltenham's April meeting. The horse went on to win the 1963 Gold Cup and Tim played an important part in his path to glory. On his first run over fences at Hurst Park, Mill House had taken a crashing fall. You'd think his trainer, Syd Dale, would have then taken his charge to an easier course for his next run, but instead he decided to throw him in at the deep end at Cheltenham. Tim was entrusted with the job of restoring the horse's confidence. He gave Mill House a wonderfully sympathetic ride. 'He made two terrific mistakes at the first two fences and I had to pick him up off the floor,' he recalled later, as cited in Chris Pitt's biography. 'He had absolutely no confidence in himself, so I took him away from the others on the wide outside and started to school him as I would at home.' Mill House gradually regained his confidence, and began to jump 'super', but Brookshaw purposely kept his horse on the wide outside so he would not be distracted by the other runners. Brookshaw only made his move as he came down the hill the last time. In the end, Mill House won by 2 lengths, and the rest, as they say, is history.

In the weather-affected 1962/63 season, Brookshaw rode thirty-six winners. There were two major highlights. In March he rode his first winner at the Cheltenham Festival, Happy Arthur, in the George Duller Handicap Hurdle. Then, in April, there was victory in the Scottish Grand National on Pappageno's Cottage, who, like Happy Arthur, was also trained by Ken Oliver. Brookshaw was usually a fine judge of equine talent but when he had ridden the chaser to a victory at Perth two years earlier, he had said to Ken Oliver, 'I think he's just a moderate selling plater.'

The horse duly went to the sales at Kelso but was let out unsold at 420 guineas. Oliver, who also doubled up as an auctioneer, went to the bar after the sale and found, in his own words, 'two of the drunkest men I have ever seen'. John D. Sheridan, Pappageno's Cottage's owner, had managed to sell his horse to local hotel owner and cattle dealer Willie King for 500 guineas. King said he couldn't afford Oliver's training fees and was taking the horse home as a hunter. Rhona Oliver then intervened. 'The pair of them were so drunk that I took the horse home and eventually persuaded Willie that we should run him in a race at Carlisle in which we had already entered him.' Pappageno's Cottage won that race and never looked back. Willie King backed him down from 50-1 to 20-1 when he won the Scottish National, the richest race in the jump racing calendar north of the border, so his 500 guineas, drunkenly agreed to in the bar, had paid him a very nice dividend. We're told by Ken Oliver's biographer Dan Buglass that at the time of the race, Tim Brookshaw had 'revised his opinion of the horse'. The irony is that the 'moderate selling plater' gave him the most valuable win of his career.

In the 1963/64 season Tim had already ridden thirty-three winners by the end of November. Another victory was added to the tally on a horse called Bold Biri at Nottingham on 3 December. Little did he know that it was the last winner under Rules he would ever ride.

The fifth race at Liverpool on Wednesday, 4 December was a 2-mile 100-yards handicap hurdle. Tim was riding a mare called Lucky Dora for Ken Oliver, on whom he had won two previous races. But he was clearly not a huge fan of the mare as before the start he warned the other riders: 'Don't track me on this one, lads, she's a fxxxxng cow.'

Tim set off in front. The pair jumped the first four flights well, but before the fifth flight, Lucky Dora was joined by another horse. Whether it was that

that put her off ... but she jinked sharply to the left, and crashed through the wing of the hurdle. Tim suffered a horror fall. 'He landed on his face and chest and his legs jack-knifed over his back. The back of his head almost touched his bottom,' writes Chris Pitt.

Brookshaw was rushed to Walton Hospital and when he woke up was told that he had broken his back and that he would never walk again. He had actually broken two vertebrae. A day later, a 12-inch long piece of steel was grafted on to his spine. He was in so much pain he had to receive four-hourly injections of morphine. But when visitors arrived to see him he still kept his sense of humour. In *Fearless*, Pitt relates the story told by Elain Mellor about when she and husband Stan visited Tim in the hospital. They had barely said hello before Tim gave a 'dirty laugh' and a 'big grin' had spread across his face. 'Mellor, you've gone and done it, haven't you!' he said. Elain was only about two weeks' pregnant but Tim had known. 'A long while later I asked him how come he could tell I was pregnant. He replied, "Well, I am a dairy farmer, aren't I."'

Thanks to great medical attention and his own ferocious willpower, within two months Tim had hauled himself out of his hospital bed and into a wheelchair. He left hospital on crutches in early March 1964 and on the 21st of the month was a guest at the Grand National. There he witnessed another horrific fall of a jockey: Paddy Farrell at The Chair. Farrell, like Brookshaw, had broken his back, though his spinal damage was even worse.

The injury to Farrell led to an appeal being launched by leading owner Clifford Nicholson. It was widened to include Brookshaw and grew into the Injured National Hunt Jockeys Fund, which, in 1971, became the Injured Jockeys Fund. By 5 May 1964, almost £47,000 had been raised. As Chris Pitt notes, at the time of Brookshaw and Farrell's accidents there was virtually no compensation to help injured jockeys – so at least some good came of their career-ending injuries.

In 1964 Brookshaw competed in the Paraplegic Games at Stoke Mandeville and then later in the same year represented Britain at the Paralympics in Tokyo. The man who twelve months earlier had been one of Britain's best jump jockeys won a silver medal in the javelin.

Although disabled, Brookshaw didn't want to be reliant on others. An anecdote from Charles Chetwynd-Talbot (now Lord Shrewsbury), who helped him on the farm, illustrates this perfectly. One day Brookshaw slipped and fell when walking across the yard. Chetwynd-Talbot asked if he wanted a hand, but Brookshaw's response was to tell him to go and do something physically impossible. 'He crawled back to the house, told me to leave him alone, pulled himself up on the downspout of the gutter and started off again. He did that four times before he got over to the milking shed.'

In 1966 Tim was back on horseback. His recovery drew inevitable comparisons with the legendary Second World War *Reach for the Sky* airman Douglas Bader, who went back to flying after breaking both his legs. Tim schooled his horses over jumps and went hunting with the North Shropshire. He saddled his first winner as a trainer at Wolverhampton on 6 March 1967. It was only a selling chase but Dufton Pike was led in to huge cheers.

Personally there were changes in Tim's life. His marriage to Joan hit the rocks, and the pair were divorced in 1971. Tragically, Joan started drinking heavily following the separation and later committed suicide. Professionally, Brookshaw was doing OK as a trainer without setting the world alight. His flagship horse in the 1970s was Cotton Coon. Sadly, the horse broke down badly at Wolverhampton in November 1977 and had to be destroyed. Tim's stepson Wayne told Chris Pitt that was the only occasion he saw him cry. It was to be almost another year before he trained a winner.

The 1981/82 season started well, with a winner at Bangor on 15 August, but Tim would not live to see the season's end. On the morning of 2 November 1981, one of his grooms went up to Tim and told him one of the horses was being 'funny'. He said he would take him out later. 'But that wasn't how Tim operated,' says Chris Pitt. Tim saddled the horse up and took him out of the yard. The horse reared up and fired Tim over his head. 'Instinctively, being a jockey, he wouldn't let go of the reins. As he lay on the ground, the horse got to his feet and kicked him in the neck.'

Tim was rushed to hospital where it was found he had broken two bones in his neck. His son Tim went to see him with his wife and young daughter. 'He was poking her in the tummy and making her laugh,' he recalled. One day later, Tim Brookshaw died. He was 52.

The stats tell us that in his career as a jump jockey he rode 555 winners. But his legacy was much greater than that. In August 1961, a 13-year-old boy was 'dragged unwillingly' to Newton Abbot races by his stepfather. A horse fell and rolled on top of its jockey. Years later, that 13-year-old boy recalled: 'I was standing right by the rail and obviously he [the jockey] was dead as the rest had galloped all over him. And then, the great man 'stood up, very, very slowly and said "Fxxxxng hell", chucked his stick into the crowd and walked off up the track'. For the young boy it was a life-changing moment.

'I thought, "what a man" and it changed what I wanted to do in life.' The jockey was Tim Brookshaw and the 13-year-old racegoer was Sir Mark Prescott. The sporting baronet began as an amateur jump jockey and broke his back in a fall when he was 18. He went to Oswestry Orthopedic Hospital, where, lo and behold, Tim Brookshaw was an outpatient. 'It's entirely your fault I'm here,' Prescott told him.

Big race wins (as a jockey)
Grand Sefton Chase 1962 (Eternal)
Scottish Grand National 1963 (Pappageno's Cottage)

Chapter Eight

Stan Mellor

Champion 1959/60, 1960/61, 1961/62

Stan, the Man for Winners

'I was young and fearless in those days, but always enjoyed riding at Cartmel. They used to call me "Cartmellor", probably because I kept coming back on a stretcher.'

Stan Mellor, 1982

It's the last Saturday before Christmas 1971. *Ernie (The Fastest Milkman in the West)* by Benny Hill is number one in the pop charts. *Bedknobs and Broomsticks* is in the cinemas. *Bruce Forsyth and the Generation Game* and *Dixon of Dock Green* are the prime-time programmes on television … while in the first race at Nottingham, Stan Mellor enters the record books by becoming the first National Hunt jockey to ride 1,000 winners.

You could say that Stan Mellor is the neglected sixties sporting maestro. He was a mainstay in the top races of that decade, yet the modest Mancunian does not have the recognition outside of the horseracing world that he should have, bearing in mind he won three successive jockey championships and came close to adding to that on a number of occasions.

His remarkable career in the saddle, which stretched from the early 1950s to the early 1970s, encompassed great changes in British life and society. When Mellor rode his first winner, in a Wolverhampton selling hurdle in January 1954, Winston Churchill was prime minister and we still had rationing. When he rode his last, at Stratford in June 1972, the country had motorways and decimal coinage, and was just about to enter the Common Market. Rock 'n' roll and The Beatles had come and gone. Stan Mellor is the link between the 'black and white' era of Tim Molony and Bryan Marshall and the 'colour' era of Bob Davies and Johnny Francome.

If there's one word that could perhaps have summed up Mellor's riding, it is 'efficient'. He got the job done with the minimum of fuss. He never made a drama out of a mid-race crisis. His great rival Terry Biddlecombe thought Mellor was in a class of his own and that he 'was the hardest man to beat anywhere from the last fence'. Brough Scott, who knew him well, has called Stan 'the brightest and the lightest' of the top jockeys of his generation. Weighing under 9 stone, he was 20 pounds lighter than most of his contemporaries but 'he made up the physical deficit with a unique blend of horsemanship and guile'.

Mellor's model was Fred Winter. Like that 'man for all seasons', he preferred not to use his whip to get his horses over the line. 'Instead of hitting horses, jockeys should just ride properly,' he once remarked. This earned him the praise of the commentator and equine welfare campaigner Sir Peter O'Sullevan, who observed, 'Stan used his whip less in one month than some of those who followed him fifteen years later would do in a single afternoon.'

Stan Mellor was born on 10 April 1937. The son of a Manchester timber merchant, from whose yard could be heard the commentaries from Manchester Racecourse, his early CV has great similarities with that of Dick Francis, the 1953/54 champion. He began his riding career showjumping, winning plenty of juvenile competitions in his native North West. His ambition was to become a professional showjumper but attending Manchester races on New Year's Day 1948 proved to be a life-changing event. With his father he saw the subsequent Grand National winner Freebooter win the Victory Handicap Chase under Tim Molony. Molony and Fred Winter became his idols.

'I did not try to model myself on Fred physically, but I certainly did mentally,' he told the *Daily Mirror* in 1971.

At the age of 15 Mellor joined Cheshire trainer George Owen, as an amateur. He was the third of the three champion jockeys 'schooled' by Gentleman George, after Francis and Brookshaw. 'Daddy always thought a lot of Stan,' Owen's daughter Jane remembers. 'He thought he had good hands.' Mellor had his first ride in public on 2 March 1953, when he finished second in a hurdle race at Worcester on Straight Border, owned by Owen's wife, Margaret.

The same horse provided him with his first winner, at Wolverhampton, the following January, when he was still only 16. Having ridden ten winners as an amateur he received the usual friendly interview from the stewards and duly turned professional. The first paid winner he rode was Wirswall Prince, in a chase at Ludlow in April 1954.

He continued to climb the ladder professionally for the rest of the 1950s, but given the nature of jump racing, there were the inevitable ups and downs. He had six good rides booked at Bangor for his twenty-first birthday in 1958, but broke his collarbone the day before and missed them all. One of the courses where he became leading jockey was Woore in Shropshire, a most difficult track. 'I learned the hard way. Tim Molony was the leading jockey there when I started riding. I made the mistake of trying to go up his inside and he put me through the dolls. George Owen was furious, not with Tim, but for me for being so stupid,' he told Chris Pitt, as recounted in *A Long Time Gone*.

Stan won his first jockeys' title in 1959/60, when he was still only 22, in a title race that went right to the very last day of the season. Fred Winter, as ever, was the man to beat, but Mellor stayed in contention when it mattered.

On 10 November, he rode a double at Warwick, the first of which was 100-9 shot Bus Stop, owned and trained by Major John Goldsmith, a man with a very interesting background. Goldsmith had been a member of the Special Operations Executive in the Second World War and once escaped from the clutches of the Gestapo by making a daring getaway from a locked third-floor hotel room in Paris.[1]

There was another double for Mellor at Warwick on 4 January. Stan rode the first two winners on the card at Uttoxeter on 19 March, one of which was Sandy Abbot in the novices' chase. The horse, regarded as the best George Owen ever trained, went on to win the Champion Chase at the Cheltenham Festival under Mellor three years later, and also won the Victory Handicap Chase at Manchester in 1961.

The Grand National of 1960, in which Mellor rode the Lord Leverhulme-owned Badanloch for George Owen, was the first to be televised live on the BBC. Mellor and his mount were prominent for quite some way but were unable to match Merryman II and his jockey Gerry Scott's burst for glory. Mellor's second place, 15 lengths behind the winner, was to be his best finish in the National, but ironically, his association with the horse might have cost him the chance of a National win the following year. He could have ridden Nicolaus Silver for Fred Rimell in 1961, but stayed loyal to Owen and rode Badanloch again, this time to an eighth place finish.

Fred Winter was six wins ahead of Mellor in early May 1960. But as we saw in Chapter Five, with a lead of one, going into the last day of the season, the reigning champion decided to join his family on holiday in Cornwall. Mellor went to Uttoxeter and rode two winners, Chauffeur and Jules Verne, to pip him for the title.

On 11 November, on the eve of the inaugural running of the Mackeson Gold Cup, Mellor was guest of honour at the special black-tie dinner at

---

[1] Goldsmith's remarkable story is told in the book *Blown*, by Jamie Reid.

Cheltenham to laud the achievement of the champion jockey of the previous season. Wing Commander P.D.O. Vaux, the senior National Hunt steward, noted that Mellor was the youngest champion 'for some years'. 'In Stan we have all that is best in his profession,' he added.

Stan was unsuccessful in the Mackeson, which was won that year by Tom Dreaper's Fortria, but it was still a good month. On 16 November, Stan rode two chance winners at Worcester to draw level, with thirty-two winners apiece, with Tim Brookshaw. On the 29th of the month, he rode a double for George Owen at Leicester on Chela Jau (100-8) and Sir Gosland (2-1 favourite). He increased his lead in the title race after riding a treble at Aintree on 1 December, with two of his winning mounts trained by George Owen.

The year 1961 began well with a win in the Victory Handicap Chase at Manchester on Sandy Abbot, thirteen years on from the fateful day when Mellor had watched Freebooter win the same race with his father. A month later, there was another big race success for the Owen–Mellor combo when they landed the Great Yorkshire Chase at Doncaster on Chavara. On 11 February, Mellor posted a treble at Warwick, the easiest winner being Owen's Highland Dandy, who won the Stratford Handicap Chase by 10 lengths, while there was another double at Southwell two weeks later.

Although he drew a blank at that year's Cheltenham Festival, Mellor – and Owen – were back in the winners' enclosure when the front-running Peacetown landed the spoils in the Mildmay Chase at Liverpool on 24 March. Five days later, Mellor became only the third steeplechase jockey of all time to pass the century of winners for the season when 7-4 favourite Frisky Scot won the Downs Selling Chase at Sandown. It was reported that Stan received a 'great ovation' when he rode his horse into the winners' enclosure, with the jockey telling reporters, 'It's really a great thrill.' The next day it was reported that Stan was going 'all out' to try to beat Fred Winter's record of 121 winners in a season.

On 14 April, there was another milestone: he won his first race on the Flat, when Curtain Time won on a mixed card at the Scottish National meeting at Bogside. He had earlier won a chase on Lothian Princess. In the end he finished the season on 118 winners, just three short of Winter's record. Still, it was a tremendous effort.

Stan rode his first winner for Oxfordshire handler Derek Ancil at Worcester on 18 October 1961. Among the highlights of that third championship season were trebles at Uttoxeter and Market Rasen in September and an 875-1 treble at Haydock in January.

On 11 January 1962, the reigning champ rode a shock 25-1 'non-runner' winner for Owen at Liverpool. It was all down to the temporary suspension of the declared runner rule due to the postal delays at the time. Owen had decided the night before not to run Regal Flame, but changed his mind in the morning. But the horse was down as a non-runner in the newspapers, hence its big price.

Mellor was brought down on the Tom Jones-trained 7-year-old Frenchman's Cove in the 1962 Grand National, but compensation was gained a month later when the pair landed the Whitbread Gold Cup at Sandown. Mellor's third title was achieved with eighty winners, with Winter, the man he idolised, again in second place.

Since he had become champion jockey Stan found himself travelling from Cheshire more and more to ride for southern trainers. To cut back on the travelling he decided to move. 'I can remember he put a map of the country on the table marking all the racecourses looking for the most central point, which turned out to be Middleton Stoney, where Derek Ancil trained,' recalls Elain Mellor (then Stan's girlfriend, later his wife). 'At the time Derek was both riding and training his horses, and when Stan mentioned his plan in the weighing room one day Derek said in that case he would give up riding and Stan could have the job of stable jockey.'

After a slow start, the 1962/63 campaign seemed likely to result in a fourth successive title. On 22 November, Mellor deployed great tactical prowess when defeating the mighty Mill House, the great rival of Arkle, at Kempton Park. Mellor's strategy on Frank Cundell's King's Nephew relied on not alerting Mill House's jockey Willie Robinson to his challenge. He knew his horse had one great burst of acceleration, which had to be saved for the right moment. He crept up on the inside and only unleashed his challenge at the last. 'Twenty yards from the fence the champion's whip went up and, still two strides away, he asked King's Nephew to do the impossible. It was all or nothing and only a man inspired, on a truly gallant horse, could have hoped to pull it off,' reported 'Marlborough' in the *Daily Telegraph*.

Four years later, Mellor deployed almost exactly the same 'hiding' tactics when recording the most famous success of his career when he rode 25-1 outsider Stalbridge Colonist to defeat Arkle (who was conceding 35lb to Mellor's horse) in the 1966 Hennessy. Again, it was all about making his challenge at exactly the right time.

Back to 1963 and on New Year's Day it was reported that the 'smiling Lancashire lad' who had been champion for the past three seasons was engaged to marry a 19-year-old Cardiff University chemistry and botany student called Elain Williams. Elain was the daughter of a Glamorgan dairy farmer; under Stan's tutelage she went on to be a trailblazing lady jockey. Elain had written to Stan ahead of her impending first ride in a point-to-point for advice on how to ride a race. 'I was still at boarding school and these were genuine fan letters, which to my surprise he answered – and the rest is history!' Elain told me in 2020.

Many years later, when Mellor was asked to name his favourite television programme, he replied, '*Blind Date*, as I was so lucky, I proposed to my wife on our first evening out.'

The racing marriage of the year was planned for June, but first there was another championship to wrap up. The weather provided the main obstacle to Stan's quest for winners in early 1963, as Britain shivered in its severest winter since 1947. Frost had already claimed the 1962 King George, in which Stan had been booked to ride the 5-4 favourite Frenchman's Cove, on whom he had won the previous season's Whitbread. Heavy snow arrived after Christmas and was a regular feature until March. 'The snow drifts were often 20 feet deep. The average temperature for January and February was -7°C. In most stables the only way to exercise the horses was to trot round a ring bedded down with soiled straw,' recalled Brough Scott in the *Racing Post* in 2013.

Just one race meeting (at Ayr) took place in Britain between Boxing Day and the week before the Cheltenham Festival. Luckily, though, the thaw arrived just in time for Stan to ride George Owen's Sandy Abbot to victory in the Champion Chase. It was another Mellor masterclass. The red-hot favourite was the Irish-trained Scottish Memories. Mellor jumped the last about 4 lengths clear but, as he later recalled in a *Racing Post* interview, his mount was 'dog-tired' and weakened rapidly up the hill on the very soft going. Other jockeys may have been tempted to give the horse some cracks, but not Stan, who, as ever, used his whip sparingly. 'A stride after the post Scottish Memories was in front,' he recalled, but Sandy Abbot had made it.

The reigning champion was twenty ahead of Josh Gifford and on the sixty-four-winner mark for the season – quite an achievement considering the number of meetings lost to the weather – when he took the ride on the Derek Ancil-trained Eastern Harvest in the inaugural running of the Schweppes Gold Trophy at Aintree on Thursday, 28 March. The Gold Trophy was a new hurdle race. With a value of £10,000 it offered nearly twice as much prize money as the Champion Hurdle (which was worth £5,585 in 1963), and not surprisingly it attracted a very large field of forty-one runners. Mellor and his mount were contesting the lead, in a race run at a Charge of the Light Brigade pace, when they crashed out at the second flight. Eastern Harvest put his foot on his rider's head and Stan received further kicks to his face from the other runners. The bulletin from Walton Hospital reported: 'Mellor has sustained fairly severe facial and internal injuries and he is seriously ill.'

Terry Biddlecombe and Bobby Beasley came to visit their weighing-room friend straight after racing. 'We walked through the ward, which had about ten beds on either side of it, and passed Stan as we did not recognise him. His head was swollen like a football and he could breathe only with difficulty,' Biddlecombe recalled.

Stan could easily have been kicked to death at Liverpool, yet miraculously he was back in action again the following August, with a 25-1 winner. He may have lost his 1962/63 title to Josh Gifford in the most unfortunate of circumstances, but his appetite for riding winners was undiminished. Brough Scott said that Mellor's recovery from such an horrific fall to become the first man to ride over 1,000 winners over jumps was 'the most sustained piece of skill and bravery' he had witnessed in all his time in racing.

Although Mellor never won another title, he came mighty close in 1969/70 (when he lost by just one winner, coming second behind Bob Davies), and again in 1971/72. Among the many highlights in the mid to late 1960s was a first King George on Frenchman's Cove in 1964, and a fabulous four-timer at Ascot on 15 December 1965, which included winning the inaugural running of the SGB Handicap Chase on Vultrix, in the first year that jump racing had taken place at Ascot.

There was also, of course, his famous victory over the legendary Arkle on the very consistent grey Stalbridge Colonist in the 1966 Hennessy, voted the twenty-first best ride of all time by *Racing Post* readers.

Mellor rode Stalbridge Colonist in the 1967 Gold Cup, and came agonisingly close to victory. His mount had a terrific duel with Woodland Venture (ridden by Terry Biddlecombe) in the closing stages, and actually went ahead for a few strides on the run-in, but in the end went down by just three quarters of a length.

It wasn't until many years later that Stan explained, in an interview with the *Racing Post*, the background to the defeat. Stalbridge's trainer Ken Cundell, described by Stan as 'something of a perfectionist', had been concerned that the scalpings that the Cheltenham ground staff had put on the walkway from the paddock to the track to ease its slipperiness following an overnight frost might clog up his horse's hooves. So he had a lad down at the walkway to pick the horse's feet out.

Alas, in doing this, Stalbridge's off-fore shoe got loosened, and Mellor had to canter to the start holding it. It was put back on by the blacksmith but its wrenching off had made the holes for the nails bigger. At the third fence Stalbridge stumbled, and it was there that Mellor thinks his shoe came off again. 'It took the gloss off him. He still ran a grand race, but he didn't finish in the way that Stalbridge Colonist did best. I never spoke publicly about this. It would have been unkind to Ken. He didn't deserve it.'

In 1967/68 Mellor finished fourth in the jockey championship, but a year later there was another nasty injury when he dislocated his ankle when riding Game Purston in the 1969 Grand National. Later that year, he was awarded the Derby Award as National Hunt jockey of the year. 'Everyone seems to think I'm a veteran,' he said, 'at least 40 years old. In fact, I'm only 32 – bit young to be pensioned off.' He finished off the Swinging Sixties in fine style, winning the last King George of the decade on Gordon W. Richards-trained Titus Oates.

Thought out of contention in the 1969/70 title race, due to another lay-off, Mellor made an earlier than expected return to give Messrs Biddlecombe and Davies the fright of their lives, only missing out on a fourth title on the final day of dramatic action at Stratford on 6 June, which will be described in more detail in Chapter Eleven.

In 1971, his quest to surpass Fred Winter's record of 923 winners – and then become the first jump jockey to ride 1,000 winners – became a major sports story. The first target was reached in February on Chorus, a Tom Jones-trained novice chaser, at Nottingham. The second looked like it would be achieved before the year was out. 'Stan Mellor is on the brink of history,' the *Daily Mirror* declared on 9 December 1971. Prairie Dog supplied him with his 999th winner, but there was an agonising wait for the magic four numbers. After finishing fourth at Chepstow on 14 December on Centaur, his young daughters Dana and Linz rather cheekily wrote him a note: 'Dear Daddy, why are you going so slow?'

There was great relief when Mellor finally rode his way into the record books on the roan Ouzo at 12.49 pm on Saturday, 19 December. Again, he'd broken a record on a Tom Jones-trained novice chaser at Nottingham. After riding his thousandth winner, he won the next race too, on Clear Cut for Charlie Hall.

There was to be no resting on his laurels. On 17 January 1972, the *Daily Mirror*'s Tim Richards reported how 'the iron man of racing' had no immediate plans to retire even after a 'creasing fall' the previous weekend at Ascot. Mellor would be back in action at Leicester the following day, but first there was a special World Sporting Club dinner at the Grosvenor Hotel in London to celebrate his magnificent achievement.

The winners kept on coming, and on 20 May 1972, he drew level with Bob Davies at the top of the championship with seventy-nine. But Davies pulled clear again, finishing in the end on eighty-nine, five ahead of Mellor. A final total of eighty-four was still an extraordinary effort, and would have won the title for Mellor in three of the previous four seasons.

It was the perfect time to bow out.

In a nineteen-year career he had ridden 1,035 winners, and had won a race at forty-seven British racetracks. The only jumps courses where he didn't make it to the winners' enclosure were Carlisle, Catterick, Kelso and Teesside (Stockton). Six hundred and one of his wins had been in steeplechases, 434 in hurdles. George Owen (136), Tom Jones (134) and Frank Cundell (120) were the trainers providing the highest number of his wins.

Stan Mellor was awarded an MBE for his services to racing, becoming only the second jump jockey, after Fred Winter, to be so honoured. He received official recognition not just because of his career in the saddle, but for what he had done for the sport in general. As the first chairman of the Jockeys Association he oversaw great improvements to safety, including the introduction of better crash helmets with chinstraps (to replace the old cork helmets, which offered little protection), early back protectors and more effective insurance. You could liken the role that Mellor played in improving safety for his fellow jockeys to that of Sir Jackie Stewart in Formula One. 'He did more for jockeys' welfare than anyone else has ever done,' says Brough Scott.

Mellor had purchased a training yard at Lambourn, naming it 'Linkslade' after the George Owen-trained horse on which he won fifteen races between 1954/55 and 1960/61, and on 30 November 1972 he sent out his first winner, Drishaune, at Haydock.

Plenty of success followed, particularly in the period 1977 to 1987. He won the Triumph Hurdle in 1979 with Pollardstown and then again in 1983 with Saxon Warrior when he trained the 1-2 in the race. There were also two Whitbread wins (to add to his one as a jockey): in 1980 with the New Zealand import Royal Mail (who finished second behind the ill-fated Alverton in the 1979 Gold Cup and third in Aldaniti's 1981 Grand National), and the bold-jumping front-runner Lean Ar Aghaidh in 1987, who had finished third in the Grand National just a few weeks earlier. There was even a valuable win on the Flat too, when Al Trui landed the Stewards' Cup at Glorious Goodwood in 1985.

However, the big race winners began to dry up after Mellor moved from Lambourn to his own purpose-built Pollardstown Stables in Wiltshire in 1988. 'A trainer these days must be ambitious and greedy, striving hard for every winner as soon as possible. That's not me, and quite probably the reason the business has gone down the sink a bit in recent seasons. I'm too old-fashioned,' he told the *Racing Post*'s Rodney Masters in 2001.

That October, Mellor sent out his last runner, Storm Tiger, at Aintree, bringing down the curtain on an incredible fifty-year career, which had resulted in over 1,700 winners, either ridden or trained.

Stan died, aged 83, on 1 August 2020. I had planned to visit him for this book, but unfortunately he was too ill. I hope I have done this great man justice in this chapter.

Big race wins
Whitbread Gold Cup 1962 (Frenchman's Cove)
Champion Chase 1963 (Sandy Abbot)
King George VI Chase 1964 (Frenchman's Cove), 1969 (Titus Oates)
Hennessy Gold Cup 1966 (Stalbridge Colonist)

Chapter Nine

Josh Gifford

Champion 1962/63, 1963/64, 1966/67, 1967/68

The Huntingdon Cavalier

'Josh was a horseman in his own right. He had everything: style, ability, judgement and sheer guts.'

Terry Biddlecombe

When Josh Gifford died in 2012, the *Independent*'s Chris McGrath noted that he was so cherished as a warm and generous friend within the racing community that his status as one of the sport's greatest achievers seemed almost incidental.

Even when Gifford's achievements were mentioned they usually started off with reference to him being the trainer of Aldaniti, the Grand National-winning mount of the cancer-defying Bob Champion, rather than the fact he was a brilliantly talented multiple-champion jump jockey who developed his own unique style of riding.

Everyone loved the ruddy-faced Josh and his company. Anecdotes about his 'relish for life and laughter', particularly in association with his great weighing room mate and fellow cavalier Terry Biddlecombe, are legion.

Gifford showed you could be a record-breaking sportsman but still keep your sense of fun. In the 1963 Grand National, for example, he fell on Out and About at the fourth last, having led the field a merry old dance for most of the way. He saw 'TB' clearing the fence on Loyal Tan, who looked a tired horse. 'He ran towards me and the next thing I knew he was hanging on to my leg, laughing,' recalled Biddlecombe. 'Get off you silly bugger,' I said, and gave him a push. He was still giggling as he lost his balance and fell to the ground for the second time.'

Gifford was champion jump jockey four times in the 1960s and on the third of those occasions broke Fred Winter's record of 121 winners in one season. Not bad for a rider who started out as a child prodigy on the Flat and who, weight permitting, may well have gone on to rival the great Lester Piggott on the level.

The son of a Huntingdonshire farmer and point-to-point enthusiast, Joshua Thomas Gifford was born on 3 August 1941. That grim Puritan Oliver Cromwell came from Huntingdonshire too, but that's where the similarities end.

At the tender age of 5, Josh was photographed jumping a fence on his pony. Like champions before and after him, he spent his childhood hunting and competing in gymkhanas. He had a sister, Susan, and a younger brother, Macer, who also became a very good jockey, riding at the same time as Josh (he won a Whitbread in 1968).[1]

Josh's love of racing was kindled by the former jump jockey Cliff Beechener who trained just over the border in Northamptonshire. Josh's horsemanship did not go unnoticed. He began his racing career at the Newmarket yard of Sam Armstrong, famous for the way it turned talented young apprentices into champions.

While he was still 14, Josh rode his first winner on the Flat, a horse called Dorsol, at Birmingham. He rode his second winner the very next day. His progress was so rapid that in his very first season (1956), he was booked by trainer Towser Gosden, father of John, to ride Trentham Boy in the Manchester November Handicap. 'Even more remarkable, Gosden had sufficient confidence in this cool, capable 15-year-old to back his horse, who duly obliged at odds of 100/6,' says Fitzgeorge-Parker. What made Gifford's performance in the saddle that day all the more laudatory was that he only just got to the track in time having been involved in a car crash a few hours earlier.

Gifford rode thirteen winners that first season, and in 1957, twenty-eight more, including a victory in the valuable Chester Cup.

What he might have achieved on the Flat after such a sensational start one can only imagine, but Gifford was tall for his age and was putting on weight. Armstrong consequently got him schooling over hurdles. In 1959, his Flat wins tally was only three, but in 1959/60 he had twelve wins under National Hunt Rules. Terry Biddlecombe recalled that the first time he set eyes on Gifford was at Hurst Park on 18 December 1959, when the teenage recruit fell at the last flight in the Christmas Rose Hurdle. He broke his collarbone in that fall and broke it again not long afterwards. 'I remember when it happened, laughing it off and telling everyone not to worry about him. I thought to myself, "Well, this is a good, brave sort of guy."'

---

[1] Macer's Whitbread win came on Larbawn, and twelve months later, in 1969, Josh rode the same horse to victory in the race when he deputised for his brother.

Most of Gifford's rides were coming from Captain Ryan Price and when Price moved to Findon in Sussex from Newmarket, Gifford joined him.

The great Fred Winter was the first jockey at Findon, but it took Gifford only two years, as number two jockey, to take the title. The way he was able to switch so seamlessly from Flat to jumps was analysed by Tim Fitzgeorge-Parker. He noted that Gifford's success was hard for jumping experts to understand because he rode over hurdles as if he was 'windy': in other words, like an old jockey who had lost his nerve. Crack hurdle jockeys, Fitzgeorge-Parker explained, were meant to crouch low over the horse's withers and go with their mount 'all the way over the obstacle', landing in the same galloping position. 'Later, frightened of a fall, their bodies might swing upright on landing as though they were negotiating a big drop fence.' Gifford, however, always seemed to swing back on landing. So how come he rode so many winners? It was Sam Armstrong who eventually solved the puzzle:

Josh developed an entirely new technique, which was all his own. … He went with his horses and against them at one and the same time, sort of picking them up before they touched down. As a result they landed balanced and straight into their action. They jumped far quicker for him than for other jockeys. It was extraordinary.

Having already made an impact over the smaller obstacles, Gifford rode for the first time over fences in public at Wye in March 1960. Sam Armstrong had forbidden him to ride in chases, but Fred Winter had a bad fall in an earlier race and Price needed a replacement to ride a steeplechaser of his called Bribery. Gifford told Chris Pitt many years later:

He [Price] asked several other jockeys but they weren't available so Ryan said I would have to ride. Going down the back straight for the last time, Bribery fell and I gashed my leg badly on the inside. I hid the injury from Sam for a long time but he eventually found out and I got a real telling off for disobeying his instructions.

Terry Biddlecombe said it was not until Gifford had thrashed him in 'Biddlecombe country' (Hereford) in November 1961, on a horse called Red Alley, that he came to know him very well. 'There was a small party in the weighing room after racing and it was then that we realised that we were somewhat birds of a feather.' The pair became bosom pals, forging one of the strongest friendships in the racing world. Together with fellow jockey

David Mould, Josh and Terry became known as the 'Three Cavaliers' for their attitude towards life and their sport. Gifford was treated as one of the family when he stayed at the Biddlecombes', and it was the same when Terry went to stay with Josh's parents in Huntingdon.

In the 1961/62 season Gifford came fourth in the jockeys' championship with sixty-one wins from 421 rides. But it was a very good fourth: he was only four behind that year's runner-up, Bobby Beasley, and just one behind Winter. Victory in the Topham Trophy at Liverpool on the Bobby Renton-trained Dagmar Gittell showed anyone who still had their doubts what a star of the winter game Gifford was going to be. He was only fourth two fences out, but he joined the leaders coming up to the last. It was still anyone's race, but Gifford rousted his mount in a stirring Liverpool finish to get the better of Johnny Lehane and College Don by a length, with Stan Mellor, on Peacetown, in third. Just 3 lengths separated the first three. Gifford, even after he had retired from the saddle, said that the win provided him with 'the greatest thrill' of his life.

Another highlight of 1961/62 was a win on Ryan Price's Beaver II in the Triumph Hurdle, run for the last time at Hurst Park. The lovely course at West Molesey, Surrey, which opened in 1890 and hosted races on the Flat and over jumps, sadly closed down in 1962, with the Triumph Hurdle later transferred to the Cheltenham Festival. Fred Winter chose to ride Price's other, more fancied runner, Catapult II, in the 1962 race, and when he reciprocated Gifford's wishes of 'Good Luck', Gifford replied, 'I've got no chance.' His mount – who earlier in the season was thought only good enough for selling company[2] – won comfortably.

At the same meeting he also rode the winner of the last steeplechase ever run at Hurst Park, a horse called Hedgelands, trained by Cyril Mitchell. There was further big race success in April, when Gifford rode the Earl Jones-trained 8-year-old Forty Secrets to victory in the Welsh Grand National.

Earlier that season, Gifford was involved in a funny – if painful – incident, which in the words of Graham Sharpe, author of *500 Strangest Racing Stories*, was literally hard to swallow. He was riding a horse called Timber in a novices' hurdle at Birmingham. Tim Brookshaw was on Joss Merlin. The two jockeys were chatting away merrily, with Gifford's mount going much the better. As he went past Brookshaw at the second last, with the race at his mercy, Gifford turned round and laughed. But he overdid it and his dentures fell down the back of his throat. 'I was choking. It was a frightening experience and as a result Tim got up to win. I always rode without teeth after that,' he later recalled.

---

[2] The lowest class of race, in which the winner is put up for sale at auction afterwards.

Gifford's title challenge in 1962/63 was anything but toothless. On 15 October, there was a hat-trick of wins in the last three races at Plumpton, all trained by Ryan Price. Stan Mellor was going for his fourth successive title and despite Gifford's efforts looked likely to achieve it for most of the campaign. There was only one race meeting (at Ayr) held between Boxing Day and the Cheltenham Festival on account of the Big Freeze, but when both Mellor and Gifford headed up to Liverpool at the end of March for the Grand National meeting, the reigning champion was twenty wins ahead of the challenger. The story of Mellor's nightmare fall on Eastern Harvest – which put him out of action until August – was told in our previous chapter. Gifford won the race on 20-1 shot Rosyth (a horse we shall hear a lot more about), and after a strong finish to the campaign, pipped his stricken rival to the title by six. He was only 21, and remains the youngest champion of the last hundred years. 'He was very gracious and acknowledged that he won the title by default, and that Stan would have won had he not been injured at Liverpool,' says Elain Mellor.

Gifford celebrated that summer by flying out to Majorca on holiday with Terry Biddlecombe and Johnny Lehane to join Fred and Mercy Rimell and their daughter Scarlett, trainer Neville Crump and his wife, and Ken and Rhona Oliver. It seems to have been some party. One night Johnny Lehane was driving Terry and Josh to a restaurant out in the sticks when he had to swerve to avoid a man standing in the middle of the road. Around the next bend the car hit a wall and burst a tyre. The trio carried on driving to the restaurant, where they charmed the locals so much they came out and changed the totally burnt-out tyre. On another occasion, Josh and Terry went waterskiing for the first time, sitting on wooden lavatory seats. No one records where they got the seats from.

Gifford had undoubtedly been fortunate in 1962/63, but in the following season he showed his success was no fluke by winning his second title very easily. However, that only tells half the story of what was a dramatic campaign. Having got off to a good start, a double at Cheltenham on 16 October put him on thirty for the season, sixteen ahead of his nearest pursuers, Roy Edwards and the amateur rider Jim Renfree.

At Kempton on 20 November, he picked up a lucky winning ride on 11-8 favourite Magic Orb in the Wimbledon Handicap Chase. Terry Biddlecombe had been booked to ride Alec Kilpatrick's horse, but he had fallen on Eagle Don in the previous race. The ambulance bringing him to the racecourse hospital took a longer than usual route – and Biddlecombe didn't get back in time. Magic Orb won by 8 lengths.

By 22 November 1963, the day that US President J.F. Kennedy met his end in Dallas, Gifford had reached his half-century. The odds of him breaking Fred Winter's record of 121 winners in a season were just 3-1. But Gifford told John Bromley in a *Daily Mirror* interview on 25 November: 'Please don't talk to me about records. They really don't bother me.' The reigning champ also said he had no worries about injury. 'That's the last thing you worry about. I'm only concerned if I have a bad race.' While admitting that the travelling was tiring, he added: 'How can you possibly get tired of something you love so much?' Readers were told that Gifford 'likes a pint and a cigarette' and when asked how long he planned to stay 'in one of the world's most difficult jobs', he replied: 'Indefinitely. I shall never slow up on the pace. The more rides I get, the better.'

On 7 December at Lingfield, with the Queen Mother in attendance, Josh narrowly avoided serious injury when his mount Odysseus crashed out at the third fence in a novices' chase. Gifford lay motionless on the ground as other horses thundered past him. Fortunately, he escaped with 'just' a lacerated thigh and was only stood down for the rest of the afternoon.

More wins followed, but then in February came the Rosyth scandal, which undoubtedly took some of the gloss off an excellent season. As mentioned earlier, Ryan Price's hurdler had won the inaugural Schweppes Gold Trophy at Liverpool the year before. In 1964 the race was switched from the Grand National meeting to Newbury Racecourse in February, and Rosyth was lined up for a repeat bid. Having failed to win in five races over hurdles since his 1963 win, he was only carrying 2lb more. Nicely handicapped, he won by 2 lengths. The Newbury stewards referred Price to the National Hunt Committee to explain the horse's improvement in form. Had he been running on his merits in his earlier races?

Price said Rosyth broke blood vessels, which made training him difficult. Furthermore, as an entire, he didn't put his best foot forward until the spring. The Committee wasn't convinced by the explanation and stripped Price of his licence for the rest of the season. Gifford was suspended for three weeks, up to the end of March, which meant he missed the Cheltenham Festival and the Grand National.

Back in action at Sandown on 1 April he showed that his enforced lay-off had made him even more determined to ride winners. In his first four days back he rode nine, which included victory on 4-1 shot Goodness Gracious in the selling hurdle at Leicester on 4 April. At Wye, on 6 April, a double brought his seasonal tally up to ninety-one. The first of the wins on the 13-8 favourite Stainsby in a novices' hurdle was particularly well received as the horse's trainer, 'Britt' Gallup, was in hospital as a result of breaking his pelvis in a schooling accident the previous day. As soon as the horse passed the line, Gallup's wife ran off to look for a telephone to tell her husband the good news.

On Saturday, 11 April, though, there was more drama when Gifford fell in the first at Cheltenham on Gorse Hill. He had two further rides at the meeting. That night after racing he went along with Stan and Elain Mellor, Terry and Tony Biddlecombe and Michael Scudamore for a meal. 'I remember seeing him in the car park and he didn't look well,' recalls Elain Mellor. Elain sat in the car with him and tried to nurse him. At the restaurant Gifford ordered Chicken Maryland, but only picked at his food. He went to the gents and Elain told Terry Biddlecombe to see how he was. It later transpired that Josh had fractured a bone in his neck. How brave he must have been to still have agreed to go out for a meal and not complain about how he felt. The following Friday he turned up as a spectator at Fontwell, swathed in plaster and bandages.

By the time the season ended, Gifford, despite his suspension, and his neck injury, had ridden ninety-four winners from 408 rides, translating into a very impressive 23.03 per cent strike rate. He finished thirty wins ahead of his nearest challenger, David Mould, and thirty-six clear of third-placed Terry Biddlecombe.

He went into the 1964/65 season the obvious favourite to win his third title in a row. But Gifford's luck ran out at Nottingham in November when he broke his thigh following a fall on Reverando. Doctors said he probably wouldn't be fit enough to ride until the following season, but on 8 January 1965, the *Birmingham Daily Post* reported that Gifford had left Nottingham General Hospital on crutches and had returned home to Little Stukeley in Huntingdonshire. 'There is just a chance I still may be able to ride What a Myth in the Grand National. I am certainly going to have a try,' he told reporters.

He never made it. Having been forced to miss the whole of the season, Gifford was still able in the summer of 1965 to indulge his other great sporting passion, cricket. He played opening bat in a team of jump jockeys captained by David Nicholson.

On Saturday, 26 June, Gifford took part in a charity cricket match between jockeys, owners and trainers at Alscot Park, near Stratford-upon-Avon. He had dinner at a hotel and visited the home of David Nicholson. Then tragedy struck. While driving on the Oxford to Stratford road later that evening, he overtook two cars in his Mercedes on a slight bend at Tredington, and collided with a Ford Anglia. He broke his right leg again, but even worse, the driver of the other car, 21-year-old Roger Field, was killed. That weekend no fewer than five people were killed in separate road accidents in Warwickshire. Gifford faced a charge of causing death by dangerous driving, to which he pleaded guilty. He had been following a car in front which had successfully overtaken the two cars, and the judge pronounced: 'It was a grave error of judgement but that was all it was.' Gifford was fined £5 and disqualified from driving for a year.

The *Coventry Evening Telegraph* reported on 20 January 1966 that the former champion was 'raring to go chasing again' after a fifteen-month lay-off. 'I am fit and ready right now,' Gifford said. 'My injured leg feels as good as ever and I have no worries at all.' He added, 'My first few rides will be over hurdles again. But I don't mean to hang around. I want to get back to racing over fences almost immediately.' He rode his first winner back at Windsor eight days later.

Despite his late start to the 1965/66 season he still managed to ride forty-nine winners from just 153 rides – translating into a 32 per cent strike rate. The title was won again by Terry Biddlecombe, with Stan Mellor in second place.

Season 1966/67 could be said to be Gifford's annus mirabilis. He not only won his third title but also broke Fred Winter's 14-year-old record of 121 winners. It seemed that everyone wanted Josh to ride their horses. Trainer David Gandolfo was very surprised when he saw in the press reports that Gifford was to ride a horse of his called Java in the 1967 Triumph Hurdle. 'He had only won a couple of races and I didn't think Josh had even heard of me. I had never had any contact with him. So I rang him up to ask if he knew anything about it. He couldn't stop laughing. It transpired that the owner of Java, who was a bit of a nut, had rung him up and said, 'See how my horse won with Bill Shoemark up. Think what more he could do if you rode him!'

But despite his success, the 1966/67 season was again not without controversy for Gifford. On 18 February, Hill House gave him and Ryan Price their fourth victory in five years in the Schweppes Gold Trophy at Newbury. But the 12-length 8-1 winner had barely been unsaddled before Price was hauled before the stewards. As in 1964 with Rosyth, Gifford too was reported to the National Hunt Committee. Again, it was the horse's 'abnormal improvement' – to quote the stewards' exact words – which was the issue. He had refused to start at Kempton, and just a week before the Newbury showcase, he had run disappointingly to finish fourth at Sandown, where he made jumping errors. It was only on the Wednesday before the race that Price had announced that Gifford would ride Hill House and not his other runner, Burlington II. The *Reading Evening Post* reported that there was 'loud booing' before Hill House crossed the line in front and that the boos continued as Gifford rode into the unsaddling enclosure. Punters obviously thought they'd been put away, but those who were 'on' thought differently. Peter O'Sullevan admitted he took some of the 10-1 on offer and tipped him to *Daily Express* readers.

Price's defence was that the horse's improvement wasn't abnormal, but then came a bombshell. Hill House tested positive in a dope test. The question was: was the level of Cortisol found in the runaway Schweppes Gold Trophy winner self-created or administered? In March, the Newbury stewards referred the case to the National Hunt stewards. It wasn't until August that Price and Gifford were exonerated. 'We were made to feel like criminals in London,' Gifford recalled of the inquiry. 'We sat there all day without even being offered a cup of tea.'

While he was under the shadow of the Hill House inquiry, Gifford was looking forward to riding Honey End in the 1967 Grand National. He rode the 10-year-old to victory over the Queen Mother's The Rip at Folkestone on 22 March, the first leg of a double that put him on ninety-four winners for the season, which equalled his previous best in 1963/64. Honey End was the subject of a big gamble on Grand National Day, which saw his odds shorten to 15/2. Gifford would have been optimistic of landing his first National. His horse was in form, had a nice weight (10st 4lb) and was trained by a maestro (Price), who had won the big race just five years earlier with Kilmore. But at the fence after Becher's on the second circuit, with a large number of runners still in contention, the riderless Popham Down cut right across the fence (the smallest on the course), causing a multiple pile-up. The only horse that missed the melee – because he was still some way back – was the 100-1 shot Foinavon, ridden by John Buckingham, who found himself with a clear lead. Honey End refused, but Gifford turned his mount round and the pair, having cleared the 23rd at the second attempt, set off in pursuit. At one stage it looked as if they might catch up but Foinavon still had plenty of petrol left in the tank and won by 15 lengths. It was one of the greatest National upsets of all time. It was so unexpected that neither the horse's trainer nor owner were there to witness it.

Gifford was convinced he would have won and it was the closest he came to winning the National as a rider. He broke Winter's record of winners by one, finishing on 122 for the campaign, with Ryan Price also winning the trainer's title for the second year running, and fourth time in all.

The year 1967 and its 'Summer of Love' was the height of the Swinging Sixties and Josh was very much part of the zeitgeist. An iconic television programme of the time was *The Avengers*, and the champion jockey posed with the delectable Mrs Emma Peel, the actress Diana Rigg, for a fashion shoot promoting the series. Josh, together with his fellow weighing room cavaliers, could be seen regularly at London's best night spots, partying the night away before heading to the Savoy Turkish Baths in Jermyn Street the next morning and getting on the train to ride winners in the afternoon at Folkestone or Wye.

Unfortunately, the Summer of Love was followed by the autumn and winter of foot-and-mouth. The highly infectious viral disease, which affects cloven-hoofed animals but can be spread by horses, people and dogs, was first noted on 25 October and wasn't officially over until the following June, by which time 400,000 cattle had been destroyed. Josh won the Mackeson on Charlie Worcester in November, but racing was suspended from the 25th of that month until 5 January, meaning no Hennessy or King George. 'The current outbreak of foot-and-mouth disease reminds us that there is one great plague virus as menacing as ever,' reported the *Illustrated London News* on 2 December. Even after resumption, racing was still disrupted until mid-March. Up to 14 February, seventy-two racing days were lost.

The title race was unsurprisingly a lot closer than in 1966/67, but in the end, Josh got home with eighty-two wins, five ahead from Brian Fletcher, who put in a strong challenge from the North. Fletcher won the 1968 Grand National on Red Alligator, whose Bishop Auckland-based trainer Denys Smith took the trainer's title from Ryan Price. As we'll see later, it was perhaps the first sign that the centre of power in the National Hunt world was moving northwards.

Gifford rode on for another two seasons. In 1969 he married the leading showjumper Althea Roger-Smith. His last ride in the Grand National came in 1970, when he finished seventh on Assad. The race was won by another top-class, retiring jockey, Pat Taaffe, who won on Gay Trip, who was winning the race fifteen years after his first success on Quare Times, in 1955. The Irishman, who was most associated for his partnership with the legendary Arkle, on whom he won three Gold Cups, was 40 in 1970, while Gifford was just 28, but his boss Ryan Price had provided him with an opportunity that was too good to turn down. The Captain decided to shift his focus on to the Flat and offered his stable jockey the chance to take over his National Hunt string at Downs Stables, which he did officially the day after the National.

In his career in the saddle Josh rode 642 winners. Although he never won a Grand National, nor even had a ride in the Gold Cup, he was only beaten by 1½ lengths on Major Rose in the 1970 Champion Hurdle, behind in the three-time winner Persian War. He trained over 1,500 winners in the thirty-three years that followed, and in 1987/88 came close to the trainers' title. He was just pipped by his great mate David Elsworth. The pair had arranged a side bet that the winner would deliver to the loser a case of whisky. 'Elsie' delivered in person and there was, in Gifford's words, 'quite a party'. A year later, he was awarded an MBE for services to racing. A sadness of these years was the death in 1985 of Josh's brother Macer, aged just 40, from motor neurone disease.

As a trainer Gifford won a Champion Chase (with Deep Sensation), a Hennessy (with Approaching) and back-to-back Mackesons (with Bradbury Star), but his most famous success was with Aldaniti in the 1981 Grand National. It wasn't just that the horse's jockey, Bob Champion, had to overcome cancer, but Aldaniti himself had to recover from serious injury that saw him off the track for a year. Gifford's loyalty towards both horse and jockey was richly rewarded. The story was told in the film *Champions* but Josh wasn't entirely happy with the way Aldaniti's trainer was portrayed. 'I wouldn't walk into a ruddy hospital with my hat on, or drink champagne in the ward, or swear at owners,' he told son Nick, who took over the reins at Findon when Josh retired in 2003. Gifford's daughter Tina became a three-time Olympic medalist at three-day eventing.

David Gandolfo remembers the last time he saw Gifford at the races:

> We both had a condition called Dupuytren's Contracture (Mrs Thatcher had it too), which is when one or more of your fingers bend inwards towards your palm. When you give someone a handshake they think you're giving them a Masonic one, but that's different. Josh had surgery on it and he held his hand up to me to show me his fingers were straight.

Almost a decade on from his passing, this wonderful racing personality – and professional cavalier – is still greatly missed.

Big race wins
Welsh Grand National 1962 (Forty Secrets)
Whitbread Gold Cup 1969 (Larbawn)

Chapter Ten

Terry Biddlecombe

Champion 1964/65, 1965/66, 1968/69 (tied)

The Blond Bomber

'Terry rode for us for nine years. He has always been a generous, cheerful fellow, universally popular in the weighing room.'

Fred Rimell, *Aintree Iron*

Not many jockeys feature on a tea towel but the late Terry Biddlecombe did. The Injured Jockeys Fund's 'Cost of Riding' towel illustrates all the injuries Terry incurred in a career that lasted from 1957 to 1974.

Working from top to bottom, his head suffered from concussion on 'numerous occasions'. He broke his nose twice, his collarbone once. He smashed his right and left shoulder blades three times each. He broke five ribs and damaged his liver. He broke his left elbow and left forearm, and his right and left wrists were broken five times. He cracked his vertebrae and had two vertebrae compacted. He broke the thumb on his left hand three times and fingers on his left hand twice. He severely damaged his kidneys. He broke his left leg and had his shin chipped. He dislocated his right ankle and broke his left one. In retrospect it was probably easier to tell you what bones he didn't break.

Tim Fitzgeorge-Parker said of Biddlecombe: 'His bravery is all the more amazing, because as his injuries show, he falls heavily. Although he has ridden more than 700 winners in thirteen years, he had had more than 300 falls in that time.'

It is important to remember that 'TB' was having his 300-plus falls at a time when jockeys were statistically more likely to suffer really serious injuries than they are today. We have already mentioned Tim Brookshaw and Paddy Farrell, who were left badly crippled. Even worse, from 1964 to 1970, three of Terry's weighing room colleagues were killed in racecourse action. As John Wayne memorably put it: 'Courage is being scared to death, but saddling up anyway.' Terry admitted he did think about the risks, of course he did, but he *always* saddled up anyway.

He came from solid Gloucestershire farming stock. His father Walter farmed near Newent and rode, and later trained, point-to-pointers. Terry's brother Tony, three years his senior, became a successful point-to-point rider, a champion amateur jockey and a prize-winning showjumper. Terry took part in showjumping classes too. At the age of 12, though, he became 'sick and tired' of horses. But a winning ride in a flapping race[1] not only restored his enthusiasm, but set him on the path to be a jockey. He regularly went to Hereford races with his dad. On one occasion Michael Scudamore, who was riding a close finish on the rails, nearly sliced his head off with his whip.

Terry was a countryman through and through. When he wasn't riding horses, he enjoyed the traditional pursuits of huntin', shootin' and fishin'. In 2004 I interviewed him for the *Racing Post* about his passion for shooting for my series 'My Other Life' on the hobbies of racing personalities. Terry said he went out with a gun for the first time when he was 6. 'I was out with my grandfather and we saw a rabbit sitting by a hole. I took a shot at it with a 12 bore, missed it, and the recoil knocked me over.'

Having seen his father and his brother ride winners at local racecourses, it was only natural that Terry would want to follow suit. His first ride in public came at Hereford on 23 February 1957, when he rode a grey mare called Balkan Flower and finished unplaced.

His first winner came just over a year later, on 6 March 1958, on Burnella at Wincanton. It was a photo finish between Terry's mount and a horse called Piper, ridden by Fred Winter.

'Riding alongside Fred Winter and oblivious to his grim expression I said, "I've won, I've won",' Terry recalled many years later. 'But he only gave me a cold look and never once said "Well done". At that moment I could not have cared less. At 17 years of age I had won my first race on a 20-1 outsider and beaten the champion jockey by a head.' Later he learnt that a considerable sum of money had been lost on Piper, which might have accounted for Winter's bad mood.

Biddlecombe rode twenty-two winners as an amateur before turning pro during the 1959/60 season. At the time the rate of pay was £7 10s a ride, with no percentage of the prize money. His first winner as a professional was the appropriately named Blonde Warrior at Market Rasen on 5 March 1960. He rode eighteen winners in his first full season as a licensed jockey.

---

[1] A horse race not held under Jockey Club Rules.

He started to ride for Fred Rimell and at the end of the campaign the Master of Kinnersley asked him if he would join his yard the following season as number two jockey to Bobby Beasley, with a retainer of £200. Biddlecombe was to spend his next nine years with the Rimells. While inevitably it had its ups and downs, it was for most of the time a strong trainer-jockey relationship. 'I liked Fred's easy-going manner and, if we had a disagreement, which was rare, we would forget it within a couple of days,' Terry later wrote.

For the 1963/64 season he was promoted to Rimell's first jockey as Beasley left. That allowed him to increase his win tally from forty-one to fifty-six and set him up nicely for the 1964/65 season. With his natural talent and determination to ride winners it was only a matter of time before Terry became champion jockey, but the injury his close friend and reigning champion Josh Gifford suffered at Nottingham in November, which put him out for the rest of the season, undoubtedly enhanced Terry's chances.

Biddlecombe made a flying start to the campaign on the West Country circuit in August but also made trips to the North to ride winners for the likes of Denys Smith and John Barclay. It was now possible for jockeys to cover a wider geographical area because of the advent of motorways. Terry could be riding in Devon on one day and at Sedgefield in County Durham the next.

On 27 October, he had two falls at Worcester. But it was only a minor setback as five days later he returned to action to win his first race back.

At the beginning of November, Terry was leading the title race, but Josh Gifford, Roy Edwards, David Mould and Stan Mellor were all snapping at his heels. He increased his lead with a double at Leicester on the 9th, which put him on thirty-five winners for the season. Gifford also had a winner on the card, but the reigning champion's season was over on 30 November when he broke a leg at Nottingham. Terry chalked up his half-century of winners at Aintree on 3 December when he rode Quick Approach to victory.

The year 1965 started well with wins on Ken Oliver's Scottish National winner Pappageno's Cottage in the 4-miler at Cheltenham on 7 January, Spartan General at Haydock on the 9th and Quick Approach at Leicester on the 11th. Given the nature of jump racing, though, it was still a case of up one minute and down the next. On 30 January, Biddlecombe experienced what he later called 'one of the saddest moments' of his life when one of his favourite horses, Red Thorn, which he thought capable of winning one or even two Grand Nationals, broke a leg at Doncaster in the Great Yorkshire Chase and had to be put down. After that depressing end to January things had to pick up in February, and they duly did.

Terry celebrated his twenty-fourth birthday on 2 February by riding a treble at Nottingham. One of them was on a horse called Tibidabo trained by Arthur Freeman. One morning, Biddlecombe was riding out for Freeman at Newmarket and the owner of Tibidabo, one Mrs A.M. Gibson, asked her trainer: 'Who's that girl you've got riding out for you, Arthur?' 'I'm afraid that's our jockey – Biddlecombe,' Freeman replied. 'Oh' said Mrs Gibson, looking surprised, 'with those golden curls he looks just like a little girl.'

The Blond Bomber – or the Blond Beatle, to give Terry his other nickname – was, like his musical namesakes, on a roll. At Wolverhampton on 25 February, he rode another treble, at odds of 11-8, 13-2 and 4-1. He was beaten by a length in the 1965 Champion Hurdle on Spartan General, a race he thought he should have won, but bounced back with a win on Coral Cluster, trained by David Gandolfo in the George Duller Hurdle just half an hour later.

At a wet Wolverhampton on Monday, 16 March, Biddlecombe rode a treble (two trained by Fred Rimell), putting him on eighty-seven for the season – thirty ahead of his nearest challenger Stan Mellor. He was champion in all but name.

On Easter Monday (19 April), there was a double at Hereford, and a day later, Biddlecombe enjoyed big race success at Chepstow when he won his first Welsh National on the Denzil Jenkins-trained Norther. It was his ninety-ninth winner of the season. The century was achieved four days later, when he partnered the Doug Francis-trained Dundalk to victory in a chase at Bangor. Ironically, the horse used to be trained by Fred Rimell, who had provided Terry with so many of his winners.

Biddlecombe had become only the fourth National Hunt jockey to ride 100 winners in a season. The question was now: could he break Winter's record of 121 from 1952/53? He gave it a jolly good try – winning his 101st race at the same Bangor meeting, but in the end came up short by seven. His final win of the season came on Joe's Girl at Stratford on 12 June. 'It was such a wonderful feeling,' he reflected. 'I knew I would be a permanent part of racing history by becoming champion jockey, which was a great thrill.'

The continued absence of Josh Gifford made Terry clear favourite to win the title again in 1965/66. The *Coventry Telegraph* of 17 September 1965 reported that TB had two main objectives: to retain his title and to break Fred Winter's record. The article noted that Terry did have weight problems – a recurring theme in his career – and recently had to put up 3lb overweight to ride a mount at 10st 10lb at Fontwell. His weight – and clashes of meetings – also meant that he was unable to ride all of Rimell's runners.

To get his weight down Terry would regularly have to shed 10lb in twenty-four hours by sweating away in Turkish baths, although being Terry he always tried to make the experience as enjoyable as possible. His weighing room mate and fellow 'Musketeer' David Mould recalled: 'I spent a lot of my time in Turkish baths all over the country, and in particular I remember spending many hours in the baths in Gloucester with Terry Biddlecombe, who would always take a bottle of champagne with him, since he maintained that nobody could sweat properly without drinking.'

On 27 October 1965, Terry had two falls at Worcester, but just five days later returned to action at Wolverhampton, and once again won on his first race back. He rode another winner at Stratford on 4 November, but that day had rather more significance than that as after the race he saw, in the paddock, Bridget Tyrwhitt-Drake, the woman who one year later was to become his first wife.

At the time Terry was dating a model called Vivienne, whom he described in his autobiography as 'strikingly pretty'. Truth was, the Blond Bomber always had an eye for the fillies. He later reminisced:

It is well known that I have been very fond of the opposite sex from an early age. As a jockey, travelling round the various race tracks, I soon realised that, as in other sports, racing had its own band of admiring female followers. I would be lying if I denied taking advantage of the pleasures offered to me. I indulged my passionate nature to the full, and loved every moment of it. Women have given me lots of enjoyment and laughter. A man has to be mad not to like them!

On the night before the 1963 Grand National Terry invited his 'attractive' hotel receptionist out for a drive. He borrowed Johnny Lehane's car and drove down to the beach for 'a night of passion in the back seat'. After a while the two lovebirds drifted off to sleep. Terry was awakened by a slapping sound on the front wheels. The tide was coming in! He tried to start the engine but it croaked and so he had to run about a mile to gather a rescue team together to pull the car out of the sea. 'When we got there the water was up to the car bonnet and I was out of favour, both with my new girlfriend and Johnny afterwards.'

In the Grand National later that day Terry finished seventeenth on Loyal Tan. It's hard to imagine any of today's jump jockeys getting up to similar shenanigans on the eve of such a big race, but that's how the sport was in those days. Terry lived life to the full, on the racetrack and off it. On 12 November he was the toast of the annual champion jockey dinner at Cheltenham. He was nervous about making his speech, sat between such august personages as 'Ruby' Holland-Martin and Lord Willoughby de Broke, but he got through it all right. 'Afterwards, everyone let their hair down, the bread rolls started to fly and we had a great evening,' he recalled.

But while he certainly knew how to party, there was, as trainer David Gandolfo says, a serious side to him as well. 'Like all the other champions who rode for me Terry was very switched on. He had a good head. He was intelligent. He wouldn't have achieved all that he did otherwise.' Graham Thorner, who later pipped Terry for a jockey's title, agrees:

> He may have had a drink problem later on after he retired but not when he was riding. People forget the wasting he had to do in the Turkish baths and how thirsty this made him. I remember seeing the bottles of Schweppes in the weighing room, and him and David Mould having a drink on the train to Folkestone and Wye but it was moisture that was needed for the dryness. He couldn't have had the success he had if he had been a 'pxxx artist'.

Terry began 1966 – the year of England's historic football World Cup victory – in splendid form. At Cheltenham on 6 January he won a novices' hurdle on Jupiter Boy and then rode Woodland Venture in a 3-mile 1-furlong novices' chase. The horses' form figures were 'PUP', leading fellow jockey Jimmy Morrissey to remark jokingly to Terry, 'I see you're riding a pup today!' Biddlecombe, however, was confident he would win. He had carefully been nursing Woodland Venture, a very talented horse, to iron out earlier jumping issues. He had got him to fence well on his previous outing at Worcester, but pulled his mount up before the last ditch as he saw Stan Mellor still on the top of the fence. So the 'PUP' form figures were not as bad as they seemed.

At Cheltenham, Woodland Venture beat Woodlawn (ridden by Willie Robinson) by a head. Terry followed up that success with another win on the same horse at Newbury on 19 February. Before that day he had gone twenty-five rides without a winner, and David Mould was just two behind him in the title race.

He rode the hurdler and former very smart performer on the Flat Trelawny to success at Warwick on 5 March and then in the Spa Hurdle at the Cheltenham Festival on 17 March. 'That was something beautiful,' he later recalled. 'I just sat on him for 3 miles, never changing hands as he jumped from hurdle to hurdle. It was the most fantastic feeling.'

Biddlecombe and Trelawny won again that month, taking the Coronation Hurdle at Aintree on 25 March. In the 1966 Grand National, which took place on the following day, Terry rode The Fossa, a 20-1 shot, to fourth place. His mount jumped superbly, but the 50-1 outsider Anglo surged right away from his nearest challengers, winning by 20 lengths.

With a commanding lead in the title race, Terry had his second title all but wrapped up. But his quest for winners remained unquenchable. He flew up to Ayr on 16 May to ride Pretentious to victory for Bishop Auckland trainer Denys Smith, and two days later won at Perth on another Smith-trained horse, Wifes Choice. On 30 May he rode a four-timer at Uttoxeter. He registered his 100th winner of the season at the same Staffordshire track on 11 June, when piloting Honey End to victory in a 3-mile chase. He had become the first National Hunt jockey to ride a century of winners two seasons running.

In claiming his second championship Biddlecombe had travelled some 80,000 miles. 'Unlike the Flat race jockeys, my travelling was mostly by road and rail, but I was so keen to be champion again that it did not seem to affect me,' he wrote.

Now he had won back-to-back titles, it was time to party. But it didn't exactly go to plan. After riding at the evening meeting at Market Rasen, Terry had arranged for him and his jockey pals Josh Gifford, Michael Scudamore and Roy Blandford to go into Lincoln. They drove all round the cathedral city trying to find somewhere to eat, but ended up in a Chinese restaurant – which did not serve alcohol. The next drink they had was at Stratford railway station – and that was cocoa obtained from a slot machine. Their failure to find any alcohol was, as Terry later acknowledged, quite unbelievable. Probably a 100-1 shot.

That summer Terry celebrated with a luxury holiday in Sardinia with girlfriend Vivienne, Mercy and Fred Rimell, and trainer Martin Tate and his wife Edna. Lord and Lady Chelsea were also staying there. There were late-night card games and Terry lost more than he could afford to lose – but generously both Fred Rimell and Lord Chelsea refused to allow him to honour his debts.

Terry had to wait another three years before he won the title again. But while he had to play second fiddle in the 1966/67 season to the returning Josh Gifford, there was still plenty to enjoy that year, including a fabulous five wins from five rides at Ludlow in September, and the considerable consolation prize of winning his first and what was to prove his only Gold Cup.

Woodland Venture, who had begun 1966 with the form figures PUP, started at 100-8 for the 1967 Cheltenham Blue Riband. The race was described by Tim Fitzgeorge-Parker as 'like Hamlet without the Prince' because of the absence of the legendary Arkle – winner in 1964, 1965 and 1966 – who had been injured in the King George on Boxing Day and never raced again.

Woodland Venture's Gold Cup year didn't start at all well, with a bad attack of ringworm early in the season, and then in the King George at Kempton it looked to be back to the drawing board after he suffered a heavy fall when well in contention. But Fred Rimell trained him to the minute for Cheltenham, and the ground – which had firmed up due to wind and sunshine – had come just right. The fall at the last open ditch at the top of the hill of the hugely popular 1963 winner Mill House left Terry and Woodland Venture in the lead. But Stan Mellor on Stalbridge Colonist was steadily closing the gap. 'It put fear of God into me because Stan was the last man I ever wanted to see taking me on in any race, let alone the Gold Cup – he was so good from the last fence,' Biddlecombe recalled. There ensued a terrific battle between the two great champion jockeys and their horses. At one point on the run-in it looked like Mellor and Stalbridge Colonist were edging ahead but Biddlecombe and his mount fought back to win by three quarters of a length in what was one of the most exciting finishes ever seen in a Gold Cup.

Terry was euphoric. 'The ovation we received was unbelievable. I dismounted and unsaddled, standing by the horse and hearing the acclaim, knowing but not quite believing what I had done.'

While Terry's greatest ambition had been achieved, he could so nearly have missed the race. The previous day he had been kicked so hard on the knee following a fall in the Cotswold Chase that he could barely walk afterwards. He went round to see his old friend Dr Bill Wilson. He told him that he feared the course doctor would pass him unfit to ride in the Gold Cup. Wilson agreed to sneak into the weighing room before racing and give the champion jockey a pain-killing injection. It worked. Terry even experienced a fall in the second race of the day without feeling any pain.

In the Grand National of 1967, made famous by the mass pile-up at the fence after second Becher's and the victory of Foinavon, Terry was on Greek Scholar. His mount ended up stuck in the fence where all the trouble occurred, but Terry managed to extradite him and eventually finished fourth. Biddlecombe believed that if he had been knocked over, and then remounted, he would have won.

He finished the 1966/67 season on eighty-three winners, a very decent total, but that was almost forty behind Josh Gifford, who beat Fred Winter's record of 121 wins by one. For the third year running, the champion jump jockey had ridden over a hundred winners.

The 1967/8 season was badly affected by the outbreak of foot-and-mouth disease and then frost and snow, and as a consequence the competition was a lot closer. In any case, Terry was out of action from mid-November to mid-January with injury, having broken both his right shoulder and the outer end of his collarbone from a fall in the Mackeson Gold Cup. Although he slipped to third place in the final table, with sixty-eight winners, behind Gifford (82) and Brian Fletcher (77), his strike rate of 24.28 per cent was actually higher than when he had won the title.

Terry married Bridget, the girl he had first seen at Stratford races two years earlier, in July 1968, just before the start of the new season. It was to be the closest title race since Mellor pipped Winter by one in 1959/60. Biddlecombe thought Josh Gifford would once again be the man to beat, but there was a new kid on the block, Bob Davies, whose story is told in our next chapter. Davies got off to a flyer on the West Country circuit but Terry had a good August too.

The Rimell yard had been boosted in the 1967/68 season by the addition of the horses of successful owner Bryan Jenks. One of the new arrivals for the 1968/69 season was Coral Diver, who was sent novice hurdling. Biddlecombe rode him to victory at Doncaster in November. Another recruit was Normandy, who was also an impressive hurdle winner for Terry at Kempton in February.

The season itself was badly affected by frost, snow and heavy rain. Ninety-four meetings were lost in total, with abandonments as early as 2 November and as late as 5 June. Among the big races lost were the King George and the Schweppes Gold Trophy. At one point, even the Cheltenham Festival looked to be in jeopardy due to waterlogging.

Luckily for Terry the rain finally stopped and Cheltenham went ahead. He rode three winners at the 1969 Festival. Normandy took the first division of the Gloucestershire Hurdle, Chatham the Arkle Chase and Coral Diver the Triumph Hurdle. What had been a memorable week could have been even better, but in the Gold Cup, Terry was unlucky for the second year running. In 1968 his saddle had slipped on Stalbridge Colonist (whom he had beaten into second a year earlier) at the business end of things and he was unable to give the horse the strong handling it required. In 1969 he was on board the joint 7-2 favourite, the Bryan Jenks-owned Domacorn. As they approached the second last, Terry and his mount looked the likeliest winners. But Domacorn ploughed through the fence – and Terry lost his whip. He attempted to roust his horse to one last effort with his hands and reins, and Domacorn started to run on up the hill, narrowing the gap on the leader What a Myth, ridden by Paul Kelleway, all the time. But the finishing post came too soon and Terry went down to a frustrating length and a half defeat.

At Aintree on 27 March, Terry was concussed following a fall on Table Mountain in the Lancashire Hurdle. That put him out of action for one day, but it was an even worse day for his title rival Bob Davies, who suffered a bad fall at Wincanton which put him on the sidelines until 12 April.

In the 1969 Grand National, the first to be televised in colour by the BBC, Terry was booked to ride Fearless Fred. He wasn't looking forward to it – he later described the horse as a 'frighteningly unpredictable jumper'. After a late night playing pontoon and poker, he had nightmares of crashing out at the first, but Fearless Fred took to the Aintree fences well. Just as Terry's pessimism had evaporated and he thought he might actually be going to win, 'Fred' landed on his head and the pair were out of the race.

Three weeks later, the partnership was reunited in the Scottish National, but they suffered a heavy fall at the fifteenth. Biddlecombe was amazed Fearless Fred hadn't been hurt; he himself went off in the ambulance with a fractured shoulder blade. Out of action for a month, he could only watch on as Bob Davies closed the gap in the title race.

Terry returned with a win at Wolverhampton on 22 May and that set things up for a nail-biting finale in a season that had been extended due to the earlier abandonments. He posted wins on Normandy at Uttoxeter on 27 May and Quick Polish at Newton Abbot a day later, and then rode two winners at Stratford on 30 and 31 May. Davies rode a double at Uttoxeter on 27 May and was only two behind Biddlecombe when the two men both headed to Devon and Exeter on 11 June. The score there at Devon and Exeter was 2-1 to Davies, meaning Terry's lead was just one going into the decisive final evening meeting at Uttoxeter on 12 June. Terry's advantage was wiped out when Davies won the novices' hurdle on Swing Along, and he found himself one behind when Davies won another hurdle race. Terry urgently needed one more winner but he didn't have a ride in the last. However, John Cook, who had been injured the day before at Devon and Exeter, and didn't feel like taking up his rides at Uttoxeter, said that if owner and trainer agreed, he'd give up his ride on the favourite Golden Berry. Owner Mrs Brotherton and trainer Bobby Renton did the sporting thing and Terry saddled up knowing that he simply had to win. 'I do not remember many occasions when I have ridden so hard but I drove Golden Berry with everything I had from about two out in the third division of the Season's End Hurdle to win by three quarters of a length from Michael Dickinson on Kilpatrick.'

Terry had tied for the title, with both he and Bob Davies finishing on seventy-seven winners. It was a great effort, but for Terry an added satisfaction was that Fred Rimell and Bryan Jenks finished as leading trainer and owner for the season.

Terry was 'dying' for a celebration bottle, but as in 1966, he didn't get the post-championship party he envisaged. 'Everything was closed,' he later recalled. 'We eventually stopped at a service station where they offered us fried eggs swimming in grease, which none of us could face, so we went straight home.'

Terry might have won his fourth title in 1969/70 had he been luckier with injuries. He won the 1969 Mackeson on Gay Trip and the Lansdown Hurdle at Cheltenham on the same day on Normandy. But when winning a race at Ascot on 22 November he experienced a pain in his back. A couple of weeks later, when he was lowering some hay bales from the barn to feed cattle at home, he jumped down from the loft and collapsed in agony. Doc Wilson couldn't find anything broken and could only presume that Terry had damaged the nerves at the foot of his spine while riding.

At that time Biddlecombe was seven ahead of Bob Davies in the title race but was advised to rest. He was put out of action for just over three weeks, returning at Christmas. He then rode what in Fred Rimell's view was one of his best-ever races for the Kinnersley stable when, keeping to the inside throughout, he steered Normandy to victory over Orient War and Champion Hurdle winner Persian War in the valuable Irish Schweppes Hurdle, run for the first time at Fairyhouse on 27 December.

Terry began the 1970s in the same form as he ended the 1960s. He won the National Spirit Hurdle at Fontwell on 11 February on Persian War, and in Tim Fitzgeorge-Parker's words, 'literally lifted French Excuse past the post' to win his second Welsh Grand National ten days later. Terry had wasted hard to do 10-9, and became exhausted. Blood was pouring from his nose and he almost collapsed. 'I felt giddy and I couldn't see. It's happened two or three times in long-distance races. But a couple of Guinness afterwards and I'm "flying again", especially after a win,' he said.

He was on seventy-seven winners for the season with a comfortable lead in the title race. But on 27 February 1970, in a hurdle race at Kempton, disaster struck. Between the third and second last flights, his mount, King's Dream, for whatever reason, went down on his knees. Terry was thrown over the horse's head. King's Dream then knelt on him with his full weight. 'I can remember crying out with the excruciating pain,' he later recalled. Terry scrambled under the rails – tried to get up but only fell down again. In the ambulance room at the racecourse he started coughing up blood. It was obvious he was in a very bad way. He was rushed to hospital, where he was sedated. When he came to the following morning the specialist told him he had been very lucky to still be alive. X-rays revealed multiple injuries, including three broken ribs and a ruptured right kidney.

In his autobiography *Winner's Disclosure*, published in 1982, Terry reflected that if he had died due to his Kempton injuries he would have gone doing the very thing he enjoyed the most – and would have had no complaints.

The champion jockeys' Grand National hoodoo struck again in April, when Gay Trip, a horse Terry had partnered to much success in the past, won the Grand National under substitute rider Pat Taaffe. Terry had told Pat everything he knew about Gay Trip, and admitted his emotions were very mixed when he saw the horse he should have been riding win.

He could quite easily have been demoralised but it is the measure of the man that he not only returned to racecourse action by the end of April, but also made a wonderfully spirited attempt to retain his title. He had an excellent run in May, which put him just two behind Bob Davies and level with Stan Mellor when it came to the final meeting of the season, at Stratford, on 6 June. But Davies rode a winner to clinch the title, while Terry drew a blank. He finished a close third (89) behind Davies (91) and Mellor (90), but it had been an amazing effort considering what he had been through. And, as he later acknowledged, the tragic death of young up-and-coming jockey Fred Dixon at Chepstow, in May 1970, made him realise how lucky he had been.

In the 1970/71 season, Terry was pipped again for the title, this time by Graham Thorner. Again, he lost out by just two wins. Once more, he was affected by injuries, and was out of action from 9 November to Boxing Day. It was to be the last time he would challenge for the title. In 1971/72 he had a good first half of the season, winning a second Mackeson on Gay Trip and the Christmas Hurdle at Kempton on Coral Diver. But his time as first-choice jockey for Fred Rimell was coming to an end.

The 1972 Cheltenham Festival was not a happy one for Terry. The Rimells blamed him for the defeat of Comedy of Errors (a future dual Champion Hurdle winner) in the Gloucestershire Hurdle. They had told him not to come before the last, but Terry found himself in the lead after the second last and decided to go for home. He was overhauled in the last few strides and lost by a neck. The next day the newspapers published the story that Biddlecombe was going freelance and that Bill Smith – whom he had recommended to Rimell – would be first choice jockey at Kinnersley the following season.

In April 1972, Terry came close to Grand National glory on Gay Trip (the 1970 winner) but had to make do with the runner-up position behind Graham Thorner and Well To Do. Terry believed it was the weight that made the difference (the runner-up was giving the winner the best part of 2 stone (11-9 to 10-1), and only went down by 2 lengths), though as we'll see in Chapter Twelve, he did receive implied criticism for going wide in search of better ground, in contrast to Thorner, who kept to the shorter inside route throughout. For one young 'TB' fan, his Grand National defeat was hard to take. Hugh Massingberd, the future Obituaries Editor of the *Daily Telegraph*, wrote:

> My regard for Terry Biddlecombe redoubled as the mange began to show on the ageing lion. His courage in the saddle, as he battled against increasing weight and injury, and his cheerfulness were inspiring.
> As Peter O'Sullevan observed in his television commentary after the jockey, controversially seeking better ground on the stands-side of the run-in to the Grand National, just failed to 'get up' on Gay Trip: 'You can't wipe the smile off Terry's face.' For my part, I was in tears. The combination of vulnerability and devil-may-care were irresistible.

It must have been a strange experience for Terry to begin the 1972/73 season as a freelance, but he still rode regularly for Rimell, as well as Fulke Walwyn and his old weighing room mate, Josh Gifford, who had started training in 1970. After piloting the very talented but rather idiosyncratic Hennessy winner Charlie Potheen to victory in the 1973 Great Yorkshire Chase, Walwyn asked Terry to be his first jockey the following season, as Barry Brogan was stepping down.

The 1973/74 season was Biddlecombe's swansong. His partnership with Walwyn meant him riding the Queen Mother's horses, and he donned her famous light blue colours for the first time at Chepstow on Saturday, 6 October 1973 when he rode Colonius to third place. He rode his first winner for the Queen Mother (Isle of Man) in the Yuletide Hurdle at Kempton on Boxing Day. Three days later, he won a handicap chase at Newbury on another of her horses, Game Spirit. With wife Bridget expecting another baby, Terry decided in early 1974 to retire after the Cheltenham Festival. He was optimistic of winning his first Champion Hurdle on Brantridge Farmer, but the horse faded badly. Could there be a fairytale ending for Terry in his last Gold Cup, riding Game Spirit?

It was an eventful race. The 13-8 favourite Pendil was brought down at the twentieth fence, and the leader, the Irish novice Captain Christy, ridden by the back-from-retirement veteran Bobby Beasley, ploughed through the last. Terry admits he rather unsportingly thought, 'Oh good – fall and bring down the other one [The Dikler],' but the front two stayed on their feet. Terry and Game Spirit finished 25 lengths behind the winner in third. He got a tremendous reception from the crowd when he came in. He was congratulated by the Queen Mother and his weighing room colleagues presented him with a watercolour of a 'two-horse match'. When he came to ride in his last-ever race, the Cathcart, the ever-sporting Richard Pitman, who was on board the favourite, insisted that Biddlecombe rode out first to parade before the stands. Terry recalled:

> I had no idea that so many people had stayed to watch me ride in my final race. It was such a surprise to me and when they caught sight of me the cheering was deafening. I could not believe it. Why on earth should anyone care that Terry Biddlecombe was retiring from racing that afternoon?

But people did care. For a decade and half, Terry had thrilled fans of National Hunt racing. They warmed to his devil-may-care courage, his endurance, his brilliance. They loved his honesty and his cheerfulness. So the least they could do was to give him a proper send-off. Terry finished fifth in his final race (which was won by Pitman on Soothsayer), but the shouts and the cheers from the crowd as he came in were – in his own words – 'tumultuous'.

It was the end of a wonderful career, during which Biddlecombe had ridden 905 winners, stretching back over seventeen years. A month later, when sitting in a Turkish bath, he was surprised by Eamonn Andrews with his 'Big Red Book', who told him he was the subject of the popular television programme *This is Your Life*. All his jockey pals took part in what Terry later described as a 'great evening'.

Writing in 1971, Tim Fitzgeorge-Parker had described Biddlecombe as 'the complete National Hunt jockey'. He further elaborated:

> His judgement and timing are superb. He gains lengths through a race by going the shortest way. He goes with his horses over their obstacles, jumping with them with tremendous confidence … Utterly fearless and unequalled in determination, he picks a horse up and gets it balanced again quicker than any other jockey riding today so that he can rally its failing resources and drive it with all his great strength and his champion's will to win.

The shrewd judge had just one criticism of this 'magnificent horseman-jockey': 'he rides unnecessarily short'.

Biddlecombe's long, powerful legs deserved longer stirrup leathers. However, Fitzgeorge-Parker did acknowledge that Biddlecombe sat so lightly on a horse, with 'such a patently firm independent seat', his 'idiosyncrasy' was obviously no handicap to him.

In 1976, a new career for the three-time champion beckoned when he was approached by Gary Newbon, a presenter on Midlands ATV, to do a racing slot on his weekly sports programme. In the 1980s, though, the former champion hit a sticky patch. His marriage with Bridget broke up, and two years later he married again, to Ann Hodgson, whom he had met at a party. He had three children with Ann and in 1985 they emigrated to Australia. But alcoholism destroyed the marriage. Terry returned to Britain in the early 1990s and with the help of the Injured Jockeys Fund, 'dried out'. In 1995 he married his third wife, the trainer Henrietta Knight. They seemed to some to be 'the Odd Couple': the earthy and jovial ex-jockey and the rather prim and posh former schoolmistress. But the 'chalk and cheese' way they were usually portrayed wasn't quite accurate as Hen and Terry had much in common, in addition to their love of horses, and they forged a great partnership.

Thirty-five years after his famous Gold Cup victory on Woodland Venture, Terry was in the winners' enclosure after the Cheltenham Blue Riband again, when the Knight-trained Best Mate landed his first Gold Cup. Two more were to follow. In 2004, when the hat-trick was achieved, Knight ran and embraced her husband. Terry was in tears. 'I think Terry was a great help to Henrietta,' says David Gandolfo. 'They were my neighbours at Wantage and I saw a lot of him on the gallops.'

Biddlecombe was universally loved in racing. 'He was just a great, big-hearted, very genuine guy,' says Graham Thorner, who pipped him to the title in 1971. Unfortunately, Terry's health began to fail as he approached 70 and in 2011 he suffered a stroke. Hen retired from training a year later to look after him. The three-time champion passed away on 5 January 2014, aged 72. A message on Knight's Facebook page announced: 'Sadly, Terry died peacefully after breakfast this morning with Henrietta by his side.'

As one of the most unforgettable characters in the history of National Hunt racing, the Blond Bomber will be remembered as much for the way he lived his life as for his remarkable accomplishments in the saddle.

Big race wins
Grand Sefton Chase 1964 (Red Thorn)
Welsh Grand National 1965 (Norther), 1970 (French Excuse)
Stayers' Hurdle (then the Spa Hurdle) 1966 (Trelawny)
Gold Cup 1967 (Woodland Venture)

Chapter Eleven

Bob Davies

Champion 1968/69 (tied), 1969/70, 1971/72

A Degree of Success

*'Bob is among the quietest and most sympathetic of jockeys, and has been
in the top bracket for many years now.'*

Jockey Jeff King on Davies, 1980

Bob Davies only turned professional at the start of the 1967/68 season, yet by
the end of the following season he was champion. Not bad for someone who
never set out to be champion jockey, nor indeed planned to be a professional
jockey at all. Sometimes when a sporting ascent is so rapid, the descent is
equally so, but not in the case of Davies. He won two further titles and, in
1978, landed the Grand National, a feat that, as we've seen, has eluded many
great champions of the past.

Like Tim Brookshaw, Bob Davies was a Shropshire lad. His father Eric was
a sergeant instructor at a cavalry school who later farmed and trained a few
of his own horses as a permit holder. Bob, his eldest son, was born on 14 May
1946. Brought up around horses, he followed the usual path of gymkhanas and
hunting. He was out with the South Shropshire at the age of 5 on lead rein
and won his first point-to-point on one of his father's horses while still only 14.

After eleven more point-to-point wins (he rode against the Brookshaw
brothers Peter and Tony), he took out an amateur rider permit in the 1963/64
season. That year he had his first ride over the Grand National fences, when he
fell at Becher's in the Foxhunters. It was another two years (9 April 1966) before
Mr B.R. Davies rode his first winner under Rules, Ellen's Pleasure at Newton
Abbot. Not that he was wasting his time. He attended Wye Agricultural College,
graduating with a BSc. In the 1966/67 season he finished fourth in the amateur
jockeys' championship, becoming trainer Les Kennard's first jockey in January
1967, when he was still at Wye, after John Cook was injured. He also rode for
permit holder and rider Billy Williams (father of Ian) after Williams was injured.

After the usual 'encouragement' from the stewards, Davies turned professional for the start of the 1967/68 season, riding his first winner as a pro at Devon and Exeter on 9 August. He enjoyed great success on the West Country circuit, riding plenty of winners at Newton Abbot and Devon and Exeter. In addition to riding for Kennard, in the second half of the season he started riding regularly for David Barons, a trainer very much on the up. He finished the 1967/68 campaign in eighth place in the championship, having ridden forty winners.

While his progress had been noted, he was still considered an outsider for the following year's championship, which was thought to be between those two great rivals Josh Gifford and Terry Biddlecombe, and the consistent David Mould. Davies was regarded, in the words of Tim Fitzgeorge-Parker, as 'the West Country's good little gaff jockey' – a reference to the tracks where he did most of his winning – but would he be able to get enough wins away from the gaffs to land the title? Probably not, was the consensus view.

Davies had a good August, as might be expected, and led Gifford by three. But David Barons' horses were not only able to win at the gaffs; on 19 September, Davies partnered Barons' Deaconsbrooke, whom he had already ridden to six straight victories since August, to an 8-length success at Cheltenham. You could read that as a statement of intent.

In addition to great skill and bravery all champion jockeys need a measure of luck to land the title. Often, it is simply avoiding serious injuries – or that injuries occur to others. In Davies's case, a bad injury to Colin Davies's stable jockey (Brough Scott, the future TV presenter) meant him taking over the ride on all Davies's horses, excluding the champion hurdler Persian War, who was Jimmy Uttley's mount.

From 24 October 1968 to the February 1969 freeze-up, Davies rode twelve winners for his trainer namesake, and those dozen winners proved absolutely crucial in what proved to be a very close title race. On 25 November, there was a three-way tie at the top of the table, with Terry Biddlecombe joining Davies and David Mould on the twenty-nine-winner mark. On 2 December, Davies was level at the top with David Mould. But a week later, after six more wins, he was four clear of Biddlecombe and Mould. As mentioned earlier, the 1968/69 season was badly affected by abandonments due to the weather, although the Cheltenham Festival did go ahead and Davies rode Specify, a future Grand National winner, to victory in the Mildmay of Fleet.

On the same day in late March that Terry Biddlecombe suffered concussion following a fall at Aintree, Davies had an even worse fall at Wincanton. He broke two vertebrae and was off until 12 April. That not only meant him missing out on the Grand National, in which he was booked to ride The Inventor, but gave Biddlecombe the opportunity to steal a march in the title race. However, TB himself was injured in the Scottish National in April, which allowed Davies to regain lost ground. On 11 June, he was just two behind Biddlecombe, and two winners to Terry's one at his 'home' fixture of Devon and Exeter that day cut the lead to just one. The title would be decided on the final meeting of the season, at Uttoxeter on 12 June. Two wins in hurdle races that evening put Davies one ahead. But Biddlecombe, as related in the previous chapter, rode like a demon to win the last race on Golden Berry, so the title, after so many twists and turns, was shared. Most agreed it was the right result. It was a good night for Bob in more ways than one. Biddlecombe had taken his sister Sue to Uttoxeter as she was determined to see the young jockey who had been 'such a nuisance' to her brother in the title race that year. As soon as she clapped her eyes on Bob, her expression changed. 'Something told me this likeable rival would somehow end up as my brother-in-law. He did,' wrote Biddlecombe.

Davies's holidaying with Biddlecombe and his wife Bridget that summer on the Mediterranean island of Elba, along with other racing friends, demonstrates once again that however strong their rivalries were on the racetrack, the leading jockeys of the era were like a band of brothers when they were away from it. 'I travelled to the races with Terry,' Bob says. 'I stayed overnight with him and with Stan [Mellor] too.' That's how it was in those days.

Tying with the great Terry Biddlecombe may have been regarded by some as a 'flash in the pan' but the next season Davies showed it was no fluke. The 1969/70 season saw another thrilling title race, which once again was only decided at the very last meeting, only this time there were three jockeys still in contention. Davies, as usual, rode plenty of winners in the West Country gaffs in the early part of the campaign: he was already on the eight-winner mark as early as 20 August, when he rode a four-timer at Devon and Exeter. But as the season progressed he was winning top Saturday televised races too, which helped boost his profile.

On 22 November at Ascot, he piloted the John Bower-trained Cool Alibi, the 100-6 outsider of the field, to an impressive victory in the 2-mile Black and White Gold Cup, worth £4,331 in prize money. Both Bower's regular jockeys, Roddy Reid and Roy Davies, had broken their collarbones and so it proved to be a lucky spare ride for Davies. 'Cool Alibi jumped perfectly to take the lead just after entering the home straight and ran on strongly to win comfortably by 4 lengths from the favourite Even Keel,' the *Coventry Telegraph* reported.

Terry Biddlecombe led the table by seven, but a back injury, which he first noted at that Ascot meeting, put him out for three weeks in December. Davies missed a week too in December due to injury but returned to action at Ascot on the 19th.

Another big race win for him that season was on Solomon II in the Imperial Cup in March. David Barons' progressive handicap hurdler had already won four times since the summer, but had a 10lb penalty for beating Coral Diver and Clever Scot at Wincanton.

It was a typically competitive renewal. The Ryan Price-trained, Josh Gifford-ridden Potentate was the heavily backed favourite. Pendil, a subsequent King George winner over fences, was also in the field. Pendil (ridden by Paul Kelleway) took it up from the third last, but Davies, on Solomon II, swept past the leader over the second last and kept going strongly up the Sandown hill to hold off Gifford and Potentatate by a neck. 'It was an extraordinary performance by the farmer's son who had taught himself so much in such a short time that he could hold his own from the last with the Flat-trained former champion, who was acknowledged as the strongest finisher in the business,' wrote Fitzgeorge-Parker. That ride perhaps dispelled any doubts that Davies couldn't beat the best jockeys at the top venues, but he still faced a renewed late challenge from two old maestros for the jockey's title. After his horrific injury at Kempton in February, which could have claimed his life, Terry Biddlecombe returned to action at the end of April and enjoyed a great run in May. Stan Mellor, also returning from injury, was in the hunt too for his first title for eight years. The final drama was set for Stratford on 6 June. Davies led the table on ninety wins, but was only one ahead of both Mellor and Biddlecombe. Mellor then joined Davies on ninety wins, but couldn't add to his tally.

The selling hurdle proved decisive. If Biddlecombe won on Mrs Wentworth, it would be an incredible three-way tie for the title. Davies was on the 100-8 chance Kaliking. He gave the horse a confident ride, taking the lead after the last to beat Biddlecombe on Mrs Wentworth by 1½ lengths. He had won his second title, and his first outright championship, by just one winner. While it's true that having better luck with injuries than his main rivals had been a decisive factor both times, he had still ridden a total of 168 winners over the two seasons, which was no mean achievement.

Fitzgeorge-Parker analysed what had made Davies a champion. Helped by his natural light weight, he could ride comfortably at 10st 3lb. 'He has beautiful hands and his shy, confident, quiet, gentle temperament travels down the reins so that horses seem to be happy and produce their best for him,' he wrote. Davies was rarely a rider who would make you get up and say 'wow' but he was intelligent and made very few mistakes. Davies himself also pays tribute to some of the great riders he was racing against: 'Jeff King was probably the best jockey never to be champion. Probably the most stylish was Johnny Haine (who never won a title either). He was amazing. You'd never know how well he was travelling by watching him. If the horse wasn't going well, he'd never show it.'

In the 1970/71 season, Davies, for once, was not so fortunate with injuries and dropped to sixth place in the championship. He could have closed the gap but had a bad fall on Foxtor in the Hennessy Gold Cup at Newbury on 28 November, which left him with two cracked bones in his spine, a broken shoulder blade and a damaged jaw. He finished on fifty-six winners for the season, eighteen behind the new champion Graham Thorner.

In 1971/72, though, it was a very different story. With the David Barons yard in cracking form, he had a great run of success in the summer and autumn of 1971. The fifty-winner mark was passed when he rode treble at Wincanton on 18 November, the earliest time in the season he had achieved the half-century. But he later missed five weeks with injury and also went through a lean patch in February, which enabled Stan Mellor to gain ground.

By the time of the final two-day meeting of the season at Stratford in early June, Davies was four ahead. But after Davies beat Mellor in a tremendous finish to the 4-year-old hurdle on the evening of Friday, 2 June, Mellor, at the end of his illustrious career, graciously conceded and said he wouldn't be riding the following day. 'It's almost a relief I have been beaten fair and square by a great fellow and gentleman,' he declared. Davies, for his part, told reporters: 'It's been a long season. After tomorrow I shall be pleased to have nothing to do with horses until we start schooling again for the next season.' He confirmed that once again he would be riding for David Barons.

He had won his third title with eighty-nine winners, five clear of Mellor. His number of rides in 1971/72 (487) was the highest total since Mellor's 608 in 1960/61. But his strike rate of 18.27 per cent was over 4 per cent lower than when he had won his first title in 1968/69.

Davies never added to his third title. His finishing positions in the next three seasons were fourth, fourth and sixth. In the 1975/76 season, though – when he was riding for David Morley – he did push John Francome close, finishing five behind in second place with ninety-one winners. It was a total good enough to land him the championship in 1969/70. 'It was a great season but at the end I just didn't have the ammunition,' he says.

Two years later, on 1 April 1978, he enjoyed the biggest payday of his career when he rode the Gordon Richards-trained 14-1 shot Lucius to victory in the 1978 Grand National. It was a lucky spare ride as Lucius's regular partner, David Goulding, had badly pulled a muscle a few days earlier, and Davies, who had expected to spend Grand National day riding at Towcester, was drafted in as a late replacement. He had never sat upon the horse until twenty minutes before the off.

The late withdrawal of the legendary three-time winner Red Rum due to an injured foot provided the ante-post drama but the race itself wasn't short of it either, treating racegoers and television viewers to what Aintree historian Reg Green has described as 'one of the closest and most thrilling climaxes the race has ever produced'.

The brave, front-running 25-1 shot Sebastian V, ridden by Ridley Lamb, led for over 2½ miles. Davies on Lucius, having travelled well throughout, was just a stride behind going over the fifth last, but was keen not to hit the front too soon. Richards had told him, 'Always try and have some company with this fellow.' So he waited. Waited while a whole host of other challengers began to join in the action at the head of the field.

It would have been so easy for Davies to panic but he didn't. He finally made his challenge after the last, and up the long run-in he and Lucius took on Sebastian V in a fantastic duel. They only gained the upper hand in the final 100 yards and then had to resist a very late burst for glory from the 50-1 Irish-trained outsider Drumroan. Davies and Lucius won by half a length from Sebastian V, with Drumroan just a neck away in third. Only 3 lengths separated the first five horses. As he was led in with the traditional police escort, Davies joked, 'I hope you buggers never arrest me for anything.'

In the *Racing '78 Highlights of the Year* Stud & Stable annual, Monty Court reported:

> After the race it was definitely a case of ice-cool at Aintree for owner, trainer and jockey. Richards and Davies answered questions from deadline-harassed racing correspondents as though they had been rehearsing them. There may be more spectacular winning rides in the Sun Grand National than that of Bob Davies on Lucius at Aintree this year – but I don't expect to see a better display of cool-headed professionalism.

With his victory described as 'the best spare ride in history', a year later Davies quite remarkably almost did it again, when he finished a close-up, and rather unlucky, second on Zongalero, another late call-up. It remains the closest six-time champion trainer Nicky Henderson has come to winning the great race.

Davies's last ride in the National came in 1982 when he was on the 17-2 second favourite Royal Mail, trained by Stan Mellor. This time, though, he failed to deliver, falling at Becher's. He retired that same year having ridden 912 winners. He planned to farm – after all, he had a BSc degree in Agriculture, but says, 'Changes to the CAP[1] in the days of Maggie Thatcher changed the economics of farming,' and so he moved into high street banking, dealing with pub mortgages instead.

But it was in racecourse administration where Davies's future lay. He began working as Clerk of the Course at Ludlow and then became general manager and Clerk of the Course. His work at the Shropshire track for a period of thirty-five years earned him the sobriquet 'Mr Ludlow'. It also led to him meeting his second wife, Dorcas, who was the course's accountant.

Davies was also, at various times, clerk of the course at Bangor, Assistant Clerk and Secretary at Hereford and Assistant Clerk of the Course at Aintree under John Parrott, during which time important safety changes were made to the course, which included modifications to Becher's Brook following two equine fatalities there in 1989. Davies says:

> It's a very different game then and now. The fences are a lot softer than they were in the 1960s. Then there's helmets. I remember the first jockey to use one with a chinstrap was Laurie Morgan, an Australian, who won the Aintree Foxhunters on Colledge Master in 1961 and 1962.

While he lauds improved jockey safety, Bob doesn't believe every change in the last half-century has been for the best. 'All the good horses nowadays go to a very few yards. In the 60s, they were spread about more. So the honours were shared more evenly.' One only has to look at how a small number of trainers and owners mop up at the Cheltenham Festival each year to see his point.

There's also the role of agents, says Bob. 'When I was riding no one had agents. I never rang up to get rides. To my knowledge the first agent was John Hanmer, who represented Steve Cauthen in the 1970s. Now I think they've too much control and influence over where trainers decide to run.'

---

[1] Common Agricultural Policy.

Davies's points, you could argue, apply just as much to football as they do to racing. A concentration of riches at the top is how society has generally gone since the 1970s, and sport, which of course doesn't exist in a vacuum, reflects this. The era in which Bob Davies operated was certainly ultra-competitive, which makes him winning the championship three times all the more creditable.

Big race wins
Imperial Cup 1970 (Solomon II)
Grand National 1978 (Lucius)

Chapter Twelve

Graham Thorner

Champion 1970/71

Oh Captain! My Captain!

*'I broke most of the bones in my body but I never dreaded coming off.
I believe it is a tough business and I didn't mind that side of it at all.
Life is too soft.'*

Graham Thorner to journalist Alan Lee, 1980

Graham Thorner was the only champion jump jockey from 1959 to 2019 who won the title 'just' once, but that should in no way detract from what he achieved in 1971, bearing in mind the disadvantages he had to overcome. Not the least of them was that the decidedly 'old-school' ex-military trainer whom he joined straight from school and for whom he rode for fifteen years, Captain Tim Forster, never ran his horses on the firm ground at the start and end of a jumps season, when the races were usually less competitive, for fear of them breaking down. Forster was a top-class trainer (he won three Grand Nationals with three different horses in a thirteen-year-period) and Thorner served him loyally, but his stable still wasn't the ideal base for someone chasing the champion jockey title.

'It was fate how I won it,' Thorner says as we discuss his championship season.

> Terry [Biddlecombe] would go somewhere and have four or five rides as he was very well established, and I'd only have one, as I'd only been around a short time, but mine won. I was very fond of Captain Forster and I had great respect for him but he was a hard person to ride for. I never knew until quite late where I was going, so it was hard to fix up outside rides. I once asked him (after I was champion) if he could let me know earlier about his plans but he said, 'I pay you and it's my privilege to fxxx you about.' I found it all very stressful.

Thorner was only 22 when he won the title. His championship success came just three years after turning professional.

Born in Somerset in 1949, his father farmed 80 acres near Axbridge. Thorner was bought his first pony by his father at the age of 10 and won numerous prizes on the West Country circuit. With his heart set on becoming a jockey, at the age of 15 he joined Captain Forster's Old Manor House stables at Letcombe Bassett, near Wantage, as a stable lad. He had got the job via his Uncle Jim, who worked as a groom at the Cirencester stud owned by one of Forster's owners, a Mrs Henriques. Nietzsche's adage 'that which does not kill you makes you stronger' springs readily to mind when reading of Thorner's baptism of fire (and water) at Old Manor House in the mid-1960s.

'There were many times when I was really scared, and I used to walk away from the hostel and cry my eyes out. The lads would sleep in the afternoons and drink heavily at nights; they would pick on the young kids and bully them,' he told Henrietta Knight for her book *Starting from Scratch – Inspired to be a Jump Jockey*. Twice Thorner had his testicles blackened with shoe polish and hoof oil; he also received regular duckings under cold water. But he stresses that such things went on in most yards at the time and that Forster's wasn't an outlier:

> That's how it was. There was a pecking order in all yards. I was bullied by one particular lad because he thought I was jumping the queue. I was this greenhorn farmer's son from Somerset and the others were tough, street-wise lads from places like London, Liverpool, Manchester and Dublin.

'He wouldn't even know the lads' Christian names,' he says of 'The Captain'. 'It was the Head Lad who dealt with all of that. Once I remember him saying to him, "I don't want to know about the lads' fxxxing football kit. You concentrate on that, I'll concentrate on training my horses."'

Thorner says Forster gave him a rollicking every single day yet the hard-to-please trainer must have seen something in his young recruit, as years later, he said: 'It was perfectly obvious from the beginning that he was going to be a fine rider. He immediately displayed natural ability, horsemanship and a racing brain.' While he would never praise Thorner to his face, Forster did tell others that his stable jockey would win twenty-five races a year that another rider wouldn't. 'Why didn't he say it to me just once?' Thorner asks today. 'I suppose it was the way he was brought up,' he continues. 'Everyone had to know their place. David Mould told me Cazalet was the same. I joined Captain Forster as a scrawny 15-year-old kid from Somerset and that's how he saw me throughout. But I have to stress that I had great respect for him.'

In his first season riding as an amateur, Thorner posted three wins, his first coming on a novice hurdler called Longway at Newton Abbot in 1966. But it wasn't his employer who gave him his first opportunities on the racetrack but permit-holders Herbie Payne and Lawrence Potter. He acknowledges the great help he received too from Ron Vibert, Forster's stable jockey who became a trainer. 'He was like a mentor to me,' he says. 'I'd look up to him a lot. His advice really went beyond normal help.'

Thorner turned professional in 1967, with his first success coming on Sandy Saddler in a selling chase at Plumpton. He lost his claim riding a horse called Multigrey, which later provided future champion John Francome with his first winner. In 1969/70, Thorner posted a very respectable forty-four wins, tying for sixth place with Barry Brogan and Brian Fletcher.

Then came the championship season – which even today you get the feeling that Thorner still can't quite believe actually happened. Certainly the bookies didn't give him much of a chance, making him a 33-1 shot at the start of the campaign. Those odds probably didn't change much even after he got the season off to a flyer with a double at Market Rasen on the opening day. On 13 August, riding Zermatt he beat three-time champion Terry Biddlecombe, who was on the favourite Clear Wood, at Newton Abbot. 'It was not until things got well under way that I and others realised Graham was a force to be reckoned with,' TB later wrote.

When I asked Thorner what he thought were his greatest strengths as a jockey he replied:

> I never gave up and had a tremendous will to win. I was a pessimist – like Captain Forster – before the race but an optimist once it had started! Marcus Armytage[1] said I was the 'AP McCoy of my day'. I wouldn't call myself a 'great' jockey like Terry Biddlecombe was but I think I was as good as anyone from two out.

Thorner earned the nickname 'Whanger' for his arm-held-high-above-his-shoulder whip style and admits there wouldn't have been 'much juice' left in most of his mounts after the race. But while he could be hard on his horses, Thorner knew when not to use his stick.

---

[1] The 1990 Grand National-winning amateur rider and racing correspondent.

I was known as a 'whip jockey' and I wouldn't dispute that. But you have to remember the type of horses I was riding for Forster. They were like big boats. Old-style National Hunt chasers. Most needed some strong handling. I always believe that when a horse is at the peak of its fitness and well, it can take a few cracks. I would never hit a horse once I got no response.

But it wasn't just forceful riding that Thorner brought to the table. There was tactical awareness too. David Gandolfo, another trainer for whom Thorner rode, says that he also had a very good brain – as indeed Captain Forster acknowledged. 'Graham always talked about "It" jockeys; to have "it", you had to be in the right place at the right time in a race. He had a lot "up there" as all champions have to have.'

The winners continued to mount up in the autumn of 1970. At Chepstow on Saturday, 5 December there was a Forster-Thorner double with Bonnie Highlander in the Quarry Steeplechase and Zermatt in the Marksman handicap hurdle. The reports noted that the latter 'never really put a foot wrong' but the former put in a couple of sketchy jumps and 'needed all of his jockey's skills before he finally landed the spoils'.

Thorner's title chances were boosted by the fact that while he didn't miss a single day through injury in 1970/71, some of his rivals had spells on the sidelines. Terry Biddlecombe injured his back after a fall at Newbury in November, from which he returned too soon and then was out again until Boxing Day. Reigning champion Bob Davies was out of action for most of December following a bad fall.

Although he was lucky in avoiding lay-offs, Thorner had difficulties in another direction. It's not that his employer purposely obstructed his title challenge; the set-in-his-ways Forster wasn't going to change his routine for anything or anyone. He certainly wasn't going to risk any of his horses on hard ground just to help his stable jockey win a title, or make it easier for him to get outside rides.

Thorner remembers how he was never allowed to go up to, or return from, the gallops – which were some way out from the stable – in Captain Forster's Land Rover. On one occasion during the final weeks of the season he had arranged a lift with Richard Pitman to go to Plumpton. He had to ride up and back from the gallops and only made it by seconds. Yet when John Francome came to ride out, Forster gave him a lift in his Land Rover, which Thorner felt was humiliating. 'He got me so low,' Thorner says today.

What should have been a happy time for Thorner chasing an unlikely title instead became something of an ordeal. 'Forster was a nice man but he was very different to how "Joe Public" saw him which was someone who was very laid-back,' says David Gandolfo. 'I always say Graham would have made a great diplomat because he was very diplomatic in the way he handled things with Tim.'

Journalists adored National Hunt racing's greatest pessimist, who could always be relied on to provide them with highly amusing copy, and the Old Etonian ex-11th Hussars army officer was charm personified when I went to see him about a book I was writing in the early 1990s. The confirmed bachelor was also a huge favourite with his relatively larger number of lady owners. But it's clear that Forster didn't have too high a regard for those he thought of as his inferiors – and jockeys fell firmly into that category. In *Hot Cherry*, Marcus Armytage relates how on his first morning riding out for Forster on secondment from the army, Dominic Alers-Hankey was bucked off a horse at the bottom end of the gallops and severely winded:

> In the distance he could see the Captain's Land Rover heading his way – to pick him up, he presumed. 'Dom' was still crumpled up on the floor when rescue arrived. The Captain wound down his window, leaned out and said, 'And to think I put you on the quietest bugger in the yard,' before driving off and leaving Dom still gasping for air.

One of Forster's favourite sayings, as cited in Graham Sharpe's *Book of Racing Characters*, was, 'There are 60 million people in this country and 20 million of them are idiots. And every single one of them has worked for me.' He also regularly bemoaned that he would have been champion trainer many times – had it not been for jockeys. Only one type of racing mattered to Forster: steeplechasing. 'One day I'm going to stand for Parliament and if I get in, my first Bill will be about abolishing Flat racing and my second about doing away with hurdlers,' he declared.

Back, though, to Thorner's unlikely title bid. On 8 March 1971, the *Daily Mirror* reported how the race for the championship was really hotting up, with only nineteen winners separating the top eleven. At that point Thorner was third in the table, with fifty-one wins, seven behind joint leaders Terry Biddlecombe (who had just returned to top form by riding a treble at Newbury on 6 March) and Barry Brogan.

'I never gave the championship a thought until the last month – and then not seriously – as the Guv'nor's horses had all run themselves out and I had very few outside rides lined up,' Thorner said afterwards.

On 3 April he had a great first ride in the Grand National for Captain Forster on the 66-1 shot Bowgeeno, who finished a close-up fourth in a thrilling race in which five horses were still in contention after the last.

With seven days to go he and Terry Biddlecombe were tied at the top of the jockey championship with sixty-nine winners apiece. Barry Brogan was also in close contention.

The Sportsman's Club for the first time was putting up a prize fund of £2,000 for the champion jockey and £1,000 for the runner-up, and Thorner and Biddlecombe agreed with Brogan's suggestion that the money be split equally three ways. 'Then Barry just disappeared and I ended up beating Terry, so looking back it was a mistake!' he says today.

Going into the last dramatic day of action on 5 June 1971, Thorner led Biddlecombe by one. Both men rode a winner at Stratford in the afternoon (Thorner won on Red Hugh for Ron Vibert), before they flew up to Market Rasen for the evening meeting.

Thorner won the title by two after beating Biddlecombe on Tam Kiss in the Summer Chase. 'Terry was wonderful. He said, "Well Done" and "Great" and he really meant it. He had ordered two crates of champagne and said come on, let's celebrate! But I was the one who picked up the bill, but I was only too pleased to!'

The very next day he received a telephone call from Barry Brogan saying he needed his share of the money urgently.

'I'm a man of my word, so I had to pay him, but I made sure I made him wait!' Thorner recalls.

After he had become champion, Thorner asked his 'guv'nor' for a retainer. 'Why?' was The Captain's perplexed response. When Thorner pointed out he was now champion jockey but was still on a lad's wage, Forster replied wearily, 'Oh, fxxxing hell. I suppose I shall have to write to all the owners.'

In an interview published on 30 July 1971 in the *Daily Mirror*, Thorner reviewed his championship season and looked forward to the new campaign, due to begin the following day. The article was entitled 'I've always had luck on my side', but that proved to be tempting fate, as on the very next day, he was brought down and injured on his first ride of the season on the Ron Vibert-trained Royal Feathers at Market Rasen. The same thing had happened to Fred Winter, when reigning champion in 1953. Thorner's injury – he cracked a bone in his right ankle – was nowhere near as serious as Winter's, but it did put him out of action for about a fortnight and allowed his rivals to steal a march in the title race. 'In those days most trainers, even the smaller ones, had their own jockeys so it was hard to get spare rides,' he remembers. And as we've seen, Forster wouldn't risk his horses on firm ground.

This helps explain how, as reigning champion in the summer of 1971, Thorner only had ten rides in August and eleven in September. In the end, he did manage to finish third in the championship, and actually bettered his 1970/71 total by one, but the disappointment of relinquishing his title was arguably more than made up by his win on Well To Do in the 1972 Grand National. This made him the first reigning champion jump jockey to win the National since Fred Winter, rider of Sundew, in 1957.

Well To Do, in the words of Aintree historian Reg Green, 'was caught in one of those extraordinary twists of fate which for so long have been the lifeblood of the National'. He was bequeathed to Captain Forster in the will of owner Heather Sumner, who had died of cancer in June 1971. Forster only confirmed Well To Do's Grand National entry with fifteen minutes to spare as he was unsure about risking the horse in the race.

The 9-year-old was backed in from 33-1 on the Friday evening to 14-1 before the off, with the race, which started at the proper National time of 3.15 pm, run in driving rain and against a strong headwind. Despite, or perhaps because of, the testing conditions, it was a terrific renewal, with four horses still in contention at the second last. Thorner, heeding advice from the 'Inside Maniac' Bryan Marshall, kept to the extreme inside all the way (as he had done with Bowgeeno twelve months earlier) and although his mount pecked at Becher's both times, and might have come down, the strategy was vindicated. Taking the lead from Black Secret just after passing the Elbow, he came with a tremendous run. Terry Biddlecome, riding the 1970 winner Gay Trip, put in a renewed challenge on the stands side but Thorner prevailed by 2 lengths. TB believed weight was the decisive factor (his horse carried the best part of 2 stone more than the winner) but Thorner maintains that going on the inner was probably worth 25 lengths. He points out that his view was endorsed by Mercy Rimell who believed she and husband Fred would have won five Nationals had Biddlecombe not gone wide in search of better ground. 'The drops were much bigger on the inner and there was a much greater chance of falling. But I rolled the dice and it came off,' Thorner says today. 'The fractions were very small, but I knew my horse was very nimble footed and so it proved at Becher's.'

There were to be no more titles for Graham but he remained in the leading group of National Hunt jockeys for the rest of the 1970s. He was seventh in the championship in 1972/73 but would have finished a lot higher had he not had a lay-off of over six weeks after cracking two vertebrae and breaking his wrist in a fall at Nottingham on 11 December. In another fall he fractured his skull and was laid up in hospital for several days. On another occasion he broke three ribs in a fall at Leicester, but still rode in the next race. 'When the adrenalin is rushing you don't feel the pain,' he says. 'But on the drive back home with the lads I was in terrible pain. I said "Stop! I think I'm going to die." I had to be taken to hospital.'

In 1973/74 Thorner finished sixth, but in 1974/75 he tied for second with John Francome, just twelve behind the winner, Tommy Stack. In 1973, he won the Arkle on the Forster-trained Denys Adventure – a win that meant a great deal to him as the horse was owned by Mrs Henriques, who had helped set him on the road to becoming a jockey. 'He was I believe in many ways the best horse I ever sat on but he had terrible leg trouble so he was never able to prove it,' he says.

There was another Arkle success in 1978 on the ill-fated subsequent Gold Cup winner Alverton, a decisive 10-length win on Royal Marshal II in the 1974 Hennessy and a King George victory on the same Forster-trained horse two years later, when he went off at odds of 16-1. Two all-time great National stars he rode were the lightning-fast 2-mile chaser Tingle Creek and Night Nurse, the legendary Peter Easterby-trained dual Champion Hurdler who embarked on a chasing career in the late 1970s. He says of Tingle Creek, whom he rode in America in the Colonial Cup: 'He was the most exuberant jumper I ever sat on by a country mile. He either had a stand-off or an exceptional stand-off when he came to jump.' Thorner rode Night Nurse when the horse was hotly fancied in the 1979 Gold Cup but ran no sort of race. 'He was lifeless. I don't believe in Dick Francis stories, but if ever a horse was doped it was him that day,' he says, pointing out Night Nurse won next time out at Aintree.

In 1978 he again showed his great skills at Aintree after staging a remarkable recovery in the Grand National. His mount, Tamalin, was literally on the floor at Becher's, with his forelegs crumpled and his back legs gone, but somehow Thorner managed to hang on to the horse's neck. The partnership got going again, and made up plenty of ground, eventually finishing twelfth. When Tamalin's trainer, Gordon Richards, who won the race with his other runner Lucius, was being congratulated by reporters he kept saying to them 'Tamalin' and insisting Thorner would have won without the Becher's mishap. 'He was quite obsessed about it,' Thorner remembers, 'but I think he was right seeing all the ground I had to make up.'

Photographer Harry Ormesher, who captured Thorner's incredible fall and rise on camera, and who had been taking pictures at Becher's for twenty years, said of the incident: 'It is the most incredible recovery I have ever seen. Miraculous.' His 'astonishing and instinctive feat of riding' won Thorner the prize of a £700 videocassette recorder for the best riding performance of the race, apart from the winner. Ironically enough, he secured his prize when

Fred Rimell (nearest) on Avenger at Newbury. His future brother-in-law Gerry Wilson jumps over in second on Custom House.

Jack and Betty Dowdeswell with a painting depicting Jack winning the Queen Elizabeth Chase at Hurst Park on Limb of the Law on 30 May 1955.

Jack (on Bob's Your Uncle) and Betty at East Wittering Sands during the harsh winter of 1946/47.

Bryan Marshall (left) with trainer Vincent O'Brien.

Bryan Marshall (on the inside, of course!) just holding off the late challenge of Tudor Line to win the 1954 Grand National on Royal Tan.

Tim Molony and wife Stella, early adapters of the jet-set lifestyle, on their way to Milan races.

Stella and Tim Molony at a ball in the 1950s.

'The Magnificent Molonys': Tim (second left, standing) and brother Martin (right, standing)

A lucky escape for Tim Molony (on ground) at Aintree as a following horse falls over him.

Dick Francis, the 1953/54 champion, on M'as-Tu-Vu.

The brilliant Fred Winter (left) swerves to avoid the leader Waistcoat before going on to win a chase at Windsor on Carton.

Tim Brookshaw with trainer George Owen.

Tim Brookshaw winning on Punch Bowl Hotel at Carlisle, 13 April 1963.

Stan Mellor with Stella and Tim Molony, and their dog Laddy.

Stan Mellor, three-time champion and the first man to ride 1,000 winners.

Sixties icons: Josh Gifford with Emma Peel aka glamorous *Avengers* actress Diana Rigg.

Josh Gifford en route to winning the 1969 Whitbread Gold Cup at Sandown on 26 April. (L to R): Titus Oates (Ron Barry); Brough Scott at back; Larbawn (Josh Gifford); head only, Graham Thorner; Excess (Bill Rees).

Terry Biddlecombe on the Bryan Jenks-owned chaser Domacorn.

The winning team: Graham Thorner and The Captain, Tim Forster.
(Photo: Fiona Vigors/Marner)

Graham Thorner (on the extreme inner) jumps the fearsome Becher's Brook second time round in the 1972 Grand National on Well To Do. He almost comes down but makes a great recovery and goes on to win.

Champions all: Champion Jockey's Dinner, Cheltenham, November 1972. (L to R): Davies, Biddlecombe, Mellor, Rimell, Marshall, Thorner, Dowdeswell, Winter, Francome, Brookshaw. *(Photo: Bernard Parkin)*

Ron Barry canters to the start on the Queen Mother-owned Earls Castle, before winning at Ayr in 1973.

Tommy Stack on Young Ash Leaf, on the way to victory in the 1972 Greenall Whitley at Haydock.

They won fifteen titles between them, and even shared the championship once: Peter Scudamore (left) and John Francome (right) with Lord Vestey at Cheltenham. *(Photo: Bernard Parkin)*

The record breakers: 'Scu' and trainer Martin Pipe. *(Photo: Bernard Parkin)*

One Man, one champion: Richard Dunwoody on the popular Gordon Richards-trained grey en route to a hugely impressive 14-length victory in the 1995 King George (run at Sandown on 6 January 1996). *(Photo: David Hastings)*

Dunwoody on Sound Man on his way to winning the Tingle Creek Chase at Sandown, 2 December 1995. *(Photo: David Hastings)*

'The Prince', aka Richard Dunwoody, after winning the 1996 Arkle at the Cheltenham Festival on Ventana Canyon. *(Photo: David Hastings)*

A young-looking AP McCoy having won a novices' hurdle at Stratford on Moonlight Air on 16 March 1998, with owner Mrs Peter Badger and trainer John Spearing (right).

Three champion jump jockeys: Stan Mellor (left), Jonjo O'Neill (third from left) and AP McCoy, with legendary Flat jockey Lester Piggott (second left) and former trainer Michael Dickinson (right). *(Photo: David Hastings)*

Dicky Johnson (second from right) and trainer Noel Chance (fourth from right) having just been presented with their trophies by HM The Queen Mother (centre) after Looks Like Trouble's win in the 2000 Gold Cup. *(Photo: David Hastings)*

Brian Hughes, the 2019/20 champion, at Aintree in December 2020. *(Photo: Author)*

Presenting the 2020/21 champion, Harry Skelton, after winning on Presenting Jeremy, his first winner of the 2021/22 season, at Worcester on 12 May. *(Photo: Author)*

he was recovering from a badly broken leg, received following a fall in a novice hurdle at Worcester a few days later.

Thorner's 500th winner, recorded at Huntingdon on his birthday, was also Forster's 500th winner as a trainer too. For good measure he rode a treble on the card.

Thorner's sudden retirement in 1979, at the age of just 30, was shock to many in the racing community, but in truth he was burnt out with all the years of working round the clock for Forster taking their toll. 'I was riding on the Monday, thinking I might go on for another two or three years. By Tuesday, I had decided to pack up,' he said. Thorner appeared to be riding as well as ever but he wasn't feeling – indeed or looking – at all well. Rather worryingly, he had lost a lot of weight, weighing in at 8st 9lb, about a stone under his normal minimum. 'I felt so ill I could not enjoy life, let alone riding,' he told journalist Alan Lee a few months later. Thorner thought he had an ulcer but it transpired that he had coeliac disease, a chronic digestion disorder, which necessitates the sufferer going on a gluten-free diet.

On his last day as a professional jockey he rode a horse for Jenny Pitman at Nottingham. They finished third. Four years later, the same horse won the Grand National. Its name: Corbiere.

The day after Thorner's retirement was announced he received a phone call from Fred Winter, urging him to reconsider and take a break instead. He really appreciated Winter's concern, though how disappointing it must have been that his employer didn't make the same suggestion.

Thorner's was a relatively short career, compared to the likes of Stan Mellor or Fred Winter, but his star shone brightly when it mattered and plenty was achieved. He tried his hand at training, but winners proved hard to come by. He quit just before his fiftieth birthday in 1999, after a nightmare season in which his horses had been hard hit by a virus.

Coincidentally that same year, Captain Forster, the man whom Thorner had become so associated with in the 1970s, but who very rarely gave him a lift to or from the races, passed away, aged 65, just a few months after receiving an OBE for services to horseracing. After Thorner's retirement he won two more Grand Nationals, with 40-1 shot Ben Nevis in 1980 (his instructions to the horse's amateur jockey Charlie Fenwick were 'Keep Remounting') and in 1985 with the aptly named 50-1 shot Last Suspect. Forster told its owner, Anne, Duchess of Westminster, before the race: 'I'll meet you at the back of the stands, after they've caught him.'

When remembering his old boss today, with whom he had such a complex 'master-servant' relationship, Thorner says:

I just feel mad at him because he missed out on so much. He was actually working against himself. It was surely in his benefit to keep his stable jockey sweet, fit and healthy. But it didn't matter where I was riding in the afternoon, I had to ride out every day and was never allowed to leave for the races early. I just accepted that's how it was, but looking back I was under so much pressure and stress driving flat out to get to the racetrack on time often just with minutes to spare.

For all his criticism of how Forster treated him, there is also a sadness that the trainer simply couldn't loosen up more and enjoy the success he had.

I remember coming back after Royal Marshal had won the King George and opening the door to his living room. He was sat there alone in front of the fire with a drink. I said to him, 'That was a good day, wasn't it?' And he replied, 'It wasn't bad.' Then I asked if there'd be anything for the lads. 'I am sure they've made their own arrangements,' he replied. He wasn't interested in conversation or celebrating what had been a great win. I shut the door (almost slammed it!) and went off to Jenny and Richard Pitman's for egg and chips and opened a bottle of champagne.

Despite the periods of depression he had working for 'The Captain', Thorner never left Forster to join another yard, which he could easily have done. Moreover, while he believes it was his prerogative to criticise his old boss, and tell it how it was, his loyalty to Forster meant he didn't like it if anyone else did. 'It was my privilege to criticise him but if anyone else did I'd say, "Shut up, you're talking about my guv'nor."' He also stresses that the non-gambling Forster was 'as straight as a die' when he ran his horses; they ran on their merits every time.

A Grand National theme runs through the Graham Thorner story – and so it was appropriate that he played an important part in the career of Tiger Roll, who went on to be the first back-to-back winner of the race since the legendary Red Rum. Jumps trainer Nigel Hawke, with whom Thorner had worked at the sales for several years, bought the son of Authorised for £10,000 when the ex-Godolphin horse came up for auction as a 3-year-old at Doncaster. But it could so easily have been different. Thorner, acting for Flat trainer Dean Ivory, was the underbidder and thought he'd put in the winning bid at £9,500. But Hawke came very late and didn't see Thorner, who was hiding. Afterwards Thorner went up to Hawke, admitting he was 'mad'. Hawke said, 'You have him,' but Thorner said, 'I'm a believer in fate,' and insisted the

Devon trainer keep his new purchase. 'If I had said yes, he would probably have ended up running in claimers at Windsor on the Flat as he was very slow,' he says today. Hawke subsequently sold Tiger Roll to his present Irish connections for £80,000 after he had won a juvenile hurdle at Market Rasen, and the Grand National hero has ended up winning over £1.4 million in prize money.

Thorner certainly has a shrewd eye for an equine bargain. Probably his best acquisition – bought for just £2,500 – was Tropics, who went on to win over half a million in prize money as a leading sprinter for Dean Ivory, the man who almost got Tiger Roll!

The 1970/71 champion is not a fan of the way many of today's jockeys have a tendency to bump up and down in the saddle without using their legs, nor is he at all pleased with the current vogue for omitting fences and hurdles in races due to 'low sun' if any jockey makes a complaint.

> I think it's ruining the sport. Obviously I don't want to see jockeys or horses injured but can anyone show me the evidence when four fell at the last because of the sun? Not only are the fences a lot less stiff today, they are now being omitted. It's stupid and a sign of a snowflake society. Will the jockeys be getting a reduced fee because they are not jumping fences?

Like Bob Davies, he looks back at an era where competition was at its peak:

> At one point in the early 1970s, you had nine champions, or future champions riding. Stan Mellor, Terry Biddlecombe, Josh Gifford, John Francome, Ron Barry, Jonjo O'Neill, Tommy Stack, Bob Davies and myself. But there were also great jockeys at that time who never became champions. The likes of David Mould, Jeff King, Johnny Haine, Richard Pitman, Eddie Harty. They would come into the weighing room pouring with sweat having given everything. What men they were, what riders!

Exactly the same can be said about Graham Thorner.

Big race wins
Grand National 1972 (Well To Do)
Hennessy Gold Cup 1974 (Royal Marshal II)
King George VI Chase 1976 (Royal Marshal II)

Chapter Thirteen

Ron Barry

Champion 1972/73, 1973/74

Big Ron

'He was a strong and beautiful horseman. All horses went so well for him, particularly The Dikler, who could be such a hard puller.'

Trainer Fulke Walwyn on Ron Barry

In an interview for the *Daily Mirror*, published on Wednesday, 1 November 1972, reigning champion Bob Davies said that even after the retirement of Stan Mellor, who had pushed him so close in 1971/72, there were at least 'half a dozen riders' in with a chance of taking his title.

There was Richard Pitman, who had ridden fifty-eight winners the previous season, when he shared the riding of Fred Winter's horses with Paul Kelleway, but was now first choice jockey at the powerful Uplands yard. There was Tommy Stack, who had come south to ride for Tom Jones, but would still pick up plenty of good rides in the North. Graham Thorner's chances would be boosted by his boss Captain Forster buying a lot of good horses, while Barry Brogan, described as a 'great worker and tireless traveller', was riding for Fulke Walwyn and, like Stack, would have plenty of rides in the North. And, of course, there was the 'Blond Bomber' Terry Biddlecombe, now operating as a freelance. The man who would take the title off Davies – and set a new record of 125 winners in one season – was none of the above, but someone who the 1971/72 champion had nevertheless mentioned as a threat. He had said of Ron Barry: 'He is riding better than ever and will benefit by this year's extra fixtures in the North.'

While the extra fixtures undoubtedly helped Barry, it's worth noting that his strike rate was a hugely impressive 28.6 per cent. We were entering a golden era for northern jump racing. Before 1972/73, no post-war champion jump jockey had been based in the North of England. But from 1972 to 1980, northern-based riders won the championship every season bar two

(John Francome in 1975/76 and 1978/79). The North's renaissance as a National Hunt powerhouse began in the late 1960s. Red Alligator's 1968 Grand National success helped Bishop Auckland handler Denys Smith win the trainers' championship that year while the horse's jockey, Brian Fletcher, pushed Josh Gifford close in the jump jockeys' title race. The likes of Gordon W. Richards, Arthur Stephenson and Ken Oliver in Scotland were all winning their fair share of races, while the 1970s also saw the emergence of Peter Easterby as a major force. The three most famous National Hunt horses of the 1970s, the legendary three-time Grand National winner Red Rum, and the hugely popular Champion Hurdlers Sea Pigeon and Night Nurse, were northern-trained.

The North's golden period continued to the mid-1980s (in 1983, Yorkshire's Michael Dickinson saddled the first five home in the Gold Cup), but in the second half of that decade southern yards began to hold sway again. At the time of writing there's been no northern-trained winner of the Gold Cup since Jodami in 1993, and after Jonjo O'Neill in 1980, no northern-based jump jockey won the title for another forty years. But back to Ron Barry. 'Big Ron' hailed not from the North of England, but like that other great champion Tim Molony, from County Limerick in Ireland, where he was born on 28 February 1943.

He started as a 6st 8lb apprentice with Mrs Ann Biddle, but in those days women weren't allowed to hold a licence, so the trainer was 'officially' Tommy Shaw. He served a five-year apprenticeship with Shaw, riding his first winner in a 1-mile handicap on the Flat at Gowran Park in May 1961.

Barry left Ireland for Scotland in 1964 to ride for the small East Lothian stable of Wilf Crawford, a former Scottish rugby international. His first winner in Britain came in a novices' hurdle at Ayr on 19 October 1964, on a horse called Final Approach, just four days after a general election brought Harold Wilson and the Labour Party to power after thirteen years of Conservative rule. Barry's first win over fences came at Catterick the following January.

It was after he first linked up with Gordon Richards that his career really took off. Richards, originally from Bath in Somerset (he never lost his rich West Country accent despite spending thirty years in the North), had just moved up to Cumbria, renting the stables at the magnificent Greystoke Castle near Penrith.

Barry's first meeting with Richards came in 1966, in the horsebox park at Newcastle races. He had driven down from Scotland when Richards shouted at him to unload his horse from the box too. 'I told him I was busy with my own horses – to which he replied: 'If you don't unload him son, you won't be riding him this afternoon.' That was news to Barry. Although he didn't win on Playlord that day, he did ride the horse to all eight of its wins over fences.

Barry became Richards' stable jockey in early 1968 and they soon became a major force in National Hunt racing. Barry rode Playlord to victory in the 1969 Great Yorkshire Chase and then in the Scottish National of the same year, when the bold jumping chaser carried 12 stone to win on ground Barry described as 'firmer than firm'. In between there was a creditable third place in the Gold Cup on ground that was much too soft. Years later, Richards said: 'Playlord will always remain my favourite because he brought me my first big success.' It was the horse who got Barry going too.

Barry tied for fifth place in the jockey's championship with forty-four winners in the 1969/70 season and went up to fourth, with sixty-five winners a year later. Sadly the season was marred when Playlord died following a fall at Doncaster. In 1971 Barry might have won the Grand National, had his mount Sandy Sprite, who led over the last, not broken down on the run-in. 'I think he would have won but I should have pulled him up earlier,' he says today.

He was then fifth in the championship with sixty winners in 1971/72, the season when he won the first of his three Whitbreads, on the Gordon Richards-trained Titus Oates. 1972/73 was to be his annus mirabilis. 'Ron Barry is flying high,' reported the *Newcastle Journal* on 12 October after the Limerickian had ridden a treble at Wetherby the previous day. He began November well with a victory on his only ride at Sedgefield on the 1st. His win on the Gordon Richards-trained The Cantabfella put him on the twenty-eight mark for the season. But Tommy Stack was right up there too and then went ahead in the title race.

'No stopping Ron Barry,' declared the *Newcastle Journal* on 7 November. The previous day Barry had gone to Wolverhampton for two rides, one in the first and one in the last, and they had both won. That brought him back level with Stack at the head of the championship. His first win that day was on Gordon Richards-trained Paddington Bear, who made all the running in the novices' chase to win by 10 lengths – Richards' thirteenth success of the season from relatively few runners.

Barry began to edge ahead of Stack and Bob Davies as November progressed. He registered up his forty-eighth winner of the campaign with a double at Southwell on Monday, 4 December 1972, which put him eight ahead in the title race. His first winner, Teddy Tudor in the handicap chase, was the fourth he had ridden for Wymondham trainer Jack Bloom since he had stepped in to replace Bloom's amateur rider son Michael, who had broken his wrist at Leicester in October.

On 6 December at Ayr, Barry chalked up his half-century of winners for the season, but such are the ups and downs of jump racing, just half an hour later he was on the deck with a broken collarbone following a fall from Merry Fox. The news that he would be out of action for probably a fortnight, and missing a possible treble at Teesside Park the following day, meant that his title odds drifted to 4-1, with Bob Davies installed as the 5-4 favourite, and Tommy Stack at 7-4. But Big Ron roared back. In early 1973 he was finding his success was causing problems of its own. At the Ayr New Year meeting he rode Ken Oliver's The Benign Bishop to victory in the Drongan Chase.

Oliver announced the 6-year-old home-bred's next target would be the Wills Premier Chase Final at Haydock on 20 January. It was reported in the papers that Barry wanted to keep the ride, but that he would most likely be claimed to ride Gordon Richards' The Spaniard for a race at Newcastle that same day.

Few champion-elect jockeys could have been riding with as much confidence as Barry in March/April 1973. He really was unstoppable and his great run enabled him to put the championship to bed.

The 1973 Cheltenham Festival was supposed to be the one when the all-powerful Fred Winter stable cleaned up the big prizes. Uplands had the odds-on favourite in the Champion Chase (Crisp), the Champion Hurdle (Bula) and the Gold Cup (Pendil). In the end none of them won. In the Champion Hurdle Barry delivered what his friend and weighing room colleague Jonjo O'Neill thought was his greatest-ever ride, to nearly steal the race from the front on 20-1 Mick Easterby-trained outsider Easby Abbey. There was another second place for Barry on Bountiful Charles that day and a third place in the Arkle when he helped The Benign Bishop recover from a bad mistake at the open ditch. 'No jockey has ridden better than Ron Barry at Cheltenham this week and yet he is still without a winner at the Festival meeting,' Doug Moscrop commented in the *Newcastle Journal* on Gold Cup Day. That was soon to change. The champion elect had got the ride on the Fulke Walwyn-trained The Dikler in the Gold Cup, replacing Walwyn's stable jockey Barry Brogan, who was unwell. Previously regarded as the 'enfant terrible of jump racing', The Dikler was a very talented, white-faced, 17.1 hands chaser, who certainly had plenty of quirks. 'Still remarkably difficult to hold and steer, prone to the odd diabolical blunder and occasionally to downright sulks, he was one of the most exasperating characters in training and one of the best loved,' was the view of Fitzgeorge-Parker. The Dikler had won the 1971 King George and had finished third in the previous two Gold Cups (a close-up one in 1972), but now aged 10, most judges thought his best chance of success had probably gone, which was reflected in his starting price of 9-1.

Barry had just one schooling session on the horse before the big race, but ten days before Cheltenham he broke his collarbone in a fall at Kelso. He confided in Jonjo O'Neill afterwards that he was worried that he wouldn't be able to control his hard-pulling Gold Cup mount as they left the parade ring. But nursing his broken collarbone, he did have a confidence-boosting win on Dark Vulcan in the Panama Cigar Final at Chepstow on the Saturday before the Festival. In the end his fears about The Dikler running away with him at the start didn't materialise, though the horse did give Walwyn's head lad 'Darkie' Deacon, who had done so much work in 'taming' him, a kick in the leg in the pre-parade ring that was so hard it almost made him faint. When the race began, Terry Biddlecombe, on board the other hard-pulling Walwyn runner Charlie Potheen, went off in front, with Barry and The Dikler settling in around fourth/fifth. The stable companions, both ex-pointers, enjoyed a good hunt round for the first 2½ miles, but the odds-on favourite Pendil, ridden by Richard Pitman, was travelling ominously well as they turned for home. Pendil and Pitman went for glory and took it up at the second last. 'The crowd are already hailing Pendil as the winner of the 1973 Gold Cup,' declared commentator Peter O'Sullevan as the odds-on favourite forged clear, but Barry had still to play his cards. The Dikler passed Charlie Potheen over the last with a tremendous leap and stayed on strongly on the run-in to pip Pendil in the last 25 yards. Poor Dick Pitman was to suffer the same fate on Crisp in the Grand National just over two weeks later.

'The irresistible combination of skill, power and outstanding guts of man and rider overhauled the favourite up the final hill and held on to win by a short head in a record time,' was how Fitzgeorge-Parker described one of the best finishes to a Gold Cup ever seen. Downing the mighty Pendil was some achievement. The Fred Winter-trained dual King George winner had been widely hailed as 'the best since Arkle' and his defeat at the hands of The Dikler and Barry was his first in eleven chases. Looking back at the race today, Barry feels that his broken collarbone may actually have helped him as it meant he couldn't take as tight a hold on his horse as he might have done.

Having won the Blue Riband of National Hunt racing it was now time to party. Ron always knew how to do that. Having provided his weighing room colleagues with the traditional case of champagne and taken part in a post-race sing-a-long in Cheltenham's Cellar Room, he headed off, with fiancée Liz, to meet friends for dinner at the Queen's Hotel. No sooner was he through the door than an 'admiring racegoer' handed him another glass of champagne. To cut a long story short, Barry got blotto. As told to Jonjo O'Neill, Liz laid him on their bed that night with his hands crossed across his heart as if he was going to die, but Ron quickly burst back to life again when he announced he was going to be sick. The next morning, not unsurprisingly, he felt awful. But he had to ride at Uttoxeter. Believing it was the 'hair of a dog', Ron drank another glass of champagne for breakfast. He felt better, but on the way up to Staffordshire, with Liz driving, he suddenly became very ill again. He somehow managed to stagger into the racecourse and change into his colours for the first race. Gordon Richards took one look at him in the paddock and said, 'Ronny boy, you don't look too good.' 'I've never felt better,' Ron replied, no doubt with his fingers crossed behind him. 'I'm pleased to hear that,' his boss said. 'We have backed Pneuma and gone for a real touch on him. Are you sure you're OK?' Richards asked again.

Ron now had to be honest. 'Not so good,' he answered. 'But there's nothing we can do about it now.' There wasn't. The stable money was down and the hopes of a Greystoke collect rested on a badly hung-over jockey. Richards instructed Barry to keep it simple and try and make all. Barry followed the plan and at the first flight kicked his mount in the belly, causing the horse to lurch forward and his jockey to almost fall off. After that scare Barry patted Pneuma and said to him, 'Son you are on your own, but please look after me.'

Pneuma did just that and the partnership won by 2½ lengths at odds of 9-1, the same price as The Dikler. Richards was relieved but his jockey still had to weigh in. Barry managed to avoid falling off the scales – and consequently getting disqualified – but was feeling so bad he asked to see a doctor. When the medic arrived and asked what the problem was, Barry replied: 'If you want to know the truth, I have got alcoholic poisoning and I'm dying. I won the Gold Cup yesterday, had a monumental party last night, and a glass of champagne this morning. I am going very badly and can't possibly ride the rest of my mounts today.' The doctor told him he couldn't put that down in the medical book. Instead he wrote just ten words in red ink: 'Off colour. Pulse 90. Headache. Should be alright tomorrow.'

There was more big race glory in store for Barry in April. The 1973 Whitbread Gold Cup had been rerouted from Sandown to Newcastle. Barry was booked to ride for Fulke Walwyn again, but this time he was on board the Gold Cup third, Charlie Potheen, who had earlier won that season's Hennessy Gold Cup and Great Yorkshire. As with The Dikler, it was the first time he had ridden the horse in a race, and it was the same result, leading the *Newcastle Journal*'s Doug Moscrop to express his doubts as to whether the unique feat of partnering two horses for the first time to win two major steeplechases would ever be repeated by any jockey. Charlie Potheen was on great form, and had to be considering he was carrying top weight of 12 stone, but as Moscrop noted:

> However great a horse he may be, the man on top is equally important, and Barry showed all the qualities of a champion, judgement of pace and his tender but positive handling of the mount. … And you could almost sense as the combination made all the running over this demanding three and three-quarter miles, that the confidence which is oozing out of the champion elect had rubbed off on his partner.

Fulke Walwyn was generous in his praise of Barry afterwards: 'Ron rode the horse as if had rode him in all his races. And I can pay no greater tribute than that.' Doug Moscrop, in his report, concluded: 'The Irishman underlined once more the general feeling that he is out on his own as a steeplechase rider. Never mind about Doctor Dolittle and him being able to talk to the animals. Ron Barry is his equal and this is no fairytale.'

Charlie Potheen was Barry's 100th winner of the campaign. Afterwards, Ladbrokes made him 2-5 to break Gifford's record of 121 winners in one season. But Barry's attempt to get into the history books was overshadowed by the death, on 3 May, of 26-year-old jockey Doug Barrott, following a fall on the Josh Gifford-trained French Colonist in the Whitbread. He was the fourth National Hunt jockey to be killed in less than three years, showing again the greater risks back then for riders of incurring fatal injuries.

On 24 May 1973, with Barry on 118 winners, he was interviewed by Tim Richards of the *Daily Mirror*. 'I've had some sleepless nights and to be honest I'll be glad when it's all over,' Barry confessed, regarding his quest to beat Gifford's record. Not that he wasn't happy about how the season had progressed. 'It has been the most marvellous time for me. So good, it's still like a dream.'

Describing Barry as 'the new nice guy of sport', Richards opined that the Irishman lacked 'the usual make-up for modern-day success'. He wasn't 'hard' in the sense of being ruthless. 'Just the opposite. Kind to the point of being soft.'

Barry did admit to being 'hard-headed' though – in a literal sense. 'I once broke a bone in my head and didn't realise I had done it until it mended.' he said. The laid-back Limerickian was pictured smiling and holding a cigarette at his digs in Cumberland.

On the same day (24 May 1973) that the piece appeared, Barry rode four winners at Perth to equal Gifford's record. The horse that gave him his 122nd win was Attaturk, on whom he rode a dead heat.

He finished the season with 125 wins. It was some year for Greystoke. Not only was Ron champion jockey, Jonjo O'Neill was champion apprentice and Richards' son Nicky was champion amateur on the Flat. In his biography of Richards, *The Boss*, John Budden estimates that Barry and Richards covered 60,000 miles from August to June in search of winners, with the trainer usually taking the wheel on the outward journey and the jockey on the way back. 'There was a lot of driving but there was less traffic on the roads than today,' Barry says now.

Not surprisingly given the success he had enjoyed with The Dikler and Charlie Potheen, Barry received an offer from Fulke Walwyn to ride for him the following season as his first jockey. It was a very tempting proposition. Walwyn had been training since the 1930s and in the early/mid-1970s was enjoying a real renaissance. The veteran Lambourn handler was also the trainer for HM the Queen Mother, meaning that Barry would be able to ride for the Royal Family. In the end, Ron decided to stay in the North. He had just become engaged to Liz and was settled in nicely at Greystoke. Gordon Richards, aka 'The Boss', was a great character but could be a tough man to work for at times as he had a fiery temper. But Barry – in the words of Jonjo O'Neill, who had a first-eye view of things there – was a 'great foil' to him:

> Ron's playful half hour helped defuse Gordon when pressures were building up and he was becoming agitated. At the same time he involved the lads in the crossfire and chitchat and we all knew it was a bit sharp. I believe everyone in the stable benefitted and Ron helped to create an atmosphere of camaraderie and to mould team spirit.

After a three-week summer holiday in Corfu, Barry came back fresh and ready for the fight to retain his crown. In a *Daily Mirror* interview published on Friday, 3 August 1973, he listed his three targets for the 1973/74 season. His first was to remain champion jockey. His second was to win the Grand National. His third, to win the Champion Hurdle. As to the first ambition, he told Charlie Fawcus he was not as confident as the bookies, who had him as short as 5-2 to retain his title. The man he feared most was his good friend Tommy Stack, third in 1972/73 and who was now riding for the prolific Arthur Stephenson yard. As it turned out, the 5-2 about Barry was good value.

The reigning champ literally couldn't have got the 1973/74 season off to a better start, winning the very first race on Fangbolt. He rode another winner at Market Rasen on the Monday and by 9 August his title odds had been shortened to 2-1 with some bookmakers.

In December 1973, Ron was out of luck in six rides at Teesside Park on the 12th, two of which started favourite – and also on his sole ride at Kelso a day later. But it was only a minor hiccup. Writing in the *Newcastle Journal* on 18 December 1973, Doug Moscrop looked back at Barry's great year and asked why the champion jockey had received no recognition for what he had achieved at the BBC Sport's Personality of the Year awards: 'He proved that a northern-based jockey can win the title – if he's good enough. And he proved that he is head and shoulders above anyone else in his profession.' Moscrop raised the possibility that if Barry had been based in the South he'd have been in the shake-up, but it's worth noting that it wasn't until 2010, and the victory of AP McCoy, that any jockey landed the prestigious BBC award. Barry, despite the lack of recognition, could only carry on riding winners and that's what he did.

The 1974 Cheltenham Festival was run in gloriously warm, sunny weather. Tim Fitzgeorge-Parker recalled how it was so hot after the last race on the Thursday that 'shirtsleeved crowds were sitting about on the grass in the enclosures and champagne corks were popping, while six brave young men stripped naked and tried to "streak" over the last fence'. Streaking was all the rage in 1974, and at the time of the Festival, Ray Stevens' song *The Streak* was climbing the pop charts.

A couple of hours earlier, Ron Barry had jumped the last fence (fully clothed, I'm pleased to say), in the lead on The Dikler in the Cheltenham Gold Cup. Would it be a second successive win in the Blue Riband? It had been another dramatic race – and in fact a dramatic twenty-four hours. Ron had suffered a horrifying fall the previous day on Well Oiled in the Arkle. That left him, in the words of Tim Richards, with a 'real shiner of a black eye', but Ron characteristically played it all down, saying, 'I'm just lovely – only a bit banged about.'

He still had to be passed by the course doctor an hour before racing on Gold Cup day if he was to ride in the race, which thankfully he was. In the race itself, High Ken fell at the second last, bringing down the favourite Pendil, who was out to avenge his short-head defeat in the Gold Cup a year earlier. That left The Dikler in the lead, but this time, with glory in sight, it was to be Ron and his mount who were overhauled on the run-in as the Irish novice Captain Christy, ridden by the returning veteran Bobby Beasley, surged to victory.

There was, though, a level of compensation for Barry when, a month later, he and The Dikler landed the Whitbread Gold Cup, following the disqualification of Proud Tarquin. It was his third win in four years in the end-of-season showpiece.

Barry won his second – and last – championship with ninety-four winners, fifteen clear of Dick Pitman in second place and Tommy Stack (76) in third.

The campaign hadn't quite reached the dizzy heights of 1972/73, which would have been very hard, but Barry had once again proved he was the man to beat.

In the 1974/75 season he dropped to fifth, his cause not helped by the repeated recurrence of an old shoulder injury. That said, he finished only nineteen winners (63) behind the new champion, Tommy Stack (82). In April 1975, he rode his old friend The Dikler to fifth place in the Grand National, won by L'Escargot. A year later, when The Dikler was 13, they finished sixth.

On 23 August 1975, the *Daily Mirror* reported what they called 'the first shock of the jumps season' – namely, the news that after nine years as stable jockey, Barry was splitting up with Gordon Richards and going freelance. Jean Richards, the trainer's wife, told the paper: 'We are very sorry for it has been a long and highly successful association. But Ron feels like he would like to be completely free.' Barry for his part said he intended to stay in the North, but if a good offer 'from anywhere' came along he would consider it.

He told the *Daily Mirror* in November that he was 'top of the pops', when asked how things were going as a freelance jockey. But he also acknowledged that the chances of winning his title back were remote as John Francome and Tommy Stack were too far ahead.

Trainer John Spearing remembers well the time he had reason to call on Barry's services: 'He was a good rider. One time he rode for me at Stratford. I needed a jockey for a horse called Greek Warrior. Ron said, "I'll ride him," he made no fuss. He won and gave him a hell of ride. It was the horse's first win.'

In February 1976 Barry enjoyed further big race success when, deputising for the flu-stricken Barry Brogan, he piloted Irish Fashion to an impressive victory in the Schweppes Gold Trophy Hurdle at Newbury. It was only the second Irish-trained winner of the most valuable handicap hurdle in the calendar and Barry, who took it up on the 16-1 shot at the third last, turned the race into procession. It was certainly a red-letter day for Ron, as later on the card he rode the Peter Bailey-trained Zeta's Son – a subsequent Hennessy Gold Cup and Mildmay-Cazalet winner – to victory in the handicap chase.

That year, 1976, also saw Barry ride Grand Canyon to victory in the Colonial Cup, the US's leading jumps race. He won the prize with the same horse again two years later, and broke the course record each time. He also won a Swiss Grand National.

In June 1977, the month of the Queen's Silver Jubilee, it was announced that Barry would be riding as stable jockey the following season for Hawick trainer Ken Oliver. There were obvious attractions for Barry with such an arrangement. He and Oliver went back a long way and Barry's wife, Liz, had formerly been the trainer's secretary. She was succeeded, incidentally, by another 'Liz' who was the wife of a champion jockey – Liz Stack, spouse of Tommy.

Riding for a yard in the Scottish Borders made plenty of sense for Ron at this stage of his career, as he was now finding all the travelling from his Cumbria home for rides down south too much.

In 1978, Barry, so unlucky on Sandy Sprite seven years earlier, could have finally realised his ambition of winning the Grand National as he was offered the ride by Gordon Richards on Lucius, following an injury to David Goulding. But Ron had already agreed to ride Forest King for trainer Ken Hogg and stayed loyal to the arrangement, thereby missing a winning National ride.

Barry was only with Ken Oliver for one season before he returned to 'The Boss'. The 'old team' marked the end of a decade in fine style, when Barry partnered the flashing grey Man Alive to victory in the 1979 Mackeson. Ron was now 36, and he continued riding for another four years. The decision to retire came quickly, and was made one night in October 1983. According to his great friend Jonjo O'Neill, Barry was sitting at home with a gin and tonic and staring into the bright log fire at his Roehead cottage overlooking Ullswater in the Lake District when he decided that win, lose or draw, he would hang up his saddle after his ride the following day on a horse called Final Argument at Ayr. It was Halloween, but the ending was a fairytale. Ron won – and wife Liz greeted him in the winners' enclosure in a flood of tears. Jonjo O'Neill and fellow jockey Colin Hawkins carried Ron out of the weighing room shoulder-high to huge cheers from the appreciative Scottish crowd. Barry had ridden his first UK winner – Final Approach – at Ayr almost twenty years before, and now he had bowed out with a win on Final Argument, on the same track. And he had told everyone to back it!

It was a fitting end to a fantastic career, during which Barry had ridden 823 winners. And, as the website Jockeypedia notes, what was particularly remarkable about his exploits in the saddle was that in almost 5,000 mounts he was only once in trouble with the stewards, and that was in itself only a minor infringement, which cost him a £15 fine.

After hanging up his boots, Barry set up his own company building timber-framed boxes and horse shelters. In 1987 he became an Inspector of Courses for the Jockey Club and stayed in that position for nineteen years. Today we remember a brilliant dual champion who greatly enriched the sport in a vintage era for National Hunt racing.

Big race wins
Scottish Grand National 1969 (Playlord)
Whitbread Gold Cup 1971 (Titus Oates), 1973 (Charlie Potheen), 1974 (The Dikler)
Gold Cup 1973 (The Dikler)

Chapter Fourteen

Tommy Stack

Champion 1974/75, 1976/77

The Business of Winners

'When the butler met me off the plane I knew nobody in racing.'
Stack, on his arrival in England to ride for Bobby Renton,
The Book of Racing Quotations

The date: 2 April 1977. The place: Aintree.

The fall of Andy Pandy at Becher's second time round when about 12 lengths clear leaves Tommy Stack and Red Rum in the lead in the Grand National. Red Rum is bidding to become the first horse in history to win the famous steeplechase for the third time, but there are still eight fences to jump and over a mile and a half to travel. Can he get home? Stack and Rummy pop over the next few fences in faultless style. 'Recrossing the Melling Road, now 4 lengths to the good, Red Rum ran into a crescendo of cheering unsurpassed on any racecourse, from crowds aware they were witnessing history in the making,' recorded National historian Reg Green.

Churchtown Boy was travelling well in second but a bad jump at the second last meant Red Rum was able to forge clear again. 'He's getting the most tremendous cheer from the crowd,' cried BBC commentator Peter O'Sullevan, 'they're willing him home now, the 12-year-old Red Rum ... He's coming up to the line to win it like a fresh horse in great style. It's hats off and a tremendous reception, you've never heard one like it at Liverpool. Red Rum wins the National!'

That day at Aintree in 1977 was arguably the greatest in National Hunt history. Unless you're a robot, it's impossible to watch the replay of the race without getting goose pimples. It's fair to say that a whole nation – and not just the enthusiastic Liverpool crowd – was willing Stack and Red Rum home.

Monty Court wrote of the immediate post-race aftermath:

> Tommy Stack, who could be relied upon to give a stride-by-stride commentary on almost every race, apologised to pressmen as his emotions threatened to check his normal non-stop delivery. He was so affected by the triumph that for days his eyes tingled with tears as he relived his own emotional action-replay.

How could Stack possibly top that experience? The answer is – he couldn't.

Just a year after his Aintree success, Stack retired, aged just 32. Injury forced his hand, but after the euphoria of Aintree in April 1977, he must have felt like a mountain climber at the top of Everest. What else was there to achieve?

The dual champion jump jockey of the mid-1970s was born on 15 November 1945 in Moyvane, County Kerry, an area where a 'racehorse wasn't seen for miles', in the words of Irish journalist John Barrett. Stack's father had a 160-acre dairy farm and as a child Tommy used to love jumping over poles on his piebald pony in a field. At the age of 12 he was sent away to the Jesuit-run Mungret College in County Limerick, as a boarder, following in the footsteps of another great Limerickian champion, Tim Molony. Tommy excelled at athletics and rugger, playing scrum half in the Munster schoolboys team.

After leaving school, he started work as an insurance clerk in a Dublin office. But the pull of horses proved too great. He was close friends at school with Barry Brogan, whose father was a trainer. He used to go to the Brogan stables at weekends to ride out. Barry took over the training operation on his father's death and one week asked Tommy to stand in for him while he was away supervising runners in England. Stack never returned to insurance.

In 1965 he left Ireland to work for the veteran Yorkshire handler Bobby Renton, who had trained the 1950 Grand National winner Freebooter. He didn't have much experience and when Renton's butler met him on his arrival he knew no one in English racing.

His first win as an amateur was on a horse called New Money at Wetherby on 16 October 1965. Yet before the 1965/66 season ended he had ridden a winner for his new boss at the Cheltenham Festival.

As a 7lb-claiming amateur he showed he was a jockey with a big future as, in the words of Monty Court, 'he conjured up a tremendous burst' out of the 8-year-old Well Packed to land the Grand Annual. He ended his first season in England with a total of five winners. A year later, he turned professional. Ironically, given what happened in 1977, one of the horses he regularly rode out when at Renton's yard at Oxclose, near Ripon, was a certain Red Rum. He didn't find the experience too enjoyable. 'He was always on his toes, jogging around the place. He was not the nicest horse to be riding out,' he later recalled. Stack rode Red Rum seven times over hurdles in the 1969/70 season without winning.

Renton asked Stack to school the horse over fences. Red Rum blundered over the first and refused to jump the second. Stack tried again, but again Rummy downed tools. Renton told Stack to call it quits for the day, before adding: 'He runs at Newcastle tomorrow, you ride him.' Stack could hardly have been ecstatic at the prospect but at the course Rummy left his schooling ground reluctance behind and jumped very well to finish third. On his next outing, in early November 1970, Stack was on board as Red Rum recorded his first win over fences, in a novices' chase at Doncaster. In ten further outings over fences that season the Stack-Red Rum partnership recorded two more wins and only finished outside of the first four on one occasion.

Bobby Renton was already in his late seventies when Stack came to work for him and when he retired aged 83 in 1971, he asked Tommy if he would like to take over the stables as trainer and jockey. Tommy said yes, and actually rode Red Rum as his trainer in two races in the autumn of 1971.

But training and riding proved to be too much work, and the arrangement only lasted a few months. Tony Gillam, a local permit holder and friend of Stack's, offered to take over the training duties, which meant Tommy could once again concentrate on riding. Red Rum won twice more for Gillam, with Stack riding, including the Zetland Handicap Chase at Catterick on New Year's Day 1972, but was suffering badly from arthritis in his feet and so in August 1972 he went to the Doncaster sales.

He was bought for 6,600 guineas by Southport trainer Ginger McCain for new owner Noel Le Mare. Beforehand, McCain had rung Stack to get his assessment. 'Tommy said the horse was an all right sort, but a bit "footy". Coming from an Irishman, that could cover a hundred things,' McCain recalled in his autobiography. Exercising on the Southport sands did wonders for Rummy's arthritis, and the rest, as they say, is history.

With a retainer from the prolific 'little fish are sweet'[1] County Durham trainer Arthur Stephenson, and a job as first jockey for Tom Jones's Newmarket

[1] Stephenson's favourite saying referred to the way he loved to farm lower grade races at northern tracks. He set a record for winners trained in Britain – 2,988, later surpassed by Martin Pipe. His biggest win came when The Thinker landed the 1987 Gold Cup, but typically, that day Stephenson went to Hexham races instead.

yard, Stack finished third in the 1972/73 jockey's championship with seventy-one winners. He was in the same position a year later with seventy-six winners, when he had more rides (458) than any other jockey.

While he didn't ride in the first Grand National to be won by Red Rum in 1973, in 1974, when Rummy won his second, he was on the 7-1 favourite, Scout. But the partnership could only manage tenth place. As he heard the cheers for Red Rum, Stack probably thought that his chance of National glory on the horse he had ridden so often had gone.

Given his progress in the previous two seasons and the number of rides he was getting, not just from Stephenson, but from other powerful northern yards like Mick Easterby's, Stack was clearly well placed to make a strong title challenge in 1974/75. It was some sporting summer. In a vintage World Cup, the free-flowing Dutch team of Johan Cruyff had earned plenty of admirers for their total football but in the final itself they lost 2-1 to the hosts, West Germany. Meanwhile, newly promoted Carlisle United, playing First Division football for the first time in their history, raised quite a few eyebrows by topping the table in August with three 1-0 wins in their first three games. Carlisle's great start soon petered out (they were eventually relegated), but Tommy Stack's didn't. A double at Teesside on 19 November 1974 brought him up to the twenty-seven-winner mark for the season, but he told *Daily Mirror* reporter Charlie Fawcus that he wasn't impressed by the odds of 6-4 on offer for him landing the title. 'It's stupid, isn't it? We're not even halfway through, and all sorts of things can happen in the way of injuries and so on.'

In January 1975 he still played down his chances even though he was now odds-on. 'I'm not so worried about the championship as jumping all those big black fences safely,' he told television crews at Doncaster.

In the 1975 Grand National, won by L'Escargot, he rode the Charlie Hall-trained Clear Cut, who had won the 1974 Topham by 8 lengths. Available at 40-1 before Stack was booked, the 11-year-old started at half those odds on the day, but they fell at the second fence. The horse did go on to win the following season's Mackeson (when trained by Maurice Camacho) in record time. Stack claimed his first title with eighty-two wins from a record 577 rides, twelve ahead of Graham Thorner and John Francome, who had 244 fewer rides.

In 1975/76, Stack slipped to third in the jockeys' championship, behind Francome and Bob Davies, but one substantial silver lining was being reunited with Red Rum. Despite having ridden the horse to two Grand National victories there had been something of a falling-out between jockey Brian Fletcher and Ginger McCain. Fletcher thought Red Rum had 'gone' after a series of disappointing efforts and that McCain had over-raced his stable star. Ron Barry got the ride in the 1975 Hennessy but then Stack took over at Haydock a few days later in the Sundew Chase and finished third.

Over Christmas it was announced by the horse's 88-year-old owner Noel Le Mare that Stack would be offered the ride on the dual National winner for the 1976 renewal. It was a tough task at Aintree as Red Rum had 11st 10lb to carry, but it looked like the hat-trick might be achieved as Red Rum landed in front of Rag Trade after the final fence. Rag Trade, though, in receipt of almost a stone, passed his rival, and looked like he would win quite comfortably before there was one late, dramatic surge on the run-in from Red Rum, who was never going to go down without a fight. The official winning distance was 2 lengths, but Red Rum was gaining all the time. A year later, he – and Stack – would gain their compensation.

Stack set a hot pace throughout in the 1976/77 season. In February 1977 he won his first Gold Trophy on True Lad, trained by permit-holder Bill Swainson. A month later at the Cheltenham Festival, he landed his second Grand Annual on Ken Oliver's Tom Morgan. That set him up nicely for his historic win on Red Rum in the 1977 Grand National. He won his second jockeys' title with ninety-eight winners.

Then, in September 1977, just five months after his Aintree heroics, Stack came down to earth in the most painful way possible, suffering an horrific paddock fall from the novice hurdler Carbon at Hexham. He broke his pelvis in ten to twelve places and also ruptured his bladder. He was in traction for twelve weeks and had to undergo several operations. That December, Stack, Ginger McCain and Red Rum stole the show at the BBC's Sport's Personality of the Year awards. Red Rum was introduced into the studio as 'the maestro himself' by compère Frank Bough, while Ginger McCain joked that his horse had been listening to applause at the back and thought it was for him. Stack appeared by video link and when he spoke, Red Rum's ears pricked up. 'I don't know what to say to him, he's much more intelligent than I am,' Stack quipped.

He faced a race against time to be fit to ride Red Rum in the 1978 Grand National, where the horse would be going for his fourth victory, at the ripe old age of 13. Spurred on no doubt by the dream of more Liverpool glory, Stack did return to the saddle earlier than expected and partnered Red Rum in the Greenall Whitley at Haydock on 4 March, where they finished unplaced. That run, as in previous years, would have got Rummy teed up perfectly for Aintree, but then in the sort of absurd twist that jump racing specialises in, Red Rum himself got injured the day before the big race and was promptly retired. Stack switched to ride Hidden Value, and came down at the third fence. That must have been bitterly disappointing compared to what he had experienced twelve months earlier and what he might have achieved on Red Rum again, but to his credit he was one of the first people afterwards to congratulate the winning rider, Bob Davies.

There was compensation of sorts when later in the month Stack landed his first win in the Whitbread, on the Peter Bailey-trained Strombolus, and received the trophy from HM The Queen. A few days later, on 2 May 1978, he brought his career total to 600 winners with a double at Sedgefield. Both horses were owned and trained, appropriately enough, by Arthur Stephenson, the man whose 'little fish' had helped fire Stack to his titles. Both wins that day showed the champion's strength in a finish. Reaghstown, backed down to 5-2 favourite in a division of the novices' hurdle, had rousted up in the closing stages, while his other winner, Super Chant, only got up by a neck in the handicap chase.

Stack announced his retirement on BBC1's *Sportsnight* programme on Wednesday, 10 May 1978, having ridden a grand total of 607 winners. He was only 32. His final winning ride came on Prince Carl for the Dickinson family at Uttoxeter.

What to do next? In his autobiography John Francome said that Stack was like himself. 'He wasn't really a jockey but a business man who rode horses.'

Stack had always been rather canny when it came to money. Barry Brogan told the story of how in his early days Tommy had bought a little black Austin for £40, then ran it for a couple of years before selling it on for £70. 'Stackie was our leader in the North,' recalled Michael Dickinson, a weighing room contemporary who went on to be a highly successful trainer. 'He would always say, "We'll go in your car and I'll drive." That way he didn't have to pay for any petrol. The rest of us were glad to let him drive because we were always so tired. Financially he always came off best.'

While he was still riding, Stack had been involved in breeding and investing in the bloodstock industry. In 1978 he became manager of Longfield Stud, the Tipperary outpost of John Magnier's Coolmore operation. Eight years after that he took out a Flat trainer's licence and enjoyed considerable success, saddling the winner of both the English 1,000 Guineas (Las Meninas) in 1994 and the Irish equivalent in 1996 with Tarascon.

In 1998, tragedy struck. Stack was rushed to hospital with meningitis just before Christmas and although he recovered, he lost his hearing. No longer would he be able to hear the roar of any racing crowd, or the thunder of the horses' hooves on the gallops, but he did learn to lip-read and continued training until 2016, when he handed over his licence to son Fozzy.

Stack was quite an unusual champion in that while he won the Grand National, his other big race wins were rare. Not only did he never win a Cheltenham Gold Cup, but he never even had a ride in the race. Ditto the King George and the Champion Hurdle. But what Stack did do was to ride an incredible number of horses each year – and win lots of races. His championships were achieved by considerable talent and lots of hard graft. We remember him for his consistency, and for the role he played in one of the most emotional sporting afternoons of all time.

Big race wins
Grand National 1977 (Red Rum)
Whitbread 1978 (Strombolus)

Chapter Fifteen

John Francome

Champion 1975/76, 1978/79, 1980/81, 1981/82 (tied), 1982/83, 1983/84, 1984/85

The Greatest Jockey?

'I doubt if there's ever been a rider with more finesse than him.'
Peter Scudamore on John Francome, 1987

The Swindon-born seven-time champion joked that most of the kids he went to school with came from a part of town that was so rough that even the Alsatians went around in pairs. Johnny Francome was like no champion that went before him or indeed after. For a start, there was his nonchalance. Francome was extremely professional – you don't win seven titles by not being so – but he always gave the impression that he thought there were other more important things in life than being a champion jump jockey.

'I like the game but I am not obsessed by it. If something came along which could earn us more money, I'd stop tomorrow,' he said in 1975.

Unlike so many of the jockeys featured in this book, Francome did not come from a racing background. His dad was a fireman on the railways who used to cut people's hair and sweep chimneys in his spare time to make some extra money, while his mum kept chickens in the garden to help pay the council house rent.

'My only connection to horses was a distant relative who went to prison for selling a blind horse to a woman as a hunter,' Francome revealed in his 1985 autobiography *Born Lucky*. Ever the joker, he put a note in the front of the book, for his friends, to explain that 'autobiography' was not the life story of a motor car.

He was bitten by the equine bug when riding a donkey on a family trip to Barry Island. On his return home he started to help his local milkman with his deliveries in return for a ride on his horse on the way home. The man who would later be referred to as 'Greatest Jockey' by fellow TV pundit John

McCririck, was almost entirely self-taught as a rider. When he was 6, and his parents had moved to a house of their own, they bought him his first pony, which had belonged to the milkman's daughter. It was called Black Beauty but doesn't seem to have had much in common with the subject of the famous Victorian novel by Anna Sewell.

The young Francome, when he wasn't lusting after girls at school, indulged his growing passion for equine activities. He spent his summer taking part in gymkhanas, and then started showjumping. Such was his progress, when he was 15 he represented Britain in France and Switzerland and won the European championships.

A career as a professional showjumper seemed the logical path but Francome was concerned about the potential financial burden on his parents. He got into National Hunt racing, which he admits he didn't have the remotest interest in, totally by chance. A friend of the family, who had some carpentry work for Fred Winter over at Uplands, suggested John went to see the famous champion jockey turned champion trainer. Winter gave him an interview, which John attended with his father, and took him on as an apprentice, starting the following month. That was 16 October 1969.

Francome would stay with Winter at Uplands for the next sixteen years, forging one of the strongest trainer-jockey relationships the sport has ever seen. Personality-wise they seemed to have little in common. Winter could be terse and was notoriously grumpy, especially first thing in the morning. Francome was a cheerful, irreverent Jack the Lad. But over the years there developed a mutual respect, and when Francome did get into trouble with the racing authorities, 'The Governor' loyally stood by him.

Francome learnt early on to try to be as obliging as possible to his new boss. Always on the lookout to make some extra money, in addition to his stable duties he did odd jobs around the place, which included washing Winter's and his head lad Brian Delaney's cars for ten shillings a week. Within three months of starting he was given his first ride schooling, and after just thirteen months at Uplands, he had his first ride in public. It was a winning one, too, on Multigrey, at Worcester, on 17 November 1970.

Francome acknowledged the great help he had from Winter's number two jockey at the time, Richard Pitman, aka 'Pip':

> Apart from getting me my first ride and later on the job with Richard
> Head and Ken Cundell it was he who drilled into me the importance
> of making what money I earned work for me. It was also Pip who

pointed out that riding ability was only part of what was needed to become a champion jockey, and that being tactful and showing trainers you are keen, are just as important. You won't get very far if you are riding for the King of Tonga and walk into the paddock and tell him what a wally he looks in a grass skirt!

After his initial success, Francome came down to earth with a bump – literally – on his next ride. He broke his wrist after a fall in a novices' chase at Cheltenham. That meant a lay-off till February, but on his return he won his second race, and the first of 575 for Winter, on Osceola at Towcester.

The horse that really helped establish him as a young jockey with a future at Uplands was Osbaldeston. The novice chaser was fast, but had fallen on his previous two runs over fences. Francome schooled him and then got the ride at Worcester where, having him settled nicely, he partnered his mount to an easy 1½-length success. They won again the following month and in the next season (1971/72) Osbaldeston was responsible for five of Francome's eighteen winners. By the time the horse died in 1978, Francome had won seventeen races on him.

Most of his early winners away from Uplands came from Ken Cundell's yard at Compton. In November 1972 he lost his claim. The early 1970s was a golden era for the Fred Winter stable, blessed with an abundance of equine talent, the likes of Bula, Pendil, Lanzarote, Crisp and Killiney. It didn't always go to plan, though. Francome says today that the Uplands horses, having had great seasons, were often just 'over the top' when it came to the spring festivals.

In March 1973 there was the agony of Richard Pitman being beaten by a short head in the Gold Cup (on Pendil) and then by less than a length in the Grand National on Crisp. In the 1973/74 season Francome broke his left arm at Wincanton (for the second time in seven months), but on his return at the end of February rode fifteen winners to bring his seasonal tally to thirty. His progress had not gone unnoticed, as in the summer of 1974 he was approached by Fred Rimell with the offer of taking over as the new stable jockey at Kinnersley. He talked it over with Winter, who told him to bear in mind that Richard Pitman wouldn't be riding for ever and that gentle hint was enough to persuade Francome to stay put. Instead of moving to Rimell's, where the job of Bill Smith's replacement went to Ken White, he took a second retainer with Captain Richard Head at Lambourn, who had some very good horses at the time.

In 1974/75 Francome delivered his first serious title challenge, falling twelve short of Tommy Stack, in joint second place, but with 244 fewer rides. It was, in his own words, 'the season when everything started to happen'. Riding with ever greater confidence he rode his first winner at the Cheltenham Festival, on King Flame, for Captain Head in the National Hunt Handicap Chase.

With Pitman retired, Francome became stable jockey at Uplands for the 1975/76 season. He was now very well placed to become champion jockey. At Christmas 1975, when Queen's *Bohemian Rhapsody* topped the pop charts, he shared the lead in the title race with Tommy Stack, the reigning champion. He would have been ahead had he not received a seven-day ban at the end of November for being held to be in breach of Rule 151 (the so-called 'non-triers' rule), for a ride he had given a horse at Plumpton. It was not the last time Francome's 'quiet' style would land him in hot water with the stewards.

On 6 January he was quoted at 2-1 for the title. Five days later, Jonjo O'Neill led him 49-48. With Bob Davies and Stack also in contention it was a close contest, but Francome eventually prevailed by five from Davies, taking his first championship with a total of ninety-six winners. Again, he had fewer rides than his main rivals (392 to Davies's 461 and Stack's 483), but his strike rate was significantly superior (24.49 per cent compared to 19.74 per cent and 16.98 per cent).

It wasn't just winning his first championship that Francome had to celebrate. He married his girlfriend Miriam on 26 June 1976, officially recorded as the hottest day ever in London, with the temperature hitting 34.8°C. Miriam had been a secretary to the trainer Patrick Haslam and on their first date John had taken her to a cinema in Swindon to see *Tales from the Crypt*, before buying fish and chips on the way back home. They were, despite the 'horror' start, an attractive pair. According to Graham Sharpe's *Racing's Greatest Characters*, they once turned up at a Lambourn fancy dress party as Adam and Eve, stark naked and wearing just four fig leaves between them. (We still don't know to this day who came as the serpent.)

Francome was a man for whom the word 'enterprising' could originally have been coined. On 12 September 1976, the *Sunday People* informed its readers that the champion jump jockey would be seen in a new role at Worcester the following Wednesday … selling hot dogs, soup, hamburgers and cups of tea to racegoers in-between races from his mobile stall. He explained:

> I've been thinking of this for 12 months. If all goes well on Wednesday I'll be able to run this service at many meetings. We aim to sell hot food and drink at low prices. Our speciality will be home-made soup for 10p a cup. We plan to make the smell of our cooking irresistible.

How many other sportsmen would even consider selling soup and hot dogs to spectators while performing at the same venue? Francome was truly a one-off.

He finished runner-up to Tommy Stack in the 1976/77 season and a year later played second fiddle behind Jonjo O'Neill, but that season (1977/78) he had the significant high of his first and only Gold Cup win, and the low of a serious run-in with the racing authorities. The trouble concerned his association with the bookmaker John Banks. The two had become chums after sitting next to each other at the Stable Lads' Boxing Dinner two years earlier. Ironically, it was when Francome was riding a horse called Stopped for Fred Winter that brought things to a head. Stopped was the favourite for the 1978 Imperial Cup, run at Sandown the Saturday before the Cheltenham Festival. He was a hard puller and so Francome kept him at the rear of the field. When he came to make his run he experienced considerable traffic problems, and by the time he had switched to the outside, the race was lost. On the second day of the rain-soaked 1978 Festival, he was called in to be interviewed by the head of racing security. He was quizzed about his friendship with Banks. 'During the interrogation I was made to feel like a criminal and I don't mind admitting that for a few moments in there I was frightened,' he later wrote. Francome admitted in the interview that he talked to Banks about the horses he had ridden but said he had no idea that doing so contravened the rules of racing.

The matter was referred to a subsequent hearing at Portman Square, the headquarters of the Jockey Club, racing's ruling body. Fred Winter followed him outside. Francome turned to his boss and assured him he had never stopped a horse in his life. To which Winter replied: 'Son. If I thought for a moment that you had, you wouldn't be standing there – you'd be lying down.'

Forty-eight hours of rain led to the cancellation of the final day of the Festival, when Francome was due to ride Midnight Court in the Gold Cup for Winter. That was one stroke of luck as the horse preferred faster ground, but when Midnight Court took up an alternative engagement at Chepstow two days later, Francome learnt that Graham Thorner had got the ride, while he was sent to ride in a novice hurdle at Lingfield. Both Francome and Thorner won their respective races, but after Chepstow things thankfully returned to normal. Perhaps it was just The Governor's way of warning his stable jockey not to take anything for granted. With going conditions in his favour, Midnight Court, with Francome back on board, won the rescheduled Gold Cup easily on 13 April. There was great rejoicing after what had been an extraordinary few weeks. Francome says today the win gave him the most satisfaction of any in his career because it was his employer's first Gold Cup, after so many near misses. It also meant that Winter became the first – and to date only – man to have ridden and trained the winners of the Gold Cup, Champion Hurdle and Grand National.

The victory was also poignant as it came just a year after Winter had lost two of his best horses, Bula and Lanzarote, following falls at the Cheltenham Festival. Even after the Gold Cup, though, the drama of 1978 still hadn't finished. Francome's disciplinary hearing took place on 30 April. It lasted all of nine hours and although the stewards failed to find any evidence that he had stopped any horses, he was brought to book for sharing confidential information with Banks. Both men were found to be in breach of Rule 220, which states that no one should do anything to cause serious damage to the interests of horseracing in Great Britain. Francome's punishment was a six-week suspension and a £750 fine.

It was a blow, but his job with Winter was secure, and the next season (1978/79), he bounced back in fine style by winning his second championship. It was the so-called 'Winter of Discontent'. A series of strikes, the impact of which was compounded with plenty of cold, snowy weather, helped bring down the Labour government of James Callaghan and usher in Thatcherism. But whatever was happening in the country at large, for Francome it was a contented time. Three winners at Lingfield on 28 February 1979 and one more there a day later brought his seasonal tally up to fifty-five. In the end he finished on ninety-five. He would surely have reached his century had not so many meetings been lost to the weather.

Despite landing his second championship Francome still didn't believe he was the best jockey riding. He knew he was the best out in the country but thought others were stronger in a finish. He said in *Born Lucky* that he only became convinced that he was number one after landing his third title, in 1980/81. That was not only the first of five consecutive seasons in which he won the title – something no jump jockey had ever done before – but the first of five consecutive seasons in which he rode over 100 winners.

The highlight of the 1980/81 season was undoubtedly winning his first, and only, Champion Hurdle on the legendary Sea Pigeon. He took the ride because Jonjo O'Neill was injured. Sea Pigeon was the reigning champion and so the pressure was certainly on. But Francome was his usual cool self. Tim Fitzgeorge-Parker described the action:

He waited and waited, like Harry Wragg in his prime. Pollardstown and Daring Run jumped the last a good two lengths in front of him, but with only a hundred yards of the Cheltenham hill to go, John picked up Sea Pigeon and flew past the pair of them to win by one and a half lengths from Pollardstown and Daring Run a neck away in third.

Afterwards Francome described Sea Pigeon as 'quite simply the best horse I have ever ridden'. Today he modestly disclaims any personal contribution to the success by pointing out that Sea Pigeon had around 12lb in hand of his rivals. But he still had to get the job done on unsuitably heavy ground. It was some day. Francome went on to complete a treble with Derring Rose in the Stayers' Hurdle and Friendly Alliance in the Grand Annual – both for Fred Winter.

With Jonjo O'Neill out injured since October, the title race that year developed into a duel between Francome and the new kid on the block, Peter Scudamore. Francome led 'Scu' by six on 1 May (96-90), but at an evening meeting at Taunton, his nearest rival fractured his skull in a bad fall that put him out for three weeks, thus ending his title hopes. Francome went on to ride 105 winners, sealing his third title after a success on Rathconrath at Warwick on 23 May. Even without Scudamore's injury, Francome would probably have won anyway as he had the advantage, but the bad luck his rival had suffered was not forgotten.

In the 1981/82 season Francome distinguished himself with one of the greatest acts of sportsmanship jump racing has ever seen. He began the season very well, and by the time the Big Freeze arrived in December – with huge snowdrifts and temperatures plummeting to -25°C, he was more than twenty winners clear of Scudamore. Then things went downhill pretty fast.

Francome was hit by a virus and in January Sheikh Ali Abu Khamsin, a leading owner at Uplands, decided he no longer required his services. Scu, meanwhile, was steadily closing the gap, and ten weeks after Christmas, Francome's lead had been cut to just three. There were still some moments to celebrate, in particular a win in the Schweppes Hurdle in February on Donegal Prince and Cheltenham Festival success on Brown Chamberlin in the Sun Alliance. But a fall at Newbury on 5 March proved to be something of a double whammy. It wasn't just that Francome was stood down for seven days with concussion, it was the fact that also injured in the melee was Sam Morshead, first jockey to Mercy Rimell. With Morshead out of action, Mrs Rimell turned to Scudamore for the rest of the season, greatly boosting the challenger's title hopes.

Scudamore raced clear of Francome and was twenty winners ahead with just five weeks to go, when he broke his arm in a fall at Southwell. Francome had been given a lucky reprieve, but on the way home from Southwell began to think about his rival and what must have been going through his mind.

For the second year running, Scudamore's hopes of winning the title had been dashed through injury. 'There are a lot of things that don't seem fair in life and this was one of them,' Francome later wrote. He decided that even though he wanted to retain his title, Scudamore didn't deserve to lose out either. So as soon as his rival was discharged from hospital he rang him up and told him what he had in mind. Francomes's plan was to draw level with Scudamore and then stop riding, so that the two could share the title. But catching the championship leader required quite an effort, especially as Francome was still suffering from a virus. He rode six winners in four days, including a treble at an evening meeting at Taunton, to reduce the deficit to fourteen, but then went three days without a winner.

Wantage trainer David Gandolfo was a particular help, providing three more winners. With a fortnight to go Francome was just six behind. The following week he literally went up and down the country to try to draw level. He had his first ride (and first winner at Sedgefield) and then did the same having driven across to Cartmel in the southern Lake District. That was an afternoon meeting, after which he drove down to Nottinghamshire, where he had another winner at the evening meeting at Southwell, for David Gandolfo.

That meant he had one more week to find just one more winner. 'By this time I had driven over 3,000 miles and could hardly wait to reach my target so I could rest,' he recalled. But four fancied mounts at Fontwell on Bank Holiday Monday surprisingly failed to produce a winner, meaning the pressure was on again when Francome headed north to Uttoxeter on 1 June. This time there was no disappointment as he piloted Buckmaster to victory in the Mayfield Novice Chase. Jim Beavis, author of *The History of Uttoxeter Racecourse*, records that Francome 'was welcomed into the winners' enclosure with a tumultuous reception from a crowd appreciative of his noble gesture'.

Whether it was good karma or not, Francome's path to the title the following season was much smoother. In addition to being first jockey at Uplands he now had another retainer with John Jenkins, who was firing in the winners. He admitted in *Born Lucky* that he only started riding for Jenkins because he wanted to chat up his 'lovely' wife Wendy – and the winners were just a bonus.

Francome was now at the top of his game. What made him so brilliant? His showjumping background was obviously a factor when it came to getting horses to jump for him. Fred Winter famously said of his stable jockey: 'He is the best placer of a horse at a fence I've ever seen. It's an education to watch him. There's no apparent effort at all.' Praise indeed considering Winter's own achievements. Close friend and fellow Uplands jockey Richard Pitman said: 'You never saw him correcting a horse coming into a fence. There was no "Come here, come here, come here", shortening up or calls of "Go on my son" to get a big one ... He was always just right.'

Veteran trainer John Spearing told me: 'He seemed to do everything very quietly. He didn't stand out when you were watching him, but he knew what he was doing. He was top class.'

While he was a joker in the weighing room, when the action was about to begin Francome was, in Peter Scudamore's words, 'as deaf as a post' and fully focused on the job in hand. He could be ruthless too on the racetrack. Richard Dunwoody recalled one time at Huntingdon he made the mistake of trying to make up ground on his inner. Francome shut the door and almost put him over the open ditch.

By 2 February 1983 he was twenty-nine winners clear of Scudamore in the title race, operating at a strike rate of 24 per cent. He finished the season with 106, thirteen ahead of Scu.

Such was his dominance in the early to mid-1980s that in the 1983/84 season Francome could even afford a five-week lay-off during October and November with three cracked vertebrae and still win the title with ease, posting a personal best of 131 winners, to Jonjo O'Neill's 103 and Peter Scudamore's 98. In June 1984 he broke Stan Mellor's all-time record of 1,035 winners after riding Don't Touch to victory at Fontwell. The BBC's Julian Wilson asked him how important it was for him to break the record. Francome replied:

> Well, I never, ever set out to break Stan's record, it just sort of happened over the years, but obviously I'm pleased to have done it.
>
> When I rode my 1,000th winner Stan was the first person to send me a telegram and say well done and I know, or at least I hope, he won't mind me beating him. I dare say Peter Scudamore or someone else will do me, but it's nice to hold the record even if it is for just a couple of years.

During this golden period the multiple champion won two King Georges (in 1982 on Wayward Lad and 1984 on Burrough Hill Lad), two Welsh Grand Nationals (Narvik in 1980 and Burrough Hill Lad in 1983), and two Hennessys (Brown Chamberlin in 1983 and Burrough Hill Lad in 1984). But Francome himself says his best ride was on board the Peter Cundell-trained Celtic Ryde at Kempton at Christmas 1981. 'I like the Celtic Ryde effort because your job as a jockey is to make everything for the horse as easy as possible,' he says.

In 1984 he was embroiled in another big news story. It transpired that his home telephone had been tapped since early November 1983, most likely by a national newspaper, hoping to record him saying something incriminating which could then be presented as a major scoop. Francome's conversation with a trainer was made into much more than it was – with again the (wrong) implication drawn that the discussion was about stopping a horse. The champion jockey went to court to try to get an injunction to stop the then Robert Maxwell-owned *Daily Mirror* from printing the 'exclusive', which the newspaper opposed. Francome never did find out who had tapped his phone (which was thought to have occurred during a house break-in), but did get awarded most of his costs.

Although he could easily have gone on for much longer, he had already decided to quit at the start of the 1984/85 season. 'Perhaps it was because I had done it all and riding no longer held a challenge for me or maybe it was because I realised that a jockey is only as safe as his last ride and I had reached the point where I had more to lose than I had to gain,' he later explained.

Boosted by the red-hot form of John Jenkins, who sent out a remarkable twenty-eight winners in just sixteen days, he got his final year off to a flyer. When Church Warden won at Cheltenham on 9 November 1984, he broke Josh Gifford's record for the fastest half-century of winners in a season by a day. At the turn of the year it looked as if he would beat Jonjo O'Neill's record of 149 winners but then the snow came and numerous meetings were lost.

Peter Scudamore believes Francome's crushing fall on The Reject in the Arkle at the 1985 Cheltenham Festival may have brought to a head his thoughts about retirement. Instead of characteristically laughing about the mishap in the weighing room afterwards he was clearly shaken. He gave up his ride on See You Then in the Champion Hurdle to Steve Smith-Eccles, thereby establishing the partnership that went on to win the race three years in a row.

On 8 April he rode a four-timer at Huntingdon and would have retired there and then, but had a commitment to ride in the World Jockeys' Championship, so the next day he went to Chepstow. There he had another fall from The Reject and the horse galloped all over him. He took it as a sign that it was time to pack it in without further delay. It was a good time to bow out, as that year, Francome helped Fred Winter regain the trainers' championship after a six-year break.

In a career that lasted from November 1970 to April 1985 he had ridden 1,138 winners, almost half of which (575) were for 'The Governor', Fred Winter. His big race record was excellent, but with the usual champion's CV omission, the Grand National. Rather like Eric Morecambe, who played all the right notes but not necessarily in the right order, Francome did ride National winners, but not in the year they won the big race. He was on Rag Trade, but in 1975, not 1976.

He rode Grittar, but in 1984, not 1982. The closest he got to Aintree glory was a distant second on Rough and Tumble behind Ben Nevis in 1980; he finished third on the same horse twelve months later. Not that Francome has any regrets. He told me during the Covid lockdown of 2020 that it doesn't bother him in the slightest that he never won the Grand National. He had a wonderful time, riding some great horses for people he liked, and that was it.

Johnny Francome can be seen as one of the last cavaliers. The sport had become a lot more 'serious' by the time he finished riding, with jockeys paying more attention to things like diet and fitness levels, but it had arguably lost some of its fun. While Terry Biddlecombe gallivanted around into the wee small hours with Josh Gifford and David Mould, Francome's weighing room partner in merriment was Steve Smith-Eccles. Writing in 1985, Francome reminisced:

> During the last seven years we have had enough laughs together to last each other a lifetime. You might be dead tomorrow was our excuse for doing just about anything and in his case anything we knew we shouldn't. We did anything from pretending to shoot cyclists from the car window with the vet's humane killer to pinning girls' tights to the coat collars of stewards, while the other one kept them distracted. Provided it never hurt anyone's feelings we were game for a laugh.

Francome says the biggest change that took place when he was riding – in addition to improved safety equipment like body protectors – was the growing use of jockeys' agents. He never had one. Yet he still won seven championships.

After hanging up his saddle he became a popular television racing presenter – a mainstay on Channel Four's *The Morning Line* for many years – and a top-selling author of racing thrillers. When I asked him if he has any photographs of himself riding for possible use in this book, he replied: 'Do you know what? I've given them all away.'

Francome doesn't look back. But when we do, and consider his career, we can only applaud a truly great champion who did everything in his own inimitable way.

Big race wins
Gold Cup 1978 (Midnight Court)
Welsh Grand National 1980 (Narvik), 1983 (Burrough Hill Lad)
Champion Hurdle 1981 (Sea Pigeon)
Stayer's Hurdle 1981 (Derring Rose)
King George VI Chase 1982, 1984 (Wayward Lad)
Hennessy Gold Cup 1983 (Brown Chamberlin), 1984 (Burrough Hill Lad)

Chapter Sixteen

Jonjo O'Neill

Champion 1977/78, 1979/80

Broken, but Never Beaten

'If I'm going to be champion jockey, it'll happen without me worrying about it.'

Jonjo O'Neill, 1978

A moment in time. Chepstow racecourse, Monday, 12 April 1982. It's a handicap hurdle that involves a tremendous three-way finish between the best three jockeys of the era.

John Francome, the subject of our previous chapter, is on the favourite, Our Bara Boy. Peter Scudamore, the man who succeeds him as champion, and breaks his record of seven titles, is on Great Developer. Jonjo O'Neill, who won two titles, but who would surely have won more if he hadn't had such rotten luck with injuries, is riding Rogairo.

Francome takes it up from the ninth flight but a mistake at the last lets Scudamore in. Then O'Neill makes his challenge and overtakes Scu. He leads until the last stride when, Francome having rousted his mount to make one final effort, comes again and pips him at the post to a neck victory. Three great champions, who dominated the sport for the best part of two decades. Consider this: from 1977 until 1993, no one apart from these three won the jump jockeys' championship.

While we can cast Francome as the court jester, laid-back and nonchalant, but determined as anyone once the tapes were raised, Scudamore was the more serious, tunnel-visioned record breaker.

Where does O'Neill fit in? The very model of Irish geniality in the weighing room, he nevertheless gave no quarter on the track. He was tough as teak and had to be, surviving a shattered leg injury which may have led to amputation, and left him in agony for over a year, and later, lymphatic cancer.

Even though he lost out that day at Chepstow, there have been few equals to O'Neill in a finish. 'His overwhelming determination to get to the line first at all costs seemed at times to inspire his mounts to do the impossible for him in a tight finish; time and again he won races that lesser riders would have lost,' was the verdict of Peter Easterby.

O'Neill was born in Castletownroche, a small town in County Cork, on 13 April 1952. His father was a cobbler by trade who would like to have become a jockey had he got the chance. His son more than made up for that. Jonjo's first association with horses came playing with donkeys and ponies on a nearby farm. At the age of 6 he begged to be thrown up onto the back of a hunter called Tom. 'The moment I was astride him, my legs at full strength, he arched his back and threw me to the ground,' he later recalled. But what happened next was the key. The young Jonjo immediately pestered to be put back on the horse again, and then rode it bareback round the field.

At school, the 'three Rs' never interested him. Writing in 1985, racing journalist Tim Richards, who co-authored O'Neill's autobiography, noted that he took longer to read the write-up of a race than he did to ride in it. What O'Neill did have was a winning smile, and bags of courage.

After leaving school, the ginger-haired teenager first joined the Mallow yard of Don Reid. When Reid quit after a year, he went, along with the trainer's horses, to the stables of Michael Connolly at the Curragh. The ambition was to be a Flat jockey, but O'Neill's weight proved a problem. Progress was painfully slow. His first winner on the Flat came in September 1970, but by 1972 he had only ridden two more – Irish Painter, over hurdles, and Stan Royal, on his first ride in a steeplechase. Connolly described his apprentice as 'always a gentleman', but felt he too often threw caution to the wind when race riding. He blamed O'Neill for the death of Irish Painter, who broke his shoulder in a last fence fall at Naas in 1972. When the young jockey went into the horse's empty box on the following Monday morning he was overcome with sadness and, fighting back the tears, asked his boss if he could leave at the end of the week. Who knows what might have happened had O'Neill stayed at the Curragh. His father's cousin, Paddy Joe Lombard, who farmed and bred racehorses, got in touch with Scottish Borders trainer Ken Oliver, who told him he had enough boys but to try Gordon Richards instead.

O'Neill arrived in Cumberland (as it was then still known) in February 1972, aged just 19. Richards, as we've seen, was now a powerful force in National Hunt racing. A hard man, famous for his fiery temper, Richards was also very fair, and gave his young apprentice every opportunity to shine. O'Neill could also not have wished for a better mentor than his fellow Irishman Ron Barry, Richards' stable jockey.

O'Neill rode his first winner in Britain, Alexandra Parade, in a selling hurdle at Stratford in September 1972. Richards must have been impressed because just seven weeks later, he gave O'Neill the ride on Proud Stone, well fancied for the valuable Mackeson Gold Cup at Cheltenham. Ron Barry couldn't do 10 stone and so the horse's owner, Jimmy McGhie, who liked to have a bet, asked Richards to engage another jockey. The Master of Greystoke insisted that his young apprentice, whom he described in glowing terms, get the ride. Sadly, things didn't go to plan. He had told O'Neill to be sure to 'wait, wait and wait', and that if he produced his horse at the last he would win. But Jonjo over-egged the pudding. Everything was going well until the last fence. To be absolutely sure of winning he asked his mount for a big one, and was promptly blasted out of the saddle. All he had to do was to pop the horse over the fence and the race would have been his. He apologised to Richards, but in the pub that evening he was confronted with an angry punter who accused him of jumping off.

That Saturday was one of the worst days of O'Neill's young life. At the time he genuinely thought his fledgling career might be over, but to his credit – and to Richards' credit too – he bounced back.

At Catterick in the week before Christmas he showed great verve to ride 20-1 shot Meerkat to victory on a cold dark afternoon when the course was shrouded in fog and racing subsequently had to be abandoned. That led Meerkat's trainer, one Tim Molony, a five-time champion jockey himself (see Chapter Three) to comment: 'He's a sure champion of the future.' As the saying goes, it takes one to know one.

O'Neill ended the 1972/73 season with thirty-eight winners, which won him the junior championship, the same year that Ron Barry took the championship with a record-breaking 125 winners.

The following season saw O'Neill partner Clear Cut, trained by the veteran Yorkshire handler Charlie Hall, to victory in the Topham Trophy at Liverpool. The front runner gave him an exhilarating ride over the Grand National fences, but in the big race itself, Jonjo, in common with many other champions, was to suffer some terrible misfortune, as we'll see later.

By the mid-1970s, the Richards/O'Neill combination had become established as a winning one. O'Neill's tallies for seasons 1973/74 to 1976/77 were 51, 64 and 65.

But tensions at Greystoke were rising. Having broken his left leg in a fall at Teesside in 1975, O'Neill smashed his right one for the first time in January 1977. His landlady couldn't accommodate him with a downstairs bed so he moved in with the Richards. That made him too available, and O'Neill felt his boss was dominating his lifestyle. He knew that quitting Greystoke would either turn out to be the best or the worst thing he could possibly do.

Fortunately it proved to be the former. O'Neill's decision to go freelance couldn't have happened at a better time. Northern racing was incredibly strong in the late 1970s and early 1980s. The fact that he was based in a regional powerhouse and everyone seemed keen to engage his services enabled him to leap from sixty-five winners in 1976/77 to a record-breaking 149 a year later. His winners were for no fewer than forty-two different stables.

Peter Easterby, three-time champion trainer, supplied nearly a third of his wins. The most famous Habton Grange horses O'Neill was associated with were Sea Pigeon and Night Nurse. These brilliantly versatile performers captured the public imagination in the late 1970s, not just because of their tremendous consistency, but because they ran so regularly, compared to today's National Hunt stars who we very often see just a couple of times before Cheltenham, if that.

Sea Pigeon, who had finished seventh in the 1973 Derby, began his hurdling career with Gordon Richards but left for Easterby's at around about the same time as O'Neill. In 1978 O'Neill rode the horse to victory in the Scottish Champion Hurdle, one of the highlights of his annus mirabilis. He reached his half-century in early December, and by the end of the calendar year was already on the seventy-six mark. Into 1978 and the winners kept coming. There was a treble at Newcastle on 14 January, including a win on Alverton, of whom we shall hear more of presently, and another treble three days later at Wetherby. On 8 February at Haydock, he registered the fastest hundred ever achieved by a jump jockey after winning on Sweet Millie, thus breaking Fred Winter's fastest hundred by five weeks. With his confidence sky-high, O'Neill passed his friend Ron Barry's five-year-record of 125 winners on Majetta Crescent at Perth on 19 April, on a day when he visited the winners' enclosure five times.

O'Neill wanted to reach 150, but just came up short. He felt he should have been awarded a race at Hexham in the last week of the season when another jockey carved him up, and then missed what would have been a winning ride at Market Rasen when the car that was taking him to the airport was delayed in heavy traffic. When he did arrive at the Lincolnshire venue, he had to watch the horse he should have been riding, Pleasure Seeker, win.

He still had one more ride but his mount in the last, Three Musketeers, who had been his 147th winner, failed to live up to the motto 'All for one, one for all' and tired on the run-in to finish second. Even so, it was a tremendous feat to break the existing record by twenty-four. John Francome later wrote that it was the equivalent in achievement and effort to winning a gold medal at the Olympics, but added that the day after O'Neill had ridden his 149th winner you had to scour the pages of every newspaper to find mention of it.

Timeform paid the new record-breaking champion a glowing tribute in their *Chasers & Hurdlers 1977/78*: 'O'Neill is the most reliable of jockeys riding over the sticks today: we cannot recall seeing him lose a race he ought to have won during the season.' They finished their valediction with the prediction: 'If he keeps clear of injury he should have a long reign as champion,' 'If' proved to be the key word. Largely due to injury he would only win one more title.

In 1978/79 O'Neill lost his title to Francome, in a season marked by great highs and lows. In fact, in a two-week period in March, O'Neill met Rudyard Kipling's twin imposters Triumph and Disaster on the same horse.

The Cheltenham Gold Cup of 1979 was epic. Raced during a blizzard on extremely testing ground, the Irish-trained front runner Tied Cottage established what looked like an unassailable lead. O'Neill never gave up though and pulled his mount Alverton to the outside in search of better ground. Two tired horses still giving it their all came to the last together, but while Alverton put in a great leap, Tied Cottage came crashing to the floor. O'Neill believes that Tied Cottage spotted his horse out of the corner of his eye and lost his concentration for a split second. It was his attacking policy on Alverton that had brought him glory. But just sixteen days later, there was a tragic postscript when the Gold Cup hero of 1979 was killed at Becher's Brook on the second circuit of the Grand National. The 13-2 favourite was cantering at the time, but inexplicably hadn't taken off at the track's most fearsome fence. O'Neill later wrote that he felt numb from the neck up as he handed Alverton's bridle in the direction of the horse's adoring stable lad Jack Warrell, who had expected his pride and joy to appear riderless at any moment. Warrell, a tough Yorkshireman, knelt on the ground and cried like a baby.

By unhappy coincidence, the two other Gold Cup winners O'Neill was associated with, Dawn Run, as a jockey in 1986, and Synchronised, as a trainer in 2012, both lost their lives not long after their heroics at Cheltenham. Synchronised, like Alverton, was killed in the Grand National, after being injured when running loose following a Becher's Brook fall.

O'Neill, you could say, was the champion jockey who had more than his fair share of bad luck. In 1979/80, though, the stars were generally shining on him. He regained his title quite comfortably with 117 winners. Peter Easterby, with fifty-one, provided the highest number of these, but he also rode winners for thirty-six other stables.

The highlight of the year was undoubtedly Sea Pigeon's win in the 1980 Champion Hurdle. O'Neill felt he should have won on the horse in the 1979 renewal, but was caught in two minds about when to kick on and his mount ran out of fuel on the run-in on very taxing ground. A year later, with the distance of the race reduced by 200 yards, and on much better going, it was a very different outcome. O'Neill and Sea Pigeon got their revenge on the 1979 winner Monksfield by 7 lengths. O'Neill, mindful of the three unnecessary cracks he had given his mount a year earlier, never picked up his whip.

That same Festival he also won the Cathcart on Peter Easterby's King Weasel. He recorded his hundredth winner of the season, Scrunch, for Bobby Brewis at Newcastle two days later, and among his subsequent seventeen victories of the campaign, there was another victory on Sea Pigeon, in the Welsh Champion Hurdle at Chepstow in April, and a win on Hallo Dandy over hurdles at Haydock in May. The horse was in the hands of Ginger McCain; four years later it won the Grand National, when trained by Gordon Richards.

O'Neill's final winner of his second championship-winning season came at Uttoxeter on 27 May, when he piloted the Philip Ransom-trained Relevance to victory. Few would then have predicted that O'Neill, clearly at the top of his game, would never win another title, but so it proved. In October 1980 he suffered an horrific fall in a hurdle race at Bangor, which shattered his right leg into at least four pieces. He was rushed to hospital, where his leg was screwed together with 6-inch alloy plate. O'Neill was determined to accelerate his recovery to get back in time to ride Sea Pigeon and Night Nurse at Cheltenham, but foolishly disobeyed doctor's orders and got back on a horse in January. Something in his leg snapped, and he found he could hardly breathe from the 'red-hot knife-like' pain.

O'Neill's rash action meant that it would not be until December 1981, a full fourteen months after his original injury, that he would return to the racing track, ruling him out of championship contention for not just one, but for two seasons. It could have been even worse. He received treatment from four different hospitals, including one in Basle, Switzerland, and at one stage it looked like his career would be finished altogether. He even faced the prospect of his leg being amputated.

When he finally returned to action, at Wetherby, and rode the mare Realt Na Nona to victory, he received a tremendous reception from the crowd.

Although he failed to win another championship, there was still plenty of success to come. In 1982/83 he forged a winning partnership with the progressive Roger Fisher-trained hurdler Ekbalco, which included two victories in the Welsh Champion Hurdle and the 1982 Christmas Hurdle at

Kempton. Sadly, the horse was killed in the 1983 Fighting Fifth at Newcastle, which left O'Neill in tears afterwards.

In 1983/84, riding better than ever, he established a commanding lead in the title race and it looked at Christmas as if, having posted the fastest half-century ever, he would be toppling Francome as champion. His total of seventy-two winners by the end of December was in fact only four fewer than in his record-breaking season of 1977/78.

But injuries once again intervened, and from the turn of the year until the end of the campaign he was only able to ride a further thirty-one winners. One of those was extremely important: on 13 March he partnered the Paddy Mullins-trained mare Dawn Run to victory in the Champion Hurdle.

Two years later, there wasn't a dry eye in the house when he rode the same Dawn Run to victory in the 1986 Cheltenham Gold Cup. This made her the first horse to pull off the big Cheltenham double, a feat that remains unequalled. Peter Scudamore later described Jonjo and Dawn Run's performance as the greatest he had ever seen in a steeplechase. Richard Austen, author of *At the Festival: Racing to Glory at Cheltenham in March*, said it was the best race he had ever witnessed. Dawn Run was relatively inexperienced over fences and had unseated her rider at Cheltenham in a far from satisfactory trial in January. In the Gold Cup itself, O'Neill got the big bay mare into a good rhythm at the head of the field with Run and Skip, but it wasn't all plain sailing as she splashed her feet at the second water jump and made a mistake at the fifth and fourth last. With four horses almost in a line, O'Neill asked for a big one two out, and got it, but nevertheless it looked as if Wayward Lad and the 1985 winner Forgive 'n Forget still had the upper hand. The latter didn't jump the last well, but Wayward Lad did. However, the three-time King George winner's stamina was beginning to wane. Let Tim Fitzgeorge-Parker describe the closing action:

> As Wayward Lad went left, Jonjo eased Dawn Run gently to her right and bravely took three precious strides to get her balanced. Then, seeing daylight and a tired horse ahead, this marvellous mare showed the will to win which had made her one of the finest champion hurdlers of all time. With her rivals stone cold, she galloped home to win by a length in a new record time for the race. As Jonjo raised his right arm in triumph, one of the biggest crowds ever to watch a Cheltenham Gold Cup roared its head off in admiration for an equine heroine and the best-loved and most universally respected jockey of his day.

It was a truly unforgettable occasion for anyone lucky to be there, but for poor Dawn Run there was a tragic postscript. Just three months after the ecstasy of Cheltenham came the agony of Auteuil when the 'marvellous mare' broke her neck following a fall in the French Champion Hurdle, when ridden by Michel Chirol. Her owner, Charmian Hill, had asked her to go to the well once too often.

O'Neill retired in 1986 having ridden 901 winners in a fourteen-year career. He had won two Gold Cups, two Champion Hurdles and a whole host of other top races, but like so many other of our champions had a poor record in the Grand National. In eight rides from 1973 to 1983, he failed to get further than the Canal Turn second time round. He was on board the 1976 winner Rag Trade in 1978, when the horse broke down and was destroyed, while a year later came the tragedy of Alverton. A year after that he fell at Becher's first time round on Another Dolly. But the Grand National apart, he must rate as one of the finest of all our jump jockeys.

His greatest strength, his bravery, was also arguably at times his greatest weakness. When you ask a horse for a big one two out, or at the last, you do increase your chances of winning, but at the same time you can also end it by falling. O'Neill never shirked it once and while his attacking, take-no-prisoners policy gave him two titles and plenty of big race success, it also brought him more than his fair share of injuries.

Yet however challenging the battles were when he was riding, when he hung up his saddle he had another, even tougher fight on his hands – against lymphatic cancer. Chemotherapy made him lose his hair, and his friends – of whom there were many – feared for the worst. But showing the same fortitude as he had shown on the racetrack, he bounced back.

His training career has had its ups and downs – with Jonjo you wouldn't have expected anything else – but by the late 1990s, and with the backing of powerful owner JP McManus, he had established himself as a force to be reckoned with. In 2001/02 he became the first person to have won 100 races in a British season as a jockey and as a trainer.

The Grand National jinx looked to have continued, particularly when Clan Royal, going so well in front, was badly baulked and carried out by a loose horse at second Becher's in 2005. Five years later, though, the hoodoo finally ended when he saddled the JP McManus-owned Don't Push It to Aintree success. That victory didn't just end O'Neill's drought in the big race, but multiple champion AP McCoy's too.

Jonjo O'Neill remains one of the best-loved people in racing. In November 2020 he added the Hennessy Gold Cup (now called the Ladbroke Trophy) to the Grand National as big races he has won as a trainer, but which eluded him as a jockey.

As we reflect on his career, we can only marvel at how many difficulties he had to overcome, and how much he achieved. That might in the future also mean him being the first champion jump jockey to sire another champion, with his highly regarded son Jonjo jnr proudly following in his father's footsteps.

Big race wins
Gold Cup 1979 (Alverton), 1986 (Dawn Run)
Champion Hurdle 1980 (Sea Pigeon), 1984 (Dawn Run)

Chapter Seventeen

Peter Scudamore

Champion 1981/82 (tied), 1985/86, 1986/87, 1987/88, 1988/89,
1989/90, 1990/91, 1991/92

'Scu': The Double-Century Record-Breaker

*'Of all the jockeys I've competed against, no one's riding better reflected
his character than Scu's. It was the will to win. Scu would galvanise a
horse that not many others could.'*

Richard Dunwoody on Peter Scudamore

Consider this: from 1945, when our book begins, until 1982, only one man,
Tim Molony, won the jump jockeys' title more than four times. In the thirty-
three-year period from 1945 to 1978, there were no fewer than sixteen different
champions. But in the forty-three years since then there have been only eight.
And three of these won the title more than four times.

John Francome might have expected his record of seven titles to last a long
time when he retired in 1985; in fact it was broken less than ten years later ...
by the man he so sportingly shared the title with in 1981/82.

You could say that Scudamore and Francome were like chalk and cheese.
Francome didn't care too much about records; Scudamore was committed to
breaking them. Francome was a laid-back Jack the Lad; Scudamore always
looked deadly serious. But appearances can be deceptive. When the race had
been won, 'Scu', as he's affectionately known across the racing world, could
let his hair down and party with the rest of them.

'People say I look miserable,' he once said. 'I don't feel miserable. It's just
concentration.' While it's true that their public personas were very different,
the two great champions, who dominated their sport in the 1980s, had a strong
mutual respect. 'I learnt a great deal from him; he was always prepared to
talk, and always had a kind word to say, whereas I was completely ignorant of
the art of conversation,' Scudamore said of Francome. Francome says of Scu:

'There has never been anyone stronger or more dedicated. Ruthless from the moment the tapes went up but after that, kindness personified.'

Scu had jump racing in his DNA. He came from a famous and hugely popular South Herefordshire farming/hunting/racing family. Grandfather Geoffrey, who rode in point-to-points, was something of a hero in the Second World War when his RAF plane, which had been on a bombing mission to Germany, came down in Nazi-occupied Belgium. With blood pouring down his face, he sacrificed his own chance of making an escape in order to help pull his stricken comrades clear of the wreckage. Geoffrey went on to train horses, while his son Michael, Peter's father, became a fearless jockey who finished second in the championship to Fred Winter in 1954/55 and won the 1956 King George on Rose Park, the 1957 Gold Cup on Linwell and the 1959 Grand National on Oxo. Ironically, Peter failed to secure any of those 'Big Three' chases, but did win eight titles.

Growing up in a racing household, and knowing all the great riders of his father's era, it is not surprising that Peter Scudamore nursed an ambition to be a champion jump jockey from an early age. He attended Belmont Abbey School in Hereford, where the teaching is done by monks, and attained A levels in Medieval History and British Constitution.

Despite learning to ride before he could walk and a childhood spent on horseback, whether it was riding to hounds, showjumping or taking part in gymkhanas, in 1978 Scudamore became not a professional jockey, but an estate agent. He had ridden five winners in point-to-points and spent six months working at veteran trainer Willie Stephenson's, and also had a spell at Jim Bolger's in Ireland. But Stephenson, who had trained Oxo, told him, 'You'll never make a jump jockey', and recommended he got a job in estate agency as a backup. So that's how the man who would become the most successful jockey in the history of National Hunt racing could be found in September 1978 licking stamps, keeping the petty cash box in order and taking For Sale signs down – or, as he later admitted, forgetting to take them down – as part of his duties for Bernard Thorpe and Partners.

The office was handily based in Stow-on-the-Wold, Gloucestershire, which enabled him to ride out in the mornings for his dad's great friend David 'The Duke' Nicholson, now training at nearby Condicote. Scu rode his first winner over jumps, Roylat, a 12-year-old trained by Toby Balding, at Devon and Exeter on 31 August. Auspiciously, they won by 25 lengths. Eight further winners as an amateur followed that season. By its end, Scudamore's brief career as an estate agent was over. He had fallen two from home on his first ever Festival ride on the Tuesday but on Gold Cup Day itself he didn't have a ride. Not expecting anyone to come into the office, he locked up and headed to the local hotel to watch Alverton win an epic Gold Cup in a snowstorm. He then returned to work and was sitting at the front desk, with his feet up and reading the racing paper, when the senior partner of the firm walked in. 'He sweetened his tactful dismissal by saying he was going to have runners at the hunter chase meeting at Folkestone and that perhaps I would like to ride them,' Scudamore recalled.

Between March and May 1979, Scu rode four winners for David Nicholson, at odds of 9-1, 10-1, 7-2 and 9-4, and at the end of the year, The Duke, obviously impressed, asked him to go back in the autumn as his assistant trainer. Scudamore accepted the offer with alacrity. The next big decision he had to make was whether to turn professional. As an amateur he was under a lot less pressure, and he admits his fear of failure was sharpened by his father's success. Suppose he turned pro and failed to make an impact? Then there would be the inevitable 'He's nowhere near as good as his dad' jibes.

Two wins on a Nicholson-trained hurdler called Oakprime in November helped make up his mind. The view collectively arrived at, following discussions between David Nicholson, Scu and his parents, was that if he was ever going to turn professional, now was the time, as he still had ten more winners to clock up before losing his 7lb claim. The allowance would help him get his career as a professional off to a flying start.

On 21 November 1979 at Worcester, riding for the first time as 'P. Scudamore' instead of 'Mr P. Scudamore', he steered Sea Lane to a 20-length success. He had started how he meant to go on. There was another victory for him that day on Toby Balding-trained Birshell. His rapid progress led to a call from Fred Rimell in early 1980 offering him a chance to become the stable jockey at Kinnersley. Scudamore counselled the advice of his father, who had ridden many horses for Rimell down the years, and his opinion was to try to ride for both Nicholson and Rimell until the end of the season, before making a firm commitment.

Eight winners in January 1980 put him on the thirty-four-winner mark by the month's end but just when things were going so well, a freak accident at Haydock ended his season prematurely. He broke his right leg when another horse and jockey cannoned into him after passing the post. He received treatment in a Liverpool hospital. 'The doctor got me talking about football,' Scudamore said when he was convalescing. 'He was on about Liverpool all the time and I wanted to put a case for Nottingham Forest, the team I follow. But as he had hold of my leg at the time, I thought better of it.'

He wasn't really considered a contender in the 1980/81 season, as everyone expected the record-breaking Jonjo O'Neill to collect again, but the reigning champion's terrible injury at Bangor in October opened things up. 'Jonjo's breaks gave me the opportunity as I took over on a lot of his horses,' Scu says today. The season developed into a compelling two-way tussle between Scudamore and John Francome.

Scudamore's surprise challenge was greatly boosted by the red-hot form of the David Nicholson yard, which was enjoying its best-ever season. By the end of November 1980 Scu had ridden thirty winners, nineteen of them for The Duke. He rode the Nicholson-trained novice hurdler Broadsword to six wins that season, describing the 'big imposing bay' as the 'first good horse' he had ridden. The partnership was pipped on the line in the Triumph Hurdle at the 1981 Cheltenham Festival by a 66-1 shot called Baron Blakeney. Ironically, what would have been Scu's first Festival success was instead a landmark for trainer Martin Pipe, the groundbreaking but still little-known West Country handler whose super-fit horses would a few years later help propel Scu to numerous titles.

At the beginning of May 1981, Scu was on ninety winners, nine behind Francome, but his title hopes ended when he cracked his skull following a fall at Taunton. Francome would still have been the favourite to hold on, but a year later there was little doubt that Scu's injury, incurred in a fall at Southwell in late April, when twenty winners ahead of the reigning champion, deprived him of winning the title outright. Francome had led Scudamore by twenty-five at Christmas but Scu had an amazing February in which he rode twenty-three winners – including trebles at Nottingham on both the 15th and 20th of the month, and four other doubles. As recounted in the previous chapter, the turning point looked to have been an incident at Newbury on 5 March, when the Mercy Rimell-trained Celtic Rambler fell, injuring Rimell's stable jockey Stan Morshead and bringing down John Francome in the process. That not only meant Francome missing a week's action, but gave Scudamore the opportunity to deputise for Morshead on the Kinnersley horses. At Wolverhampton on 31 March he rode a treble for Rimell, in the process reaching his first century.

By the time he went to Southwell to ride Prairie Master on 26 April, Scu was on the 120-winner mark, having ridden forty-two winners in the previous eight weeks compared to Francome's fourteen. Not only was the championship his for the taking, he also had an outside chance of breaking O'Neill's seasonal record of 149 winners. At that point he had already broken the record for most rides in a season (623).

Then came the break. Or rather, breaks. He smashed his left arm in two places, and was knocked out. When he came to, and still delirious, he told Steve Smith-Eccles, who had come to visit him, that he was not to be sent to fight in the Falklands War, which had started earlier that month. The Falkland Islands were, as history records, regained without him.

Scudamore said he was 'eternally grateful' for the great act of sportsmanship from John Francome, detailed in the previous chapter, which at least allowed him to share the title in 1982. He had to wait a further four years, though, until Francome retired, before he won his first outright title.

The seasons 1982/83 and 1983/84 saw him record win totals of ninety-three and ninety-eight. But the 1984/85 campaign proved to be a major disappointment. Condicote was badly hit by a virus and Scu could only muster fifty winners, the lowest of his professional career. There was, however, one good omen for the future. On 2 March he picked up a spare ride on the Martin Pipe-trained Hieronymous at Haydock. His orders from Pipe were simple: 'Make all the running and you'll win.' The pair recorded a 15-length success. It was the first winner Scudamore rode for Pipe. A further 791 would follow. Not surprisingly, he sees the win as a real turning point.

The 1985/86 season looked at the start as if it would be as disappointing as 1984/85 had been. Firm ground kept The Duke's horses out of action and by the end of August Scu had only ridden two winners. By 17 October, that total had only risen to eight. At the same time the former amateur champion and newly turned professional Simon Sherwood, riding for 'early bird' John Jenkins, whose modus operandi was to have lots of runners ready to run (and win) on the fast ground in the early weeks of the season, had established what appeared to be a commanding lead in the table. Scudamore rode nine winners in October, but his season really stepped up a gear at Chepstow on 2 November, when he and Nicholson enjoyed a fabulous four-timer. That cut Sherwood's lead to ten. One of the horses Scu won on at the South Wales venue, the aptly named 2-mile chaser Very Promising, went on to win the H & T Walker Gold Cup Chase at Ascot two weeks later. But by the time the Hennessy meeting came around in late November, Sherwood remained the pace-setter on the forty-winner mark, with Steve Smith-Eccles seven behind in second place.

Scu's title aspirations received a boost, which he would not have wanted, after a bad injury to one of his weighing room colleagues. Sam Morshead had ridden the John Spearing-trained front runner Run and Skip to second place in the Hennessy but had a bad fall at Warwick in late November 1985, which put him out for the season.

At Cheltenham on 6 December, Scu deputised and piloted Run and Skip to an impressive success in a handicap chase. It was the start of a remarkable month. Scu teamed up with Run and Skip again in the Welsh National on 21 December, and the pair led from pillar to post. If that wasn't enough, they also won the Anthony Mildmay/Peter Cazalet Memorial Chase at Sandown in early January, once again making all.

He finally drew level with Sherwood after riding a double at Windsor on 29 January. There followed a great battle between the two friends until the end of the season. At Cheltenham in March there was a welcome change of luck for Scudamore. It's astonishing to reflect that until 1986 he had not ridden a Festival winner. There had been plenty of near misses, including a Champion Hurdle second on Cima behind Dawn Run in 1984. But in 1986, the year of Halley's Comet, the stars were clearly in alignment, not just for Scu but for The Duke too, who was also on the score sheet for the first time as a trainer, although they did have to wait for the final day of the Festival for the hoodoo to be broken.

Solar Cloud's 40-1 starting price in the Triumph Hurdle reflected the lack of confidence in the juvenile hurdler, who on his previous run at Kempton had hung so badly left that he had nearly thrown the race away. Nicholson told his jockey to come late, but finding himself in front at the top of the hill after a perfect run round, Scu decided to go for home. The decision paid off, and Solar Cloud, under a typically strong Scudamore drive, held on by a diminishing three quarters of a length. At 40-1 it turned out to be the longest-priced winner Scu would ever ride in his career. Rather like buses, you wait so long for a Festival winner and two come along at once, and so it proved as later that afternoon Scu won the Ritz Club National Hunt Handicap Chase on Charter Party, who two years later would win the Gold Cup. Nowadays, two winners would give you no chance of winning the Ritz Club Trophy for leading jockey at the Festival, but it is a sign of how much more competitive things were back in the 1980s that Scu's brace on Gold Cup day were enough to make him leading rider. It was the same scenario twelve months later.

On the Saturday after Cheltenham '86, Scudamore rode another four winners at Chepstow, but Sherwood responded with a four-timer at the Newton Abbot Easter meeting. The decisive day was 17 May. Scu went to Newcastle to ride Nigel Twiston-Davies's mare Mrs Muck, and also picked up a spare ride on the 13-year-old veteran Silent Valley, who also won. Sherwood, who could have gone north to ride Mrs Muck, instead drew a blank. A treble for Scu at his 'home' track of Hereford on 26 May sealed the deal.

He was outright champion for the first time, finishing the campaign on ninety-one winners, twelve ahead of Sherwood. 'I suppose I would admit I'm not as hungry as someone like Peter Scudamore,' Sherwood said. The truth was, no one was in 1986.

Despite enjoying Festival success for the first time, the Nicholson-Scudamore partnership had, by the close of the 1985/86 season, reached the end of the road. Shareholders were being brought in to finance the Condicote operation, and The Duke no longer had sole authority. When Fred Winter rang Scudamore in April to offer him the job of first jockey at Uplands, he readily accepted. Nicholson, needless to say, was not too pleased with the way things were handled.

Winter's was not the only offer Scu received. Martin Pipe also asked if he could ride some of his lower weighted horses the following season.

With the backing of two top yards, and lots of good rides for other stables, Scudamore was in pole position to retain his title in 1986/87. That said, his first seven rides for Pipe were all beaten and Scu overheard Pipe's father David muttering that he might be an 'unlucky jockey'. Fortunately, things soon picked up.

The highlights of that season were a Christmas Hurdle success on the Mick Easterby-trained Nohalmdun, a first Scottish Grand National success on Little Polveir, who two years later would win the Aintree version at odds of 28-1, and a Queen Mother Champion Chase win on the John Edwards-trained Pearlyman (in which he beat his old friend Very Promising into second place). Scu says today that Pearlyman was 'probably the most talented' horse he ever rode.

The main challenger in the title race this time was the northern-based rider Mark Dwyer, who had been backed by the ultra-shrewd Malton trainer Jimmy Fitzgerald at 100-1 for the title. On 22 December, Scudamore was just four clear, leading 58-54, and Dwyer kept the pressure on going into the new year. Even in early March, Scudamore was only twelve ahead, although he did finish the season very strongly to put the championship to bed, recording thirty winners in April and May. That brought him a final total of 123 (later readjusted upwards by one, on account of a disqualified horse).

Fifty-one of his wins in 1986/87 had been provided by Fred Winter, and forty-two by his 'second choice' trainer, Martin Pipe. But when Pipe's first jockey Paul Leach retired in 1987, Scu took over at Pond House for the new season.

It was to be Scudamore's best season yet, but still something of an emotional roller coaster. In August, Fred Winter became critically ill following a fall in his house and although he survived, he was left confined to a wheelchair with partial loss of speech. His young assistant Charlie Brooks took over the day-to-day running of Uplands. That season Scudamore only rode thirteen winners for Winter/Brooks but one was particularly important. At the 1988 Cheltenham Festival, he partnered Celtic Shot to victory in the Champion Hurdle. He took it up approaching the third last and stayed on up the hill strongly to win by 4 lengths. He describes the win as the most satisfying of his career for what it meant for the yard. It was his first Champion Hurdle, and Fred Winter's last. He retained his title with 132 winners, eight up on the previous year, but this time Pipe contributed eighty-nine to the total – an augur of things to come. The dominance of Scudamore that year can be seen by the fact that the runner-up in the championship, Chris Grant, finished all of fifty-two winners behind.

Impressive though they were, even Scudamore's achievements in 1987/88 were put in the shade by what he accomplished a year later, when he became the first jump jockey to ride over 200 winners in a season. As to the scale of the achievement, consider this: In 1924 Fred Rees became the first jump jockey to ride more than 100 winners, setting a new record of 108. That stood for nearly thirty years until Winter rode 121 winners in 1952/53. Gifford then pushed it up to 122 in 1966/67, Barry to 125 in 1972/73. In 1978/79, O'Neill raised the bar to 149. In his annus mirabilis of 1988/89, Peter Scudamore not only surpassed O'Neill, he added to his score by an extra seventy-two winners. Scu didn't just break the existing record; he blew it straight out the water. At the time he believes he never quite got the recognition he (and Martin Pipe) deserved for breaking the '200 barrier' and for how they had taken the National Hunt game forward to the next level. 'It's not about me, but about what was achieved,' he says. He certainly has a point. If, as John Francome says, Jonjo'O'Neill's 149 winners in 1980 was the equivalent in achievement and effort of a gold medal at the Olympics, what can we say of Scu's 221? It has to be one of the greatest feats in post-war sporting history.

A number of factors aided his cause. First and foremost there was Martin Pipe, who had now strengthened his stable with the arrival of some very decent chasers. Scudamore and Pipe were made for each other. They shared the same insatiable thirst for winners, the same laser-like focus on the job in hand. In his quest to gain an edge over his rivals the Meticulous Mr Pipe left no stone unturned. He kept copious amounts of data and analysed everything. He carried out regular blood tests on his horses in his own special laboratory. He developed intensive interval training up and down his steep, purpose-built all-weather gallop. He was, in the words of Sir Mark Prescott, the leading Flat trainer, the man who 'transistorised' National Hunt racing.

Pipe got his horses, many of whom had been claimed from the Flat, fitter than anyone else's and liked them to make the running. What was the point, he said, of conceding ground at the start? You could liken the modus operandi that Pipe developed in the 1980s to the 'long-ball' tactics that became popular in domestic football at the time. That too was based on scientific analysis and getting players super-fit, and trying to get from A to B in the shortest possible time. That also brought extraordinary results, as we saw from Graham Taylor and Watford's meteoric rise through the four divisions to be Division One runners-up.

In the same way that Luther Blissett banged in the goals for the high-scoring Hornets, Scudamore was Pipe's perfect finisher – as well as starter. 'He was a terrific judge of pace,' Pipe said. 'He went out, knew the pace, knew the horses would jump and then got them jumping and going.'

New technology – and improved transportation – also played its part in aiding the Pipe-Scu win machine. The completion of the M5 motorway in the 1970s meant that West Country trainers like Pipe could send their horses far and wide. Pipe also had a helicopter in which he and Scu would travel from one race meeting to another. The advent of cellular phones in the 1980s helped with the booking of rides. Although Scudamore never had an agent, he did invest in a mobile phone in early 1985 and reaped instant dividends. He was driving up to Doncaster to ride Burrough Hill Lad, but an hour from the course he rang up and learnt the meeting had been abandoned. He then contacted trainer Rod Simpson to tell him he would, after all, be able to ride a horse called Tangognat at Cheltenham that afternoon. He reversed his car and headed off to Gloucestershire, where he rode another winner.

Back to 1988/99 and Scudamore's remarkable tally was also helped by an exceptionally mild winter, which resulted in only a small number of meetings lost to the weather. That season no jockey-trainer combination had ever been so dominant in National Hunt racing as Scudamore-Pipe.

They made a statement of intent with a win in the very first race of the season, when Scudamore rode odds-on favourite Rahiib to victory at Newton Abbot on 30 July. By the end of August, Scu was already on the twenty-two-winner mark. On 25 October he recorded the fastest fifty of all time, when Wolfhangar held on to the race after a stewards' inquiry at Fakenham. In November he added another thirty-four winners, including big race Saturday wins in the Mackeson (on Pegwell Bay for Captain Forster), the Edward Hanmer Memorial Chase (on Beau Ranger for Pipe) and the Hennessy (on Strands of Gold for Pipe). On 27 December, Scu turned the Welsh Grand National at Chepstow into a procession on board the Pipe-trained Bonanza

Boy, winning by 12 lengths, and for good measure rode another three winners on the card. He finished the old year on the 112-winner mark.

Another factor that aided him in his record breaking was improvements in racecourse safety and protective equipment. On 3 January 1989 he had a nasty fall in a chase at Cheltenham. He was thrown into the rail, which in the old days would have been made of concrete, but by the late 1980s was plastic. He notes in his autobiography that if there had been concrete posts in the vicinity, as in his father's day, he would have been lucky to have survived. In 1988/89, too, body protectors were made compulsory – and a 1lb allowance was given to jockeys to allow for the extra weight. That helped reduce the risk of serious injury as well as long lay-offs. While jump racing continued to be a risky sport, it was no longer quite as dangerous as it had been.

Thirty-two winners in January 1989 meant that at the beginning of February, Scu was already within touching distance of Jonjo O'Neill's record of 149. He broke it on the Pipe-trained hurdler Anti-Matter at Warwick on 7 February. When he won on Avionne at Newton Abbot a week later, he became only the third National Hunt jockey (after Mellor and Francome) to have ridden 1,000 winners.

It was another wonderful month. At Kempton, on the 25th, he received plenty of plaudits for the ride he gave Bonanza Boy to win the Racing Post Chase. Unlike at Chepstow, this time they looked flat to the boards for most of the way, but Scu never gave up and the Welsh National hero came with a great late run to prevail by a length.

In March there was a win in the Imperial Cup on Travel Mystery, but ironically, given the red-hot form he was in going into it, the Cheltenham Festival that year proved something of an anti-climax, with just the one win on Pukka Major in the Grand Annual. On 5 May, he won his 200th race of the season on Anti-Matter, the horse on which he had earlier broken O'Neill's record, and he rode his 221st and final winner of an extraordinary campaign on Hazy Sunset at Stratford on 3 June.

Scudamore had won on 33 per cent of his rides, a quite remarkable statistic bearing in mind the champion usually weighs in around the 23-24 per cent mark. One hundred and fifty-eight of his winners (71 per cent) had been saddled by Martin Pipe, the majority of which had started favourite. Pipe himself trained 208 winners, smashing his previous record of 129. The bookies must have been sick of Scudamore-Pipe that season but for punters there had probably never been such a reliable source of winners.

Not that there wasn't criticism. Scudamore's riding had always been vigorous, and for some, on occasions, it was too much so. Bryan Marshall, the 1947/48 champion, said of Scu: 'He still doesn't get down behind a horse enough and push with his bottom to help him. Instead he lets his enthusiasm run away with him and he brings his whip down from too high and uses it too fast.' Scu defended the selective use of the whip, making the point that horse welfare was not under threat by it, but also admitted that new Jockey Club guidelines, introduced in 1988, made him more aware of how he used his stick and this ultimately made him a better rider. He acknowledges he was riding with 'slightly more finesse' at the end of the 1980s than at the start. Speaking today, Scu says:

> It was said that John Francome was one brave man lined up at the start with idiots, and on occasions I would have been one of the idiots in the early days. You set off not knowing what you will do if you get some falls. When you get to the age of 24 or 25 you accept you are going to get the falls.

It's a sign of how high Scudamore and Pipe had raised the bar in the 1988/89 season that the champion's tally of 170 winners in the 1989/90, the second highest in National Hunt history, seems slightly disappointing. Yet Scu would have gone close to matching, or even surpassing, his record had he not sustained an injury that ended his season prematurely. He actually got off the blocks even faster than he had done a year earlier, reaching his half-century of winners as early as 12 October, thus breaking the record he had himself set in 1988/89 by thirteen days.

At Ascot, on 18 November, another landmark was achieved: he broke John Francome's all-time record of 1,138 winners. Colonel Piers Bengough, Clerk of the Course, presented him with a bottle of champagne but there was no time for celebration as immediately afterwards he was rushing into a helicopter to ride two for Martin Pipe later that afternoon at Warwick. Scudamore recorded his seasonal century on the same date (20 December) that he had achieved it a year earlier, but this time it was from forty-nine fewer rides. The highlight of the Christmas period was another, even more impressive, Welsh National win on the redoubtable Bonanza Boy. In 1988 the Pipe staying chaser, who was not over-big, carried 10st 1lb to victory; in 1989, he lumped 11st 11lb, showing he was, as the *Racing and Football Outlook Annual* later declared, the best marathon chaser in the country when the going was soft.

Scu began the 1990s with a win at Devon and Exeter on New Year's Day on the 5-2 shot Lucky Verdict. Sixteen further winners followed that month and eleven more came in February. At the Cheltenham Festival of 1990,

Scudamore rode Regal Ambition to an impressive, almost all-the-way success in the Sun Alliance Novices' Hurdle, but with his second double century in sight, he had a crushing fall at the Cheltenham April meeting, which left him with a broken rib and injured wrist. With his wrist still hurting he returned to action prematurely to ride Gold Service to victory for Martin Pipe at Devon and Exeter on 7 May, but it only made his injury worse. It transpired that he had turned a bone round and without surgery there was a danger he could lose all mobility in the wrist.

So that was the season finished. He won his seventh and eighth titles in 1990/91 and 1991/92, posting final scores of 141 and 175 winners, thus making him responsible for the three highest winning totals in jump racing history. Yes, there was a lot more racing in the early 1990s, but Scudamore's strike rate was truly outstanding, at 33 per cent (three times) and 34 per cent.

In 1990/91 he faced a serious challenge for his title from Richard Dunwoody. Yet again, Scudamore and Pipe won the first race of the season at Newton Abbot and by the time he headed to Market Rasen on 9 November, he had already chalked up another half-century and was seventeen clear of Dunwoody. But a fall on the hurdler Black Humour left him with a broken left leg and put him out of action until 24 January. By the time he returned, he was twenty behind Dunwoody. Scu, as you would expect, was determined not to give up without a fight, but although he soon got back to winning ways – riding nine winners in the last week of January – a two-week period in February, when the only racing that could take place due to the wintry weather was on the all-weather surfaces at Lingfield and Southwell, stalled his charge. At the Cheltenham Festival of 1991, two wins (on Rolling Ball in the Sun Alliance and Chatam in the Cathcart) made him leading rider at the meeting again and when old friend Bonanza Boy sluiced home by 28l in the mud at Uttoxeter in the Midlands National on 16 March, he had cut Dunwoody's lead to two. Another, rather embarrassing, injury following an unseat at Newbury (he landed so hard on his left buttock he got a blood clot in his bottom) meant another short lay-off. When he returned to action at Chepstow he had to use a longer leather, as he was unable to raise his left leg due to tightness in his posterior. He notes that he took some stick in the weighing room for looking more like Fred Archer than a modern jump jockey, but he did manage to silence his critics by riding a double. With Pipe giving him every support possible he finally moved ahead of Dunwoody with a treble at Taunton on 26 April. That was the day the championship tilted very much in Scudamore's favour, as after an evening meeting at Wincanton, Dunwoody received a five-day ban for hampering the runner-up.

In the end, Scudamore, with 141 winners, finished fourteen clear of his rival. A seventh title had been achieved, and a third for Pipe, who smashed the trainers' record with 230 winners. But the intensity of what Scudamore and Pipe were doing was beginning to take its toll. 'What with injuries, the travelling, and the constant anxiety about whether I would make the top of the table this year, I was beginning to feel a bit worn out,' Scu admitted. He acknowledges that the race for the title did become 'obsessive'. 'You find yourself listening each night to the racing results, to see if say Peter Niven has won, and whether you're going up or down the table,' he told me.

A further cause of stress was the resentment Pipe's success was engendering. 'Some slanderous and downright malevolent, never mind fanciful, explanations have been put forward for his prodigious feats,' wrote 'Hastings' in the 'Points West' section of the 1990/91 *Racing and Football Outlook's Jumping Annual*.

It probably didn't help that Pipe wasn't cut from the traditional National Hunt trainer's cloth. He wasn't an ex-jockey, nor ex-military, but the son of a bookie, who learnt his art as he went along. Things reached a head when Pipe was investigated by the ITV programme *The Cook Report*, which went on air in 1991. The thrust of the programme was the allegation that the champion trainer's success was at the expense of horse welfare, but it signally failed to prove its case.

Despite the mounting stresses of the previous year, Scudamore and Pipe were raring to go again at the start of the 1991/92 campaign. Scudamore says that the upside of the criticism that was directed towards the Pond House operation was that it helped forge a 'fortress' mentality, similar to that which existed at Old Trafford under the glory years of Sir Alex Ferguson. The more brickbats were thrown, the more determination there was to break records.

There was an audacious attempt to go through the card at the 'home' fixture of Devon and Exeter on 23 August; the first five horses won, but in the sixth and final leg Scudamore was beaten on Ever Smile. All five of the Pipe-Scu winners were odds-on favorites, and until 23 November, the longest price of a Scudamore winner was 5-1.

The Pipe stable, while still churning out winners on an industrial scale at the West Country gaffs, was gradually attracting better class horses, and this can be seen by what big races Pond House landed that season. In November, Scu won his second Hennessy, on the 10-1 shot Chatam, while in December there was a third Welsh National win, with Carvill's Hill. Originally trained by Jim Dreaper in Ireland, Carvill's Hill was a giant chaser with huge ability, but he had been difficult to keep sound. A muscle problem was identified at Pond House and a special treatment programme was constructed for him.

The results spoke for themselves. After his 20-length win in the Welsh National, there was an equally impressive 15-length romp in the Irish Hennessy in February, which saw him installed as the favourite for the 1992 Gold Cup. By the time the Festival came around, Scu had already ridden his 1,500th career winner, and had a commanding lead over Richard Dunwoody in the title race. He felt that with reasonable good luck he would win his first Gold Cup on Carvill's Hill, but it was not to be. The race was one of the most controversial in the history of jump racing's Blue Riband. It centred on the tactics that seemed to be deployed on the Jenny Pitman-trained Golden Freeze, who took on Carvill's Hill in the early stages of the race, and even when Scu let the Pitman runner go on, was reined back to sit upsides the favourite again. It looked as if Golden Freeze, who was not a confirmed front runner, was being deployed to worry Carvill's Hill out of the race, and indeed the favourite, after some poor jumping, faded out of contention approaching the second last to finish the last of the five finishers.

Scudamore admits that he afterwards felt 'very cross' about what had happened, but it was subsequently discovered that his mount had pulled muscles in his chest and also injured his tendon. Carvill's Hill sadly never ran again. 'His bad jumping probably had more to do with these problems than with any tactics employed by Golden Freeze's connections,' Scu later acknowledged. Pitman was cleared of any offence.

Despite Miinnehoma's win in the Sun Alliance, it was a disappointing Festival for Scu as in addition to his Gold Cup frustrations, he also fell at the second last on Granville Again in the Champion Hurdle, when looking a likely winner. At Ayr in April, the pair made amends by landing the Scottish Champion Hurdle, and the following day, Scu won his first Scottish National on the novice Captain Dibble, trained by his friend, and by now business partner, Nigel Twiston-Davies.

Scudamore won his eighth and final title with 175 winners, forty clear of Richard Dunwoody. His percentage of wins to rides that year was actually the best of his career, at 34 per cent. But despite arguably riding better than ever, retirement was very much on his mind. He was now 34, and had long thought that 35 was the right age for a jumps jockey to bow out. Although in his final season his win tally dropped to 129, his lowest since 1986/87, his strike rate was still a very impressive at 31 per cent. His nearest rival, Richard Dunwoody, sensed that the times were a-changing: 'In the early months of the new season, Scu wasn't the man of old. He was still competitive and professional but not as driven as before ... you could tell his heart wasn't in it in the way it had been a couple of years previously.' The reigning champion still kept Dunwoody in his sights for much of the winter but then his younger rival began to pull away. Even though he relinquished his title – finishing in the end forty-four winners behind Dunwoody – there was still plenty for Scu to celebrate in his final season. The undoubted highlight was Granville Again winning the Champion Hurdle. This time the partnership safely cleared the second last, and after a driving finish, went on to win by a length from Royal Derbi.

Scu also won the Sun Alliance Novices' Chase on Young Hustler and then on the Wednesday helped connections land a £50K bonus by steering Olympian to victory in the Coral Cup, just four days after winning the Imperial Cup at Sandown.

It was on the Monday after Cheltenham, following a defeat in a novice chase at Uttoxeter, that Scu made his mind up to call it a day at the end of the season. However, he didn't even last until then, quitting after riding Sweet Duke to victory at a very muddy Ascot on 7 April. He retired as the most successful jump jockey of all time, his place in National Hunt history guaranteed. In a fifteen-year career he had ridden 1,678 winners, beating Francome's previous record by 540; 792 of his winners (47 per cent) had been for Martin Pipe – with his strike rate on Pond House runners standing at an astonishing 37 per cent.

Revealingly, close on half (45 per cent) of his winners for Pipe had been odds-on favourites. But, still, despite his record-breaking feats Scudamore shared one thing in common with many previous champions whose story has been told in this book: he failed to win a Grand National. Nor, for that matter, a Gold Cup or a King George. The closest he came in the National was in the wonderfully thrilling 1985 renewal when he led approaching the second last on the 1983 winner Corbiere, and rallied again on the run-in. In the end, though, he could only finish a close-up third behind the 50-1 winner Last Suspect and Mr Snugfit.

In the Gold Cup, his best chance of success came and went with Carvill's Hill. After retirement Scudamore became assistant trainer to Nigel Twiston Davies, later fulfilling the same role for his new partner, Lucinda Russell, in Scotland. Although the race brought him no luck as a jockey, he did play a key part, as an assistant trainer, in the Grand National victories of Earth Summit (1998), Bindaree (2002) and One for Arthur (2017). When I asked him in 2020 if he had any regrets about not winning the National, or indeed the Gold Cup when he was riding, he was philosophical. 'I have no real regrets. I felt very grateful for achieving what I did. You can keep saying "if this had happened or if that had happened" but I was just very fortunate to find Martin Pipe.' Modestly, he adds, 'I don't see myself as a better jockey than

Stan Mellor or Fred Winter, it was just that my opportunities were different.'
John Spearing, who's seen a good few jump jockeys in his time, says that
Scudamore is 'probably one of the best jockeys there's ever been'.

Scu's two sons, Tom and Michael, have enjoyed success as jockey and
trainer respectively, carrying on the illustrious Scudamore tradition. In 2015,
Tom won the Grand Annual at the Cheltenham Festival, a race his father
had won in 1989 and his grandfather in 1961. Peter described the win as
his 'greatest moment in racing', showing how important his family, past and
present, is to him.

Even though Scu's career record of 1,678 winners was to be surpassed
much sooner than he could ever have imagined, first by Richard Dunwoody
and then by the phenomenon known as 'AP McCoy', his achievements today
remain undiminished. He was a superb horseman on the racetrack and a
true gentleman off it, a man of faith who set an incredibly high standard that
inspired those who followed him.

'If I had a hero in the weighing room, it was Peter Scudamore. What
I became was just a dream of him,' said Richard Dunwoody, whose own story
is told in the following chapter.

Big race wins
Welsh Grand National 1985 (Run and Skip), 1988, 1989 (Bonanza Boy),
1991 (Carvill's Hill)
Champion Chase 1987 (Pearlyman)
Hennessy Gold Cup 1988 (Strands of Gold), 1991 (Chatam)
Champion Hurdle 1988 (Celtic Shot), 1993 (Granville Again)
Scottish Grand National 1987 (Little Polveir), 1992 (Captain Dibble)

Chapter Eighteen

Richard Dunwoody

Champion 1992/93, 1993/94, 1994/95

The Prince

*'Richard Dunwoody was arguably the best jockey National Hunt racing
has ever seen. He was the complete article: strong and stylish with an
inborn determination to win.'*

Henrietta Knight, *Starting from Scratch –*
Inspired to be a Jump Jockey

It has been described as one of the greatest duels in sporting history. The
gripping, season-long battle for the 1993/94 jump jockeys' championship
between Richard Dunwoody and Adrian Maguire was without doubt the most
intense title race in National Hunt history. Dunwoody described it afterwards
as a 'journey through hell'. His determination to come out on top helped
destroy his marriage, while the chase for winners up and down the country
left both men physically and mentally drained. Dunwoody *v* Maguire was
jump racing's equivalent of Formula One's Hunt *v* Lauda, or boxing's Ali *v*
Foreman. Those battles were made into compelling, award-winning films,
and so too would the dramatic story of the 1993/94 season, if an enterprising
film director happens to be reading this. 'I don't really look back to it that
much but I remember how it was so intense, very up and down, with both of
us trying so hard. It just had so many twists and turns, even down to the very
last day,' Dunwoody says.

By the time he inherited Peter Scudamore's champion jockey mantle in
1993, Dunwoody had already won a Grand National, a Gold Cup, a Champion
Hurdle and two King Georges. In fact, it's hard to think of a jockey who
had accomplished so much before he won his first title. The fact that he had
already won almost every big prize there was to win made him covet the
championship even more.

In the years when Scudamore was so far ahead in terms of winners, Dunwoody had the satisfaction of knowing that, in general, he was riding better quality horses. One of the first jump jockeys to employ an agent, he tended to earn as much prize money as Scu from about half the number of rides. In the three years before he became champion he topped the prize money chart, posting a new record of £923,972 in 1991/92. In addition, unlike Scu, he also had a retainer, at first with David 'The Duke' Nicholson, and later with Nicholson and Nicky Henderson.

Many of our champions started early, but Dunwoody may have been the fastest starter of them all. Born on 18 January 1964, he attended his first race meeting in a pram. At the age of 2½, he was given a rosette, having been led round on a small grey pony at a horse show in Newtownards, Northern Ireland. At the age 5 he was riding Tony, a 12.2 pony, behind his father's string of racehorses.

George Dunwoody was a very successful former amateur rider, who trained at Ballyclare, County Antrim. His wife Gillian was the daughter of Epsom Flat trainer Dick Thrale and a talented horsewoman in her own right. Like so many other National Hunt champions, Richard was bred for the part.

When he was a child there were regular cross-border raids to racetracks in the Irish Republic, which, in the late 1960s and early 1970s, inevitably meant getting caught up in 'The Troubles'. On one occasion Dunwoody snr was coming home late at night from Navan. He was signalled to stop by men on the road. When he lowered the window a gun was pointed at his head. He was questioned as to what he was doing out. He said he was coming back from the races. He was asked his name. 'George Dunwoody, the point-to-point man?' asked the gunman. 'That's me.' 'Ah, tell us, how did yous get on today?'

There's no doubt that people living in Northern Ireland during this time developed a certain toughness. You had to in order to survive. It was no place for snowflakes, to use a contemporary term. It's surely no coincidence that not one, but two record-breaking National Hunt champion jockeys of the late twentieth century and early twenty-first (Dunwoody and McCoy) spent their earliest years in Ulster during The Troubles. 'I suppose you could say we have a certain stubbornness,' Richard says today.

Partly because of the political situation and partly for other family reasons, the Dunwoodys quit Ulster in 1972 and moved to Tetbury in Gloucestershire. George took on a job as manager of Charlton Down Stud. Young Richard got a scholarship to Rendcomb College public school, where he boarded, but he hated being away from the horses. A turning point came in 1976 when there was another move, to Newmarket, where Dunwoody snr began working for the retired jockey-turned-trainer Paul Kelleway. Richard began riding out for Kelleway during his summer holidays at the age of 12. 'Trainers wouldn't be able to get the insurance for it today,' he says.

At school, he attained ten O levels, which included an A for Classics in Translation, but then in his first year as a sixth-former he developed an obsession about his weight and became anorexic. Things got so bad he ended up in hospital. Before he had fully recovered he told his parents he wanted to leave school to become a jockey. 'You'll end up with nothing,' his mother, who had wanted him to become a vet, told him. Latin's loss was jump racing's gain. Accepting he was too tall for the Flat he joined the National Hunt yard of the genial Oxfordshire trainer John Bosley, a friend of the family.

It was, as Dunwoody later acknowledged, a perfect stepping stone between leaving home and looking after himself. Bosley was a good trainer, probably most famous for his splendid mare Eyecatcher, who finished third in consecutive Grand Nationals, but after a few months Dunwoody moved on to the larger yard of Captain Tim Forster at Letcombe Bassett as a £15-a-week pupil assistant, arriving during the very harsh winter of 1982.

The Captain, as we've seen, was a man who didn't suffer fools, gladly or otherwise. Dunwoody describes Forster as a 'daunting figure', someone whom he was never able to get close to, but his riding did improve considerably during his time at Old Manor House. He recalled schooling sessions for novice chasers where there were always plenty of loose horses because The Captain would never use lead horses. Forster would look at the skies and exclaim, 'My God, and you want to call yourselves fxxxing jockeys!'

As the stable's amateur, Dunwoody was able to gain valuable experience riding in point-to-points for The Captain's friend, Colin Nash, the Master of the Old Berks Foxhounds. His first ride under Rules came for the small Welsh stable of Dr Arthur Jones at Chepstow. He was on a 33-1 outsider, Mallard Song, and managed to finish second. He was so excited that he crashed his Morris Marina on the way back home. His first winner came on Colin Nash's Game Trust in a hunter chase at the Cheltenham May meeting in 1983. Before the season ended he was off the mark for his employer too. The famously pessimistic Forster didn't hold up much hope of success. 'He walked into the yard, his stick in one hand, his other making a gesture that suggested total despair,' Dunwoody recalled. '"Good God," he said to me. "I can't find another jockey. I've got to give you the ride on Swordsman at Fontwell. Don't fall off."'

Dunwoody not only didn't fall off, he steered his mount to a comfortable success. He even got a very rare 'well done' from The Captain afterwards.

From four wins in 1982/83, his total climbed to twenty-four the following season. The undoubted highlight was when he rode four winners, a second and two thirds from seven rides at Hereford. That received not only another 'Well done' from Forster, who thought he'd be too tired to ride in seven races, but also the additional words: 'That's great.' One wonders if The Captain had ever been so effusive in his life!

At the end of the season, having been judged 'Amateur of the Year' by *Pacemaker* magazine, Dunwoody decided it was time to turn professional. In 1984/85, riding as second jockey to The Captain and engaged by a growing number of other trainers, he almost doubled his wins tally to forty-six.

That could be considered his breakthrough season, as it saw him win two races at the Cheltenham Festival, the Coral Hurdle on Von Trappe and the National Hunt Handicap Chase on West Tip, both for Droitwich trainer Michael Oliver. Partly on the basis of that win, West Tip, with Dunwoody up, was sent off the joint favourite for the 1985 Grand National. It was his first ride in the race, and here he was, at the age of 21, just two and a half years after riding his first winner, on the jolly in the race that stopped the nation. It was quite a news story, and led to an invite on the Terry Wogan chat show on BBC1.

'Who is that handsome young jockey?' millions of women watching asked; it was, as he later wrote, his first big success with the opposite sex.

A few days later a dream debut in the world's most famous steeplechase looked like it might become a reality. West Tip, travelling extremely well, came to the front over second Becher's. But the horse crumpled on landing and Dunwoody was unshipped. The race was won by the 50-1 outsider Last Suspect, ridden by Hywel Davies for The Captain, and Richard remembers the ribbing he got when turning up at Last Suspect's return to the yard on the Sunday morning.

When he got back home on the night of the National, Dunwoody watched the video of the race and saw that West Tip had jumped the five fences before Becher's perfectly. 'His ears were pricked and what had distracted him was a combination of the crowd, the noise and the drop. Becher's was a noisy place in those days.' Doing his homework, he noted that a number of horses who had led the National at second Becher's had come down in similar fashion. If the opportunity came again next year, he was determined he would not be in front at that point again. Luckily he got his chance. Twelve months later he rode his race to ensure West Tip would get a lead to second Becher's. The result: he won the 1986 Grand National by 2 lengths. The story illustrates one of the reasons why Dunwoody became a champion. He admits that in the mid-1980s he was still not the complete rider. He started off riding too short, but then rode too long. He could be stronger in a finish. But what he did have was a seemingly infinite capacity for self-examination and willingness to learn from his mistakes. His diligence in this regard involved him keeping a riding ledger in which he would record not only his wins, but his falls. He was determined to reduce his ratio of rides to falls, and managed it.

At the start of the 1985/86 season he had accepted an offer from David 'The Duke' Nicholson to be second jockey at Condicote behind Peter Scudamore. This was in addition to still being second jockey for Tim Forster, and riding for other trainers too, when available.

Scu was already his idol and Dunwoody says he admired him even more once he really got to know him. 'While he was ambitious for himself he was always fair to others. He went out of his way to help me,' he wrote. When Scu left Condicote at the end of the season, Dunwoody was his natural successor. He finished the 1985/86 season on fifty-five winners, but that rose to seventy the following year, when he was riding as The Duke's first choice jockey.

After a dip in his fortunes from 1984 to 1986, Nicholson was making his presence felt once again as one of the country's leading trainers. One might say the turning point was the 1986 Cheltenham Festival, where he saddled winners for the first time. He wore a pair of red socks that day and thereafter was never seen on a racecourse without them. The momentum continued in the autumn of 1986. Nicholson sent five horses to Stratford on 18 October and four of them won. Dunwoody's first big race ride for The Duke came at Cheltenham in the Mackeson Gold Cup in November, and he won by 2 lengths on Very Promising. Dunwoody got on very well with his new boss, who was fiercely loyal, and together they made a great team.

The high point of the association came in the Cheltenham Gold Cup of 1988 when Dunwoody rode Charter Party to victory. The Jenny Mould-owned chaser was talented – but could be an iffy jumper. It was subsequently discovered that he had contracted navicular disease, which meant he was often lame. Richard had fallen on Charter Party in the 1987 Gold Cup but as soon as he mounted the horse in the parade ring a year later he felt he had a big chance. 'I asked the lad how he was and he said he hadn't taken a lame step all day,' he recalls. Charter Party travelled and jumped superbly and won by six lengths. Yet Dunwoody hated watching the video of the race afterwards as he felt he had hit his mount too many times on the run-in. Even at the moments of his greatest success, Dunwoody, the continually self-examining perfectionist, reproached himself for not winning better.

He accepted that the championship, at least for the time being, was out of the question, with Peter Scudamore so far ahead in terms of winners. As we've already noted, though, Dunwoody was generally riding the classier horses. And in the late 1980s there was no classier, or gutsier, chaser to ride than Desert Orchid. Simon Sherwood had won 'nine out of ten' on the hugely popular David Elsworth-trained grey, with the ninth win coming in the 1989 Cheltenham Gold Cup. A true race for the ages, it saw Dessie – on testing ground, which he usually hated, on a track where he never seemed to run at his best – snatch victory from the jaws of defeat by heroically rallying again on the run-in to overhaul the gallant outsider Yahoo. *Racing Post* readers voted it the Race of the Century in 2004. I was at Cheltenham that day and rewatching the race still gives me goose pimples.

Dunwoody had a relatively close-up view of the action as he was riding Charter Party to an honourable third place, but after Simon Sherwood retired at the end of the season, the ride on Desert Orchid became his. He recalled:

> The Duke helped me get the ride and said that nine times out of ten there'd be no clash with one of his runners so I didn't have to worry. He also helped me get the ride on Kribensis (on whom I won the 1988 Triumph Hurdle and 1990 Champion Hurdle), too.

Riding Dessie was some responsibility. After his Gold Cup heroics, the grey had acquired national treasure status. Dunwoody didn't just have to win on Desert Orchid; he had to look after him too. He acknowledged that when he rode Dessie his performance was more closely scrutinised than ever before. But, as ever, he passed the test. While arguably Simon Sherwood had the best of Dessie, who had after all turned 10 in 1989, Dunwoody still partnered him to another two King Georges at his beloved Kempton (he won four overall), and a memorable pillar-to-post win in the Irish Grand National of 1990, when he lumped 12st to victory and survived an almighty last fence blunder, which would have brought a lesser horse – and jockey – down.

In the 1990 Gold Cup Dessie was sent off the odds-on favourite to repeat his 1989 success, but he tired from the second last and finished third behind the shock 100-1 winner Norton's Coin. That would have been deflating, but Dunwoody showed his mettle by riding a storming finish on Bigsun to win the Ritz Club Handicap Chase for The Duke in the very next race. He finished the Festival as leading jockey, having won his first Champion Hurdle, on Kribensis.

It was in the 1989/90 season that Dunwoody rode more than 100 winners for the first time (he finished on 102), a feat he would achieve for ten years in a row. While he pipped Graham McCourt (the rider of Norton's Coin) for second in the jockey's championship, his first whiff of actually winning the title came a year later. As detailed earlier, Scudamore's bad fall on Black Humour at Market Rasen on 9 November put him out of action until late January. Dunwoody had a very merry Christmas, winning the King George again on Dessie, and the Feltham on Remittance Man, and by the time Scu returned to the weighing room, the challenger was twenty winners ahead.

The 1991 Cheltenham Festival, however, produced just the one winner (Remittance Man in the Arkle) but Dunwoody still led the championship until late April. He must have been optimistic of taking it to the wire but a rather harsh five-day ban for careless riding scuttled his chances. He had actually been allowed to keep the race in question following a stewards' inquiry at Wincanton, but losing connections successfully appealed to the Jockey Club. In the end he finished fourteen winners behind Scu.

In 1991/92 he was thirty-eight winners behind Scu, with his total of 137 the highest anyone had ever attained without being champion. But a year later, after three consecutive second places in the championship, there was finally a changing of the guard. He admits that at the start of the 1992/93 season becoming champion jockey was 'the' ambition in his life. He was now 28 – and the *Racing and Football Outlook's Jumping Annual* noted that in any other era of jump racing the prize would have already been his. Dunwoody told the *RFO*'s Tony Coleman: 'I have my best chance of winning the title this year.' There were solid grounds for his optimism.

It helped his cause that the Nicholson stable was poised to hit even higher levels of attainment following a move to the purpose-built, state-of-the-art Jackdaws Castle training facility. The Duke's string, like that of Nicky Henderson, for whom Dunwoody also rode, was getting bigger (in terms of numbers, the two stables just about matched Pipe's) and better. For the previous three seasons The Duke had had first call on Dunwoody's services. That had brought much success but also meant Richard missing out on winning the Champion Chase on Remittance Man in 1992. He had ridden Nicky Henderson's brilliant chaser to each of his very impressive eight victories over fences, but at the 1992 Festival he was claimed to ride Waterloo Boy for The Duke, who finished third. For the 1992/93 season Dunwoody arranged a joint retainer with both Nicholson and Henderson. 'It was quite tough as I was caught in a sort of tug-of-war between The Duke and Nicky Henderson on what to ride,' he remembers. It helped his title aspirations that Peter Scudamore in the early part of the season seemed to have lost some of his drive. He was no longer travelling here, there and everywhere for winners.

Dunwoody, with the tailwinds in his favour, established a lead in the title race, boosted by a wonderful November, during which he rode thirty-three winners. He rode six winners at the Newbury Hennessy meeting and another three on day two of the Kempton Christmas meeting.

By the end of February, he was already closing in on his previous highest total (137) of 1991/92 and by the time the 1993 Cheltenham Festival came around he had a lead of twenty over Scu. Dunwoody's only win at Prestbury Park that year was Thumbs Up for Henderson in the County Hurdle (a horse bred by AP McCoy's father Peadar), but two winners the following day at Wolverhampton restored his advantage to twenty. A few days after the 1993 Grand National, which was voided due to a chaotic false start, he was driving home when his agent, Robert Kingston (Scu's brother-in-law), called to tell him Peter Scudamore had retired. 'I put the phone down and cried,' Dunwoody admitted. 'There was relief that I would now be champion, but there was no elation, no joy now that I had what I desperately wanted.' Deep down he had wanted to beat Scu over a full season. He had been denied the 'true victory' he craved. But the following year he would be involved in a title race that went right down to the wire.

A game of musical chairs had taken place by the time the 1993/94 season started. Dunwoody had been offered, and accepted, Scu's old job as first jockey to Martin Pipe. Adrian Maguire, who had first come to public attention in 1991 when, as an amateur, he had ridden Omerta to victory at the Cheltenham Festival and then the Irish Grand National, replaced Dunwoody as stable jockey to The Duke. The scene was set for an utterly compelling ten months. What was remarkable about the 1993/94 championship race was that Dunwoody did not miss a single ride due to injury and Maguire hardly missed one either. It was as if neither man would allow themselves to be injured. Dunwoody believed that by accepting Pipe's offer it would guarantee him the championship and it was the only reason he left The Duke, but it looked by the end of October like he had made the wrong call. Maguire had made a great start, while Pipe's horses were laid low with a virus. There were already tensions between trainer and jockey. Dunwoody admits that he was close to despair. He enlisted the help of a sports psychologist who told him to focus on 'controlling the controllables'. In other words, to stop worrying about what Maguire was doing and concentrate on himself. It was wise advice but was Dunwoody ready for it?

At the end of November, Maguire was twenty-seven clear and long-odds on to become champion. A season that promised so much for Dunwoody was turning into a nightmare. At Christmas, Maguire landed the King George for The Duke on Barton Bank, but Dunwoody responded by landing his first Welsh Grand National, on the Pipe-trained Riverside Boy. Even so, when the year ended, Maguire's lead had been stretched to thirty-nine.

The year 1994 started badly. Nadir was reached in the evening of New Year's Day when Dunwoody returned home after riding at Newbury. He had fallen at the last in a handicap hurdle on Supreme Master, handing the race on a plate to Maguire, on Winter Forest. He drove home furious with himself and took it out on his wife Carol. 'By the time I got home I was fit to be tied,' he admitted. 'Carol only had to ask how the day went and I exploded. The row became vicious but one-sided; all the aggression, the malice and the anger came from me.' Dunwoody was never anything but brutally honest. That night he replayed a hundred times over a video of the race. He was so angry that he admits literally knocking and banging himself into the doors and walls in his house, in order to punish himself for his mistake. Yes, he had put tremendous pressure on himself but he was also under great strain from his huge workload, the schooling, the tens of thousands of miles driving, the debilitating hundreds of hours spent in saunas trying to make the weights on top of the rides – nearly 900 that season, more than any other year. In the circumstances is it any surprise that he was so close to a nervous breakdown?

Thankfully, things did improve in January, at least, on the racetrack. In the week commencing 29 January, he rode eighteen winners. Maguire, conversely, was having a bad run. A two-day ban for misuse of the whip in his King George win was followed by further suspensions in the new year. At Warwick he got a six-day ban for misuse in a driving finish against Dunwoody. The title race was going man to man. Literally. In the rescheduled Victor Chandler Chase at Warwick, The Duke ran his two crack 2-mile chasers Waterloo Boy and Viking Flagship. Maguire chose Waterloo Boy, Dunwoody had the ride on Viking. Dunwoody won. Two weeks later, he won the Cleeve Hurdle on Flakey Dove, and by the end of February, Maguire's lead was down to four.

The sparks were flying, and at Nottingham on 1 March they became a fire. Dunwoody was riding a horse called Raggerty in a selling hurdle. Maguire was on Mr Geneaology. Dunwoody led but on the approach to the second last drifted off the inner. Maguire sought to come through the gap, but Dunwoody moved across to his left and shut the door. Raggerty went on to win by 15 lengths. Maguire and Mr Geneaology ran out.

Inevitably there was a stewards' inquiry. 'Outside the stewards room I sat, Adrian stood,' Dunwoody recalled. 'What the fxxx were you at?' 'Where the fxxx were you going?' was the exchange. Dunwoody was given a 14-day ban for causing intentional interference, which meant he would miss Cheltenham.

It was Maguire who made the first peace offering, saying to Dunwoody that he was sorry he would miss the Festival. Dunwoody suggested they go for a drink, just off the motorway. Weighing room colleagues came too, perhaps worried that the two rivals would come to blows. But the meeting did ease tensions. 'I joked about him needing to look where he was going. He said I'd better keep watching my inner. We smiled and left it like that,' Dunwoody recalled.

His psychologist recommended that instead of watching Cheltenham at home, he went on a week's skiing holiday. Even at Val d'Isère, though, he couldn't resist a peak at *Paris Turf* newspaper – to see that Maguire had won the Champion Chase on Viking Flagship. But he was happy that a French horse, The Fellow, had won the Gold Cup, and not Maguire on Miinnehoma.

By the time he returned to racecourse action Maguire's lead had increased to twenty-five. But refreshed from the ski slopes, Dunwoody was ready to renew battle. At Aintree he rode Docklands Express and Cyborgo to victory on the Thursday and Friday, and in the Grand National itself was on board Miinnehoma. Maguire was on Moorcroft Boy, for The Duke, which started the 5-1 favourite.

Run on heavy ground, the race turned out to be one of the most exciting Grand Nationals of all time. After a number of fancied runners had crashed out, the dour stayer Just So, a lovely big black horse who had been backed in from 80-1 a week before to 20-1 on the day of the race on account of the ground, took it up at Valentine's. But Dunwoody was cruising on Miinnehoma, while Maguire was improving all the time on Moorcroft Boy. As they turned for home, the Irish mare Ebony Jane led, but then Maguire made his move. 'Looking at how well he was going I thought there's no way I'm going to beat him,' Dunwoody says. But his horse was still on the bridle. Richard took a pull on the run-in as he knew Miinnehoma didn't want to hit the front too soon. It was Maguire *v* Dunwoody, the story of the entire season. Then Dunwoody pressed 'Go'. He passed Moorcroft Boy and looked set for victory.

The race wasn't over yet, though. There was one more twist. The out-and-out stayer Just So, who looked as if his chance had gone with a mistake at the second last, rallied again and was closing with every stride on the outside. 'Just So putting in a tremendous challenge ... Miinnehoma and Just So as they race towards the line,' declared commentator Peter O'Sullevan. It was spine-tingling stuff.

In the end, Dunwoody held on to claim his second Grand National win, and trainer Martin Pipe's first. 'It was all down to the horse,' he says modestly. 'He was nearly on the floor at Becher's but he found a leg. He was so clever.' But Dunwoody too had been brilliant. He had shown great nerve to 'take a pull' on the run-in with his mount going so well but if he had gone too soon, the prize might well have been lost. It was a classic race, in keeping with a classic National Hunt season.

In the closing weeks, Dunwoody travelled here, there and everywhere to try to win his second title. In one absolutely crazy week in April he went up to Hexham for one ride for Peter Beaumont, then rode two at Wetherby the following afternoon before flying to Ascot to ride four at the evening meeting. The next day he flew to Ireland for three rides at Punchestown, before flying back for Cheltenham's evening meeting. Then he flew back to Ireland for six more rides the following day, and back to England for more rides at Newton Abbot and Bangor on the Friday. On the Saturday he rode four at Uttoxeter then flew to Plumpton by private helicopter to ride five in the evening meeting.

In the space of six days, Dunwoody had thirty-four rides at six race meetings. Those thirty-four rides had brought him eight winners (and quite a few Air Miles!). May was even madder. On one day he and Maguire rode at three different meetings: Hereford, Southwell and Huntingdon. Both men were winning on horses they had no right to. But there was a salutary reminder of the risks of the sport in which they were participating on the May Day Bank Holiday Monday when the fatal fall of Arcot in the Swinton Hurdle at Haydock left jockey Declan Murphy fighting for his life in a Liverpool hospital. Thankfully, he survived.

Boosted by Pipe's factory production line of winners, Dunwoody took the lead in the title race, but a treble for Maguire at Uttoxeter reduced the lead to just three, with two days to go. After Maguire picked up a spare winning ride at Stratford on the penultimate day, the lead was down to one. Pipe sent five horses to Stratford on the final day, and three of them won. Dunwoody was now five ahead, with only the evening meeting at Market Rasen to come. Surely he was home and dry. But Maguire won the first two races, and for a moment it looked like a remarkable late twist could be on the cards. But Maguire was unable to add to his tally and the title was Dunwoody's by three. 'I felt no elation; spiritually drained, I wondered what Adrian must have been thinking,' was Dunwoody's reaction. He celebrated his epic triumph a couple of days later – with a burger and milkshake at the McDonald's in Swindon.

His marriage to Carol was now in terminal decline and in August he moved out. The 1994/95 season looked like it would be a lot less dramatic than 1993/94, with Dunwoody establishing what appeared to be an unassailable lead in the championship. But then, in early January, he was hit with a twenty-eight-day ban after again being found guilty of intentional interference, in a very similar incident to that which had occurred at Warwick twelve months earlier. Dunwoody thanks Luke Harvey, the jockey who had tried to come up his inside, for changing his life.

He took a break to Monaco with his new girlfriend Emma. A day after he arrived there he received a phone call to say that his friend, the trainer Barry Kelly and his fiancée, had been killed in a car crash in Ireland. He flew to Dublin for the funeral and then back home. He found there was a message on his answerphone from Kelly. It said, after the greeting: 'You stupid prat getting yourself banned. It's lucky for us. Now you can come along to our wedding next week. Make sure you do.' Dunwoody had received a wedding invite from someone whose funeral he had just attended. It stunned him, but made him reflect on his priorities. 'All I had ever worried about was the next winner. For the first time in my life, there was something else to think about, something more important. Where was the sense in my little world?' he wrote. Dunwoody was never the same again. 'It was a game changer,' he says today. 'It came at a time when I was down, my marriage had broken up, I was banned, I had weight problems.' Yes, he still wanted to ride winners, but the championship was no longer important.

He did win his third title that season, with 160 winners. He was thirty clear of Adrian Maguire, whose challenge ended when he broke his arm in a fall on Easter Monday, and Norman Williamson, who tied for second. But it was the last time he chased the title.

At the end of the 1994/95 season, after he had ridden Martin Pipe-trained Cache Fleur to victory in the Whitbread, he told his boss he was leaving.

For the next four seasons, before injury intervened, he still rode over 100 winners each year, but the intensity had gone. He began to ride more often in Ireland, which he greatly enjoyed. 'Those four years were the happiest of my life,' he says. 'I was still working very hard, but the pressure was off and I could take a day off when I wanted.' Having the odd day off from riding didn't mean lying on a sofa, but allowed him to indulge his new passion: motor racing. Once, having ridden at Punchestown, he flew from Ireland to Scotland for a Formula First testing session. He then drove down to Bangor in Wales for an evening meeting, then up to Haydock for a meeting the next day, and then down to Uttoxeter for another evening meeting, before driving back up to Scotland for two Formula First races at Knockhill.

And this was Richard taking things a bit easier!

There were still plenty of red-letter days in the saddle. At the 1997 Cheltenham Festival, he rode three winners. There were also successful link-ups with Martin Pipe, such as when he rode Challenger Du Luc to victory in the 1996 Mackeson. Having won two King Georges on one famous grey (Desert Orchid), he repeated the feat on another, the Gordon W. Richards-trained One Man in 1995 and 1996. In fact, the 1995 race was postponed because of frost and run at Sandown in early January 1996, so Dunwoody became the first and, to date, only man to win two King Georges in one calendar year.

He was riding better than ever in the mid-to-late 1990s but now seemed much more at peace with himself. He was earning a very good living (around £200K a year minus tax and expenses), and not unreasonably hoped to go on riding until he was 40. He was forging a successful partnership with trainer Philip Hobbs, a real rising force, who trained over 100 winners for the first time in the 1999/2000 season. 'Richard Dunwoody whilst riding for us was an absolute gentleman but hated getting beaten and could get into a strop about it but I don't think he ever got beaten on a horse of ours that should have won,' Hobbs told me in 2020.

In February 1999 Dunwoody partnered Hobbs's Dr Leunt to victory in the Racing Post Chase, while in April he finished third on Call It A Day in the Grand National, the eighth time he had been placed in a race in which, as we have seen, many other champions had such a wretched record. On Easter Monday at Wincanton, he broke Peter Scudamore's record of 1,678 winners, becoming the most successful winning National Hunt jockey of all time. Scu was there, and was one of the first to congratulate him. Yet just four months later, Dunwoody's career was over.

His last day as a jockey, although he didn't know it at the time, came at Perth on 21 August 1999. A year earlier, in May 1998, he had fallen awkwardly at Fontwell, leaving him with what turned out to be a serious neck injury, which left him with a very weak right arm. He was forced to have a three-month rest to July 1998, but even when he returned to action, problems persisted. He rode three winners from four rides at Perth but did have a fall in the second last in a hurdle race, which left his neck and right arm sore. The last winner he rode was Twin Falls, for Philip Hobbs, in the very next race.

Afterwards he flew to California in a last-ditch attempt to get his right arm sorted, but the advice from the exercise kinesiologist after he had examined the X-rays was to 'call it a day'. Richard joked that he would have given his right arm to continue riding – but that it was his right arm that in the end stopped him.

In a seventeen-year career he had ridden 1,699 winners from 9,399 rides in Great Britain, with an additional 175 winners in Ireland. Additionally he had also won ten races in countries as diverse as Australia, Belgium and the US, where he won two Breeders Cup Chases and a Colonial Cup on Highland Bud.

He retired not only as the jump jockey who had won more races than anyone else in the history of the sport, but also with one of the best big race records of any champion. He was only the second post-war champion after Fred Winter to win the 'Big Three' races of the jump season – the Champion Hurdle, the Gold Cup and the Grand National – and, up to then, only the fourth in all, with Willie Robinson and Bobby Beasley. Just about the only major races missing from his CV were the Champion Chase (in which he was placed seven times) and the Scottish National.

'Whether you could say Richard was the best jump jockey of all time, I'm not sure, but you certainly wouldn't place anybody above him,' says trainer David Gandolfo.

Yet Richard himself says he feels that the work he did with John Reid as vice-president of the Jockeys Association, following the retirement of Scu, was as much of his 'legacy' as the winners he rode. Together with Michael 'Corky' Caulfield, the Jockeys Association's CEO at the time, he helped to introduce jockeys' sponsorship at the end of the 1990s. 'We also pushed hard to improve the standards of medical care on racecourses (with the introduction of physios and paramedics, replacing the St John's Ambulance men),' he says.

He found retirement hard to adjust to. He was for a time an insightful and eloquent racing pundit on the BBC but the job held no long-term appeal for him. Dunwoody wanted to be doing things, not discussing other people doing things. In his book *Obsessed*, one of the most riveting autobiographies you'll ever read, he penned a wonderful passage about what being a jump jockey meant, and what he missed:

Never again will I come down the hill at Cheltenham with plenty of horse in my hands, never again will I feel the thrill of flying those four fences down the back at Ascot, when it seems you are travelling at 100mph, and never again will I clear Becher's second time round at Aintree thinking 'We can win this National'. In those moments you focus, your concentration, your sense of living are pitched at a level normal life cannot touch.

To try to recapture the 'sense of living' he had when race riding, he set himself a number of extreme challenges. In 2003 he competed in the inaugural Polar

Race to the North Pole, and then headed in the opposite direction to the Antarctic. 'Walking to the South Pole was probably the hardest thing I have ever done. My teammates Doug Stoup, James Fox and I ended up in quite a bad crevasse field. We were on a glacier ridge that no one has ever walked up before or since,' he told me when I interviewed him in 2017 for the *Daily Express*. That was just before he embarked on his latest adventure, walking the length of Japan to raise awareness of sarcoma, a rare form of cancer suffered by his nephew George. Since retiring, Dunwoody has raised the best part of half a million pounds for good causes, including when he walked 1,000 miles for 1,000 hours for Racing Welfare in 2009. His love of travel has seen him taking private tours to some of the remotest parts of the world, which enabled him to indulge his other great interest: photography. In 2014 he held his first exhibition in London, for the Brooke Hospital Equine Charity. His photography (and web design) website can be found here: https://richarddunwoody.com/

Always keen for new experiences, he moved to Spain, where he now lives with his girlfriend Olivia and daughter Milly.

While he was away in Japan, the Cheltenham and Aintree Festivals were taking place, but missing them didn't bother the intelligent and engaging man who, twenty years earlier, had given so much to be National Hunt champion and whose brilliance in the saddle will never be forgotten.

Big race wins
Grand National 1986 (West Tip), 1994 (Miinnehoma)
Gold Cup 1988 (Charter Party)
Champion Hurdle 1990 (Kribensis)
King George VI Chase 1989, 1990 (Desert Orchid), 1995, 1996 (One Man)
Welsh Grand National 1993 (Riverside Boy)
Whitbread Gold Cup 1993 (Topsham Bay), 1995 (Cache Fleur)

Chapter Nineteen

AP McCoy

Champion 1995/96 to 2014/15

The Phenomenon

*'There has never been a sportsman quite like Sir Anthony McCoy ...
and there never will be.'*
Robin Oakley and Edward Gillespie, *Sixty Years of Jump Racing*

It's Wednesday, 11 March. Day two of the 2020 Cheltenham Festival. The JP McManus-owned Champ, ridden by Barry Geraghty, is 4-1 third favourite for the RSA Chase. He looks a well-beaten third after a hesitant jump at the second last and is still a long way behind the leading pair after the last, touching 100-1 in running. Then something remarkable happens. Champ suddenly produces a stunning finishing burst, which even Pegasus would have found hard to match, to split the Irish duo Minella Indo and Allaho on the line. It was a victory that never looked likely until it actually happened, but one totally in keeping with a horse named after AP McCoy, the man who was twenty times a 'champ'.

Yes, that's right, twenty times. Tim Molony won five titles from 1948 to 1955. John Francome, seven from 1975 to 1986. Peter Scudamore bettered that by one. AP McCoy bettered it by thirteen. The figures are truly staggering. Stan Mellor became the first jump jockey to ride 1,000 winners in 1971. Francome broke that record, reaching 1,138, Scudamore raised it to 1,678, Dunwoody to 1,699. McCoy rode 4,358. When Scu rode 221 winners in the 1988/89 season it was a record few thought would ever be beaten. McCoy surpassed it five times. 'AP' is the man who rewrote the record books. His greatness transcends the world of horse racing. In *Sixty Years of Jump Racing*, Oakley and Gillespie commented:

Other great sportsmen have achieved remarkable, sustained
success – but they were not competing in one of the two sports in

which participants are followed, day in, day out, by an ambulance, and in which regular and painful injury is inevitable. Nor were they driving their bodies every competitive day well below their natural weight on a starvation diet.

It must be said that McCoy did benefit from the prevailing tailwinds.

Firstly, by the mid-1990s, the UK's motorway network was very extensive. Back in the 1940s, racing was more or less regionalised; by 1995, jockeys, either by speeding along motorways or climbing into helicopters, could go anywhere for winners. Then there were the increased fixtures. Sunday racing was introduced in 1992, and the introduction of summer jumping in 1995 came just at the right time for someone like McCoy, who didn't mind riding all year long.

We also have to mention the advent of jockeys' agents, who made it much easier to get rides, and improvements in racecourse safety and medical treatments, which meant injured jockeys could return to action quicker than in the past. Jump racing remained a dangerous sport – as the tragic death of McCoy's friend Richard Davis following a fall at Southwell in 1996 showed – but, statistically, not quite as dangerous as it had been.

McCoy also benefited from riding in an age when the financial benefits for the top jockeys were much greater than ever before. He could afford to employ a PA, the former jockey Gee Armytage, to handle his admin. His great rival (and friend) Richard Johnson also pointed out in 2002 that AP had the privilege of not having to ride out in the mornings, save for a handful of times each year. That meant he could conserve his energy for the racecourse.

And, of course, finally, there was Martin Pipe – the trainer whose horses propelled McCoy, like Scudamore and Dunwoody before him, to so many titles. Consider this: from 1985/86 to Pipe's retirement, every champion jockey had, at one time or another, been his number one rider. Pipe himself was champion trainer for all but two of the years in the period from 1988 until his retirement in 2005.

Even with all these advantages, McCoy wouldn't have won twenty championships in a row without being very special. It wasn't just that his appetite for winners was extraordinary; it was that his appetite was never satiated. We've seen how seven years as champion was enough for Scudamore, and three sufficed for Dunwoody. McCoy, by contrast, was as keen to win the title in 2014/15 as he was in 1994/95.

I asked him how he managed to 'stay hungry' for such a long time. 'I loved what I was doing. I didn't see it as work,' he replied. It also helped that he was always 'in the zone'. 'I once read an article about Lester Piggott,' he tells me. 'It stuck in my mind. He said that if you're competing at the top level in sport it's a weakness to let either praise or criticism get to you.'

In the same way that Scudamore was Dunwoody's idol, McCoy looked up to Dunwoody. 'He set the standard. He was a great jockey and someone to emulate. And he became a very good friend.' The pair had much in common, both growing up in Northern Ireland during The Troubles. That meant getting used to bombs going off at any hour of the day and regularly being stopped at army checkpoints. On one occasion an IRA activist on the run sought refuge with the McCoys. He was an old friend of the family, and AP's mother Claire hid him under a bed while the nearby area was being combed by police and army men and their sniffer dogs. One night of the ordeal was enough for Mrs McCoy. The next morning she told her house guest to leave.

Anthony's father, Peadar, was a carpenter. National Hunt history was changed when he decided to construct three stables behind the bungalow he had built for himself and his family at the back of his parents' house. He had always wanted to breed horses and in 1970 he purchased his first mare, a relative of the 1962 Grand National winner Kilmore. Of his six children, it was young Anthony, born in May 1974, who inherited his father's interest. A shy and rather withdrawn boy who didn't much enjoy talking to people, he asked his dad for a pony of his own when he was 9. He then started riding in gymkhanas. On one Saturday morning every month, McCoy snr would take his son to the yard of his old friend, the National Hunt trainer Billy Rock, who became a mentor to young Anthony.

McCoy's racing foundations, you could say, were as solid as a Rock. He started riding horses on the trainer's gallops, and never stopped falling off. But that only made him more determined to succeed. At the age of 15 he'd had enough of school and wanted to become a professional jockey. He spent the summer of 1989 working full-time for Rock for £100 a week. Rock felt that McCoy was too small and too light to make it over jumps, and recommended he took out an apprentice licence on the Flat. He arranged for him to have a two-week trial at the top yard of Jim Bolger, in Kilkenny. One of racing's great characters, Bolger was a man with a droll sense of humour, but who demanded the very highest standards of those who worked for him. Stable lads were not only expected to be immaculately turned out – like the horses they 'did' – but to go to Mass every Sunday and every morning during Lent. Smoking was a particular pet hate. 'You can drink and you can smoke, I have no issue with that. You just won't be working here if you do,' was one of Jim's regular sayings. Any lad turning up for work with a cigarette hanging out of his mouth and/or wearing unpolished boots would have been out of the yard quicker than the time it took Bolger's Jet Ski Lady to win the Oaks. 'You'd get a bollocking for the slightest thing. Jim loved giving people a bollocking,' McCoy said. But he also said that he'd recommend working at Bolger's to anyone who wanted to get a good grounding in racing.

He had his first ride in public in August 1990, on a maiden called Nordic Touch in a 6-furlong race at the now defunct Phoenix Park in Dublin. McCoy claimed the maximum 10lb apprentices' allowance and finished seventh. What odds would you have got on him then of becoming the most successful jockey in National Hunt history?

He had to wait another six weeks before he got his next ride but it wasn't until eighteen months later, on 26 March 1992, that he rode his first winner, a 20-1 shot called Legal Steps at Thurles. He admits he hadn't even considered being a National Hunt jockey. He was with one of the strongest Flat yards in the British Isles and could look forward to riding Classic winners in the future.

However, he was struggling with his weight, particularly after he broke his leg and got heavier. Bolger rubbished the idea of him switching to jumps, but he did pick up spare rides over obstacles for other trainers. That said, after March 1992 he didn't ride another winner until 8 October 1993. By the summer of 1994, he knew where his future lay. His ticket to England came courtesy of Toby Balding. Son of Britain's greatest international polo player Gerald, brother of Mill Reef handler Ian and uncle of the broadcaster Clare, the benign, bespectacled Balding had won the 1969 Grand National with Highland Wedding but enjoyed his greatest years as a jumps trainer in the late 1980s and early 1990s, when he won a Grand National, a Gold Cup and two Champion Hurdles, and finished runner-up behind Martin Pipe in the trainer's championship. Toby met Anthony at Wexford races in July 1993, and offered him a job. He had only trained seventeen winners in 1992/93, a considerable drop from the year before, and his stable stars were by that time past their best. But he assured the young Irishman, who was then 19, that if he didn't like it in England he could always go back to Ireland, and that he had nothing to lose.

McCoy arrived at Balding's yard at Fyfield in Hampshire in August 1994 and found things rather different there than at Jim Bolger's. 'At Toby's everything was so much more relaxed, jeans and wellies were the order of the day. Toby was one of the lads, not this headmaster-type figure who put fear of God into you … lads smoked on horseback and chattered away to each other without a care in the world,' he wrote.

One of the best decisions McCoy made was staying at Balding's the first time champion trainer Martin Pipe came calling, just a week or so after he had arrived. It wasn't just because he liked his new boss and didn't feel good about leaving him so soon; it was that Balding had told him he would introduce him to the top jockeys' agent Dave Roberts. Roberts had helped Adrian Maguire become champion conditional in 1991/92 when riding for Balding, and also had Norman Williamson, Richard Guest and Mick Fitzgerald on his books. It was now the mid-1990s and top jockeys, like most other sports stars, relied on agents. Roberts was the best in the business, and would play a key role in McCoy first becoming champion conditional in 1994/95 and, a year later, champion jockey.

Anthony – who became known as 'Tony' as soon he crossed the Irish Sea – had his first ride in England on 13 August 1994, when he finished second on the John Jenkins-trained Arctic Life in a novice hurdle at Stratford. His first winner came on 7 September, when he rode Chickabiddy, trained by Gordon Edwards, to victory in a handicap hurdle at Exeter. He rode his first winner for Balding a couple of weeks later and at the end of the month had his first ride – and win – at Cheltenham.

He was making progress fast. In October he rode his first winner over fences, a 20-1 shot called Bonus Boy, in a selling handicap chase at Newton Abbot. He had another winner on the card and the following day the *Racing Post* hailed him as 'a rising star'. One of the trainers who thought the same was John Spearing, who noticed the young Ulsterman's 'dedication'. Other shrewd judges thought McCoy was so good he should have been giving weight to other riders, not receiving it.

Things really took off after Christmas. By the end of February he was well on his way to the conditional jockey's title. He finished the season on the seventy-four-winner mark, breaking Maguire's record by three. There was another approach from Pipe in the summer, after Dunwoody had quit as Pond House stable jockey. McCoy hesitated, as Balding said he would be riding all his horses that season, and he also had begun riding for Paul Nicholls and Philip Hobbs, two men on the rise.

The job of Pond House stable jockey went to David Bridgwater, but Pipe did use McCoy a lot in the opening weeks of the 1995/96 season and it was these early wins, in the first year of summer jumping, that gave him a head start in the championship. Everything seemed to fall right for McCoy that long hot summer. Richard Dunwoody, champion for the past three years, wasn't chasing the title. Adrian Maguire, who had pushed Dunwoody so close, and who surely deserved a title of his own, was out injured with a broken arm. By early October, McCoy had ridden fifty winners. He still didn't believe he would win the title, though, with Bridgwater being Pipe's first jockey. But the winners kept on coming. He had 120 on the board by the time the Cheltenham Festival of 1996 came around. There he rode his first Festival winner, the Philip Hobbs-trained Kibreet in the Grand Annual.

He had another big race win at Aintree a couple of weeks later, when he steered the David Nicholson-trained dual Champion Chase winner Viking Flagship to victory in the Melling Chase. McCoy had arrived at High Table. His first championship was achieved with 175 winners, a grand total (the joint third-highest of all time), forty-three ahead of David Bridgwater. At the age of 22, he was the youngest champion since Josh Gifford in 1962/63.

When 'Bridgie' unexpectedly quit as Pipe's stable jockey in September 1996, because he wasn't enjoying it, McCoy was the obvious successor, but at first he kept riding for Pipe (and other trainers) with no mention of 'the job'. Things came to a head in January 1997, with him already close to 150 winners. Pipe's Cyborgo and Paul Nicholls's Flaked Oats were entered for the same race at Newton Abbot and both trainers – who were great rivals – expected McCoy to ride their horse. McCoy decided to ride Cyborgo, even if it meant losing the ride on some of Nicholls's leading chasers, such as See More Business, who went on to win a Gold Cup and two King Georges.

In the race at Newton Abbot Cyborgo won and Flaked Oats fell at the last. The association with Pipe was now established. Just about the only thing that went wrong for AP in 1996/97 was breaking his shoulder following a fall at Wincanton on 23 January. That put him out of action for a month, but he more than made up for the absence with a fantastic Cheltenham Festival. On the opening day he rode Or Royal to victory in the Arkle. In the Champion Hurdle, the very next race, he was on Make A Stand. Martin Pipe's novice had been bought for just £4,000 out of a claimer on the Flat the previous season, but had shown great improvement over timber, winning a number of valuable handicaps. Make A Stand had one way of running, going flat out from the start and getting his rivals into trouble, before resolutely staying on all the way to the line. Could you win a Champion Hurdle in such a 'one-dimensional' way, the experts asked? The answer was an emphatic 'Yes'. Make A Stand, sent off at 7-1, made all, jumped superbly and came home by 5 lengths. Forty-eight hours later, in the Gold Cup, McCoy was on board the Noel Chance-trained Mr Mulligan, on whom he had fallen at the last fence when lying second behind One Man in the 1996 King George. Off the track since then, the 7-year-old was allowed to go off at a very generous 20-1 on Gold Cup Day. McCoy gave his horse a super ride, taking it up from Dublin Flyer after the 13th and then seeing off a challenge from One Man, to win by 9 lengths from Barton Bank.

AP had become only the second jockey since Fred Winter in 1961 to win the Champion Hurdle and Gold Cup in the same year. And all this had come less than three years after he had ridden his first winner over jumps!

For the next seven seasons the Pipe/McCoy combo proved hard to catch. In 1999 they landed the first race of the Cheltenham Festival, the Supreme Novices' Hurdle, with Hors La Loi III. Marcus Armytage relates how in the paddock McCoy told Pipe that the Irish-trained favourite Cardinal Hill had been 'catching pigeons' at work. Pipe replied: 'That's nothing. Our fellow can catch 'em, cook 'em and eat 'em.' Hors La Loi won the race by 17 lengths, while Cardinal Hill unseated.

McCoy says today that Pipe was '100 per cent' the man who turned him into a record-breaker. 'I admire him greatly both as a friend and as a trainer,' he says. He was already single-minded enough before he became the Pond House stable jockey, as his conditional title and first championship proves, but Pipe's own laser-like focus pushed AP to even greater heights. He admits his obsession with riding winners became robotic. 'Every winner was just a number, just another winner, another notch. Even when I look back now, so much of it is all just numbers,' he wrote. But what numbers they were! In 1997/98 he broke Scudamore's record of 221 winners in a season by riding 253. There was another double ton in 1999/2000 (245), the season's highlight being a thrilling photo-finish Champion Chase victory on Edredon Bleu, and in 2001/02 he rode 245 winners at a strike rate of 31 per cent. A year later (2001/02) he smashed his own record by riding 289 winners. His target had actually been to surpass Flat jockey Sir Gordon Richards' record of 269 winners in one season.

In that annus mirabilis of 2002 he also posted the most winners in a calendar year (307) and surpassed both Scudamore's and Dunwoody's previous all-time records.

'Looking back I think the 2001/02 season and the whole of 2002 is the time that stands out,' he says when I ask him which of his twenty years as champion gave him most satisfaction. 'I broke Sir Gordon's record and I honestly don't think the record of riding 307 winners in one calendar year will be broken, because there's less racing and jockeys can only ride at one meeting a day.'

Inevitably, his determination to win, particularly in the early days, meant regular whip bans. The typical McCoy treatment was rousting up, with a mixture of hard driving and cajoling sometimes reluctant horses to find hidden reserves and pull off unlikely victories. A classic example was in the Martell Hurdle at Aintree in April 1998 when he partnered Pridwell to victory over the mighty Istabraq, who had won his previous ten races. 'I do believe

I made Pridwell win that day. It might sound ridiculous but I believe that I made him want to win,' he wrote. That ride earned him plenty of plaudits, but also a four-day ban.

McCoy won on horses that other jockeys wouldn't. One of his greatest rides was on Wichita Lineman in the William Hill Chase at the 2009 Cheltenham Festival. The gelding made a series of blunders and never looked to be travelling well, but his jockey never gave up and produced him with a stunning late run up the Cheltenham hill to overhaul Maljimar on the line. If you watch the Racing TV replay of the race on YouTube the first comment says it all: 'Not another jump jockey in the world would have won that race, the horse did everything to lose until AP got to grips with it.'

His second Gold Cup win on Synchronised, another JP McManus-owned, Jonjo O'Neill-trained gelding, was very similar. He was 'flat to the boards' at the back of the field for much of the way, to use commentator Richard Hoiles' expression, and looked a well-beaten fifth as they turned for home, but again McCoy kept at it and managed to coax his mount into a supreme effort on the run to the line. Tragically both Wichita Lineman and Synchronised were killed on their very next outings, showing again the thin line in National Hunt racing between triumph and disaster.

Probably the most remarkable example of McCoy's 'never give up' philosophy came at Southwell in January 2002. He was riding the odds-on favourite Family Business but they parted company at the tenth fence. So disgusted was McCoy with what he regarded was a soft fall, he threw his skull cap into the ground. But, rather like something out of an Agatha Christie novel, the remaining five runners started falling one by one too. McCoy, hearing the racecourse commentator describe the drama, caught up with Family Business, remounted, and trotted back to the fence at which they had come to grief. He and Family Business successfully negotiated the remaining circuit to claim an unlikely victory, to the delight of favourite backers – and particularly the punter who had staked £4 with Betfair at odds of 1000-1 on McCoy winning the race.

McCoy's 1,700th winner, which made him the most successful winning jump jockey of all time, came on Mighty Montefalco at Uttoxeter on 27 August 2002. Having achieved the fastest-ever double ton by Christmas that year, he then set his sights on becoming the first jump jockey to ride 300 winners in a season. That was McCoy – every time one mountain had been climbed, there was always another. 'You need to have goals,' he tells me. 'If you don't set yourself goals you just float through life.' But – in another acknowledgement of the role played in his career by the likes of Martin Pipe and later JP McManus and Jonjo O'Neill, he adds, 'you also need to have successful people around you.'

The triple-century in 2002/03 certainly looked doable, before injuries intervened. A broken collarbone put him out of action for ten days in March and then he had a disastrous Cheltenham Festival when he hit the deck four times, missed two rides through dehydration and broke his collarbone again. He finished the campaign on the 257 mark, still the second highest total of all time. That season he had also won his first, and as it turned out, only King George, on Best Mate, the best chaser in the country.

But AP being AP, he still wasn't satisfied. 'I can't wait for the new season to start because last year was a disaster,' he said at Sandown Park on Whitbread Gold Cup Day. That's right – a 'disaster' for McCoy was winning the championship with the second-highest total of all time.

The new season started the very next day, and he was off to Hexham to ride the winner of a Class G selling hurdle. During the McCoy era just about the only chance other jockeys had of challenging him seriously for the title came when he was out injured. On 18 June he broke his arm following a fall at Worcester. That put him out of action for two months, and when he returned, on 22 August, Richard Johnson led by eighteen. There was an air of 'Fergie time' inevitability about McCoy riding a winner on his first ride back, and the deficit being turned round.

He won the 2003/04 title with 209 winners, twenty-three clear of Johnson.

Despite his success, like many other great champions before him, he still appeared jinxed in the Grand National. His first ride in the race, on Chatam in 1995, crashed out at the twelfth. In 1996, Deep Bramble went lame. In 1999, he rode Eudipe, who was killed in a fall at second Becher's. In 2000, his mount Dark Stranger fell, but at least in 2001 he did get round to finish third, after remounting Blowing Wind (on whom he had previously pulled off the Imperial Cup/County Hurdle double) in a memorable, mud-splattered multiple pile-up renewal in which only two horses, Red Marauder and Smarty, completed without mishap.

After the 2005 race McCoy probably thought he was fated never to win the Liverpool showpiece. He was 6 lengths clear of the field on Clan Royal, a horse with a terrific Aintree record, and cantering towards second Becher's, when he was driven to the edge of the fence by two loose horses. One minute he was dreaming of National glory, the next, his horse had literally been taken out of the race. Everyone, except those who had backed the eventual winner, Hedgehunter, felt sorry for him.

By now he had left Martin Pipe and signed a very lucrative retainer for top owner JP McManus, the man whose famous green-and-gold silks he wore on Clan Royal. The decision to leave Pipe in 2004 and join Jonjo O'Neill's Jackdaws Castle set-up couldn't have been easy but McCoy felt he needed a fresh challenge. He acknowledged in his autobiography that if any one of the top twenty jockeys in the weighing room had been riding for Martin Pipe instead of him at the same time, they would have been multiple champions too. Again, it was all about setting goals and climbing new mountains.

His mid-career 'change of horses' reaped immediate dividends. AP powered to his tenth successive title in 2004/05, notching up another double-century on the final day at Sandown. He was fifty-eight clear of the runner-up, Pipe's new stable jockey Timmy Murphy. McCoy's obsession with riding winners, like Dunwoody's, was bound to impact on his personal life. In 2006 he married Chanelle, but the courtship was turbulent. On one occasion McCoy told his girlfriend the relationship was over because he had caught her smoking – a pet hate that he had perhaps inherited from Jim Bolger. In an interview with the *Mail on Sunday* in 2015, Chanelle revealed how she had threatened to walk out on her husband a number of times. 'I would get home and he would be sitting there bawling his eyes out. He had become champion jockey but he was driving himself demented thinking he might not be number one the following year.' But the McCoy's marriage survived, and prospered, with Chanelle saying in 2013 that her husband had 'mellowed', having proven his 'sustainability' as a champion.

No other jockey had been so dominant for so long in the history of the sport but the remarkable thing is how little jealousy or resentment there was towards McCoy from his weighing room colleagues. On the contrary, there was huge admiration. Though, of course, there was the usual ribbing too. 'He's a miserable, selfish, spoilt, lazy, horrible bxxxxxd, a bad loser, very lucky to ride for Martin Pipe but continues to give the rest of us hope because he's useless with women. I bet you don't print that,' jockey Carl Llewellyn told journalist Marcus Armytage. Marcus did.

The way AP was perceived by the public is also interesting. In his early days he was regarded as a rather cold, austere and moody figure. A brilliant jockey but not someone you could really warm to. Did McCoy ever smile, people asked? Why did he always look so flippin' miserable?

But by the mid-2000s, with perhaps his Clan Royal misfortune the turning point, it's fair to say there was a shift in how people saw him. The public recognised that here was a man whose determination to win was quite extraordinary. The way he went through the pain barrier to ride winners also helped established the AP legend.

In January 2008 he fractured both sides of his T12 vertebrae and shattered two other bones in his back after a fall at Warwick. To hasten his recovery he underwent cyrotherapy treatment, which meant enduring extremely cold temperatures in a special chamber. When being told that the coldest anyone had ever endured in the chamber was -145°C, he asked for -150°C. He was back in action in time for the Cheltenham Festival.

In November 2012 he was kicked in the face by a horse at Wetherby. His injuries necessitated the extraction of two teeth and some plastic surgery but so keen was he to ride at Ascot the following day, he refused general anaesthetic. He arrived at Ascot with medical tape over his nose and upper mouth, prompting trainer Nicky Henderson to jape, 'I wanted a jockey, not the Phantom of the Opera.' Needless to say, 'The Phantom' won on My Tent Or Yours, his 101st winner of the season.

By that time he had finally won a Grand National. In 2009 there had been more bad luck at second Becher's when he came down on Butler's Cabin, on whom he had previously won an Irish National. The race was won by the 100-1 shot Mon Mome. I was at Aintree that day and the shock winner was met with stunned silence from most of the crowd but twelve months later it was a very different story when McCoy came home in front on Don't Push It. The horse was backed in from 22-1 to 10-1 before the off in a concerted gamble from both the public and professional punters, and after McCoy and his mount overhauled Black Apalachi on the Elbow there were huge cheers. It seemed the entire racing world and much of the nation shared in McCoy's joy at finally – on his fifteenth attempt – winning 'the big one'.

The year 2010 was monumental for AP. In addition to his National success, he also won the Champion Hurdle on Binocular (few could have seen that coming after the horse had been matched at 1000-1 on Betfair, when he was thought likely to miss the race due to muscle problems), and to cap it all off, in December he won the BBC Sport's Personality of the Year award. It was a long-overdue recognition of the contribution he had made not just to horse racing, but to sport in general.

You could have forgiven him for taking his foot off the pedal after such a tremendous twelve months but with AP there was never going to be any let-up. He not only won another five titles, but in three of the next five seasons he also registered another three double-centuries. At Towcester on 7 November 2013, just six months after suffering a collapsed lung following a fall at Cheltenham, he became the first jump jockey to ride 4,000 winners.

To celebrate, JP McManus brought everyone on the course, around 4,000 people, a free drink.

A good time to retire? McCoy was now 39, but immediately focused on his next target, beating the 4,191-winner tally posted by his old patron Martin Pipe as a trainer. He achieved that on 19 July 2014 at Market Rasen. That season, 2014/15, was McCoy's swansong. He received a rapturous reception when, at his last Cheltenham Festival, he won the Ryanair Chase on the 16-1 shot Uxizandre.

He bowed out on 25 April 2015, finishing third on the appropriately named Box Office at Sandown. In a twenty-one-year career he had ridden 4,348 winners, from 17,546 races, a total that included two Champion Hurdles, two Gold Cups, one Grand National and a Champion Chase. Every season he had competed in England he had been the champion. 'I was always the "hunted" but that's how I wanted it,' he says. While he admits it would have been nice to have broken Sir Gordon Richards' career record of 4,870 wins, it was important for AP to go out on top, which is what he did.

In 2016, he became the first champion jump jockey and only the second jockey to be knighted (after Richards), having earlier been awarded the OBE.

He broke all the jump racing records, but Sir Anthony never became arrogant: his respect for his sport – and those who came before him – never wavered. Proof of this came in August 2020 when he came to the village of Ashbury near Swindon on the day of Stan Mellor's funeral. He just stood there on his own, immaculately dressed in his suit and black tie, as the cortège went past. One racing great paying tribute to another. The sign of a true champ.

Big race wins
Scottish Grand National 1997 (Belmont King)
Champion Hurdle 1997 (Make A Stand), 2006 (Brave Inca), 2010 (Binocular)
Gold Cup 1997 (Mr Mulligan), 2012 (Synchronised)
Champion Chase 2000 (Edredon Bleu)
King George VI Chase 2002 (Best Mate)
Whitbread Gold Cup (as previously known) 2002 (Bounce Back), 2009 (Hennessy)
Grand National 2010 (Don't Push It)
Welsh Grand National 2010 (Synchronised)

Chapter Twenty

Richard Johnson

Champion 2015/16, 2016/17, 2017/18, 2018/19

The Bridesmaid who finally Became the Bride

'Richard Johnson is the best jockey I've ever seen on a front runner. He's magnificent. And I've been watching racing for over fifty years.'
Sir Rupert Mackeson, former amateur rider and racing art expert

Jimmy 'The Whirlwind' White was six times runner-up at the World Snooker Championships. Czech tennis ace Ivan Lendl was eleven times a runner-up in Grand Slam finals.

But in the history of sporting 'seconds', no one can quite match the record of Richard 'Dicky' Johnson. Before he landed his first jump jockeys' title in 2016, at the age of 38, he had been runner-up to Tony McCoy no less than SIXTEEN times.

Season after season, Johnson chased McCoy home. Sometimes he got close. In 2005/06 he was only eleven winners behind AP. Johnson admits that there were times, in his thirties, when he thought he'd never be champion. 'If I had retired without that it would have been disappointing,' he says. But when McCoy retired, the perennial bridesmaid finally made it to the altar. Not just once, but four times.

Overshadowed for a large part of his career by McCoy, at least in terms of the jump jockeys' title, it's worth reflecting that Johnson is second only to AP in the all-time winners' table. By the end of the 2017/18 season he had already ridden more winners than Peter Scudamore and Richard Dunwoody combined.

If McCoy had stayed with Jim Bolger on the Flat, then Johnson would, in 2019, have been celebrating his twentieth title.

The rivalry between McCoy and Johnson was intense but both men had enormous respect for each other. McCoy admitted: 'Without him [Johnson] pushing me, I wouldn't have achieved anything like so much as I did.' Johnson says of AP: 'He raised the level. He was a brilliant person to compete against and a brilliant person to be around. We had a very similar mindset and outlook.'

Like Richard Dunwoody, Johnson achieved an impressive number of big race wins relatively early in his career – and indeed, a long time before he became champion. By the end of the 2002/03 season, when he was still in his mid-twenties, he had already won the 'Big Four' races of the Cheltenham Festival, i.e. the Champion Hurdle, Gold Cup, Champion Chase, and Stayers' Hurdle, as well as the Welsh National – and he had come agonisingly close in 2002 to winning the Grand National.

He had also made the gossip columns of the papers – and not just the racing pages – on account of his well-publicised, three-year relationship with Zara Phillips, daughter of the Princess Royal.

Loyal, dependable and universally liked, Johnson succeeded McCoy as champion conditional in 1995/96. Whereas McCoy and Dunwoody both hailed from Northern Ireland, Johnson, like Peter Scudamore, another of our great champions, came from Herefordshire farming stock. He even went to the same school as Scu, Belmont Abbey. His ambition to become champion jump jockey came from looking up to Scu – the local hero – as a child.

Johnson's paternal grandfather, Ivor, a farmer and permit-holder who trained Bridge Ash, the winner of the 1982 Midlands National (who was ridden by Johnson's father Keith), was another big influence. Johnson said of him:

> The great thing about Granddad was that he always seemed happy. He didn't try to teach me about riding, much less about racing, but simply through watching him and following him, as I did through a number of years, he transmitted the sheer joy that horses can offer. And that was quite a start in life.

Ivor handed over his licence to Johnson's mother Sue, who trained at Madley, near Hereford. With his background, Richard was always going to end up riding horses for a career, and he was taken on by David Nicholson as soon as he left school in 1993. The Duke was now at Jackdaws Castle – and with the state-of-the-art training facilities at his disposal and a great team of horses in his care he was all set to wrest the champion trainer's title away from Martin Pipe.

The Duke could be a hard taskmaster but took a shine to his new recruit. 'The good thing about him was that he might yell at you in the morning but he'd still speak to you in the afternoon. Once it was said, it was finished,' Johnson recalled.

His first ride in public, though, came not on a Nicholson inmate, but on his family's own home-bred point-to-pointer Rusty Bridge. The first foal of Bridge Ash, Rusty Bridge had already won two points by the time Richard, then aged 16, took the ride in the Men's Open at Larkhill on 27 April 1994. They finished fifth. Next time out, it was a very different story. The race was the Next Generation Hunters' Chase at Hereford, an appropriate name seeing that it would provide a future three-time champion jockey with his first victory.

With the former Whitbread winner Brown Windsor attracting the market support, Rusty Bridge was allowed to go off at 25-1. But Johnson and his mount set off with great gusto to make every post a winning one and having jumped the last, were all of 5 lengths clear. Johnson then gave Rusty Bridge a couple of right-handers with his whip but failed to pull his stick through to his left hand to keep him straight. The race was very nearly thrown away as the pursuing The Malakarma made a straight line to the post. To Johnson's great relief, 'Number Nine', Rusty Bridge, was declared the winner in the photo finish. On the following Monday morning at Jackdaws Castle, The Duke marched towards him and said gruffly: 'Well done. But from now on, you ride out with a stick in your left hand every day.' The lesson was learned.

That solitary win in the 1993/94 season was followed by twelve in 1994/95 and then fifty-three in 1995/96 when Johnson became champion conditional. In November 1995 he had left the amateur ranks to turn professional.

Like AP McCoy, his career was boosted by having 'super agent' Dave Roberts to book his rides, as well as the advent of summer jumping. In the summer of 1996, best remembered by sports fans as when the hosts England reached the semi-finals of Euro 96 only to lose (again!) to the Germans on penalties, Johnson was in great form, riding the Peter Bowen-trained Stately Home to five chase wins and the Milton Bradley-trained mare Maggots Green to three of her five successes. By the end of that 1996/97 season he had recorded his first ton (102), the first of twenty-four successive centuries, a feat no other jockey – not even McCoy – has matched.

He could, with more luck, have been celebrating his twentieth birthday in July 1997 having won both the Gold Cup and Grand National as the respective winners of those races that year, Mr Mulligan and Lord Gyllenne, had been his rides at one point. Those disappointments apart, Johnson was very much a man on the up, as we can see from his winners total: 102 in 1996/97, 120 in 1997/98 and 133 in 1998/99.

By now there had been a falling-out between David Nicholson and his first stable jockey Adrian Maguire, of which Johnson was the beneficiary.

Before Maguire quit, Nicholson had replaced him on a number of horses with Johnson. In December 1998, Adrian Maguire quit and Johnson became The Duke's number one jockey.

The highlight of the 1998/99 season was undoubtedly riding his first Festival winner, Anzum, in the Stayers' Hurdle. It was a ride that showcased Johnson's never-say-die attitude in the saddle, an attribute he shared with AP McCoy. Anzum, a 40-1 shot who had been well beaten in the race two years earlier, was a good 25 lenghts off the leaders going to the top of the hill, about a mile from home, but Johnson says the 'optimist' in him 'insisted' the race wasn't yet over. His horse began to pick up but still had 10 lengths or so to make up on the leaders after the last. Johnson kept on pushing and up the Cheltenham hill he and Anzum passed both the weakening Lady Rebecca and then, in the shadow of the post, the leader, Le Coudray, to pull off an unlikely success. Betting in running wasn't around in 1999 but if it had been, it's likely Anzum would at one stage have been a few hundred to one. There was an added poignancy to the victory in that it was to be The Duke's last Festival winner. There was a symmetry too: Peter Scudamore had ridden Nicholson's first Festival winner, Solar Cloud, in the 1986 Triumph Hurdle, at odds of 40-1, and another Herefordshire jockey (and subsequent champion), Richard Johnson, rode his last, also at odds of 40-1.

With Nicholson retired, Johnson formed an even closer alliance with trainer Philip Hobbs, cementing a partnership that was to prove one of the most enduring in National Hunt racing. Hobbs, a former jockey based near Minehead on the North Somerset coast, had established himself by the late 1990s, with the minimum of fuss, as one of the top National Hunt trainers in the country. Another trainer with whom Johnson became associated from quite early on and for whom he still rides today is Henry Daly, the former assistant to Captain Tim Forster.

In December 1999, Daly saddled Johnson's Welsh National winner Edmond, the last big race winner of the decade – and, indeed, of the century.

Three months after that, in March 2000, Dicky won his first Gold Cup. For once, the wheel of fortune favoured him, and not his great rival McCoy. AP, who had already won one Gold Cup for trainer Noel Chance, had the opportunity of partnering another, Looks Like Trouble, who had been Norman Williamson's ride before a fall-out with connections. But McCoy decided to ride Martin Pipe's brilliant novice Gloria Victis, who had been electrifying when winning the Racing Post Chase under top weight, ironically under Johnson.

So quite late on, Johnson was booked to ride Looks Like Trouble. It proved to be a turning point in his life in more ways than one. In a dramatic race,

Gloria Victis made all the running but came down at the second last, a fall that sadly cost him his life and left his battle-hardened jockey in tears. Looks Like Trouble had made a mistake after one circuit and with about a mile to go it wasn't looking good as the big bay gelding was receiving reminders from his jockey. ITV commentator Simon Holt noted that Looks Like Trouble 'appears to be struggling', but Johnson got the response he wanted and moved up to second four out. After jumping the second last, where Gloria Victis made his tragic departure, he just about had the lead, and then, with stamina his strong suit, powered strongly up the Cheltenham hill to win by 5 lengths from Florida Pearl. 'There are days when a big winner does not register but this was not among them. I felt the surge of euphoria immediately I crossed the line and the fact that it had been the luckiest of breaks for me to be riding the horse did not detract in any way from what I felt,' Johnson said later. The association with Looks Like Trouble and Chance had another happy outcome too, as Dicky later married the trainer's daughter Fiona, who became the mother of his three children. 'I gained a wife and a father-in-law and everything else out of it,' he told the *Guardian*'s Chris Cook as he looked back at the victory in 2018. He even gained a 'family pet', as after he retired, Looks Like Trouble came to live in a field behind the Johnsons' Herefordshire home and is still being happily looked after there today. How different things might have been had Williamson, or McCoy, got the Gold Cup ride.

Johnson finished the 1999/2000 season with 142 winners and in 2000/01, that rose to 162, his highest total yet. His inexorable progress was, however, checked by breaking his right leg twice in a period of ten months. The first injury occurred in October 2001 at Exeter, when he crashed out at the fourth fence when riding Ilico II, who was sadly killed. That put Johnson out of action until January, and he celebrated his return to action with the first of his two wins in the Irish Gold Cup on the Willie Mullins chaser Florida Pearl, the horse he had beaten into second place in the 2000 Gold Cup. The second leg break occurred after an horrific fall at Newton Abbot on August Bank Holiday Monday, 2002. His horse, Lincoln Place, had the race at his mercy at the last but then flipped over in mid-air, threw Johnson to the ground, and landed on top of him. Dicky lay unconscious for fifteen minutes and many watching feared the worst.

Yet, within two days, he was out of hospital and walking on crutches without even a plaster on the fracture. While the broken legs destroyed any chance he might have had of putting in a meaningful challenge to McCoy for the jockey's title, in both the seasons concerned Johnson was back in time to enjoy big race success at the Cheltenham Festival.

In 2002, he and Philip Hobbs enjoyed a great day when they landed the Champion Chase with Flagship Uberalles. The horse – who was with his fifth trainer – didn't appear to be travelling particularly well on ground that didn't suit. He clouted the third last but Johnson refused to read the 'it wasn't really his day' script and got down to some serious work. Latalomne had a narrow lead when falling two out, but Johnson rousted his mount for a renewed effort and the pair overhauled Cenkos to win by 3 lengths. Like his Stayers' Hurdle and Gold Cup victories, it had been another example of Johnson's 'optimism', and strength in the saddle, winning the day.

The 2003 Festival was similarly memorable. There was an almighty roar from the crowd when Johnson surged to the front at the second last on the Philip Hobbs-trained grey Rooster Booster in the Champion Hurdle, and then stormed up the hill to record an emphatic 11-length success. Twelve months earlier, Johnson had won the County Hurdle, the last race of the 2002 Festival, on 'The Rooster', and the grey, by the time of his greatest victory, had become one of the most popular horses in training for rising up the hurdling ranks at a relatively advanced age of 9.

He wouldn't have believed it at the time but it was to be another fifteen years before Dicky won one of the Big Four at the Festival again. 'I think those big race wins I had relatively early in my career would have meant even more to me had I fully appreciated just how difficult it was to win them,' he says.

In the period 2004 to 2015 there were two more Racing Post Chase wins (in 2005 and 2011) to add to the three in a row he landed in 2000 to 2002, two Whitbreads (in 2006 and 2008), plus a Scottish National (in 2011), a Midlands National (2014), a Supreme Novices' Hurdle (2010) and two Triumph Hurdles (2004 and 2006), with most of his big wins coming for Philip Hobbs.

But the showcase Saturday successes were only half the story. The other half was what Dicky was doing at midweek meetings at tracks such as Hereford, Fontwell, Uttoxeter and Ludlow. A testament to his reliability is that he kept riding for the same trainers year in, year out, without any fallings-out. His popularity with trainers and owners wasn't just due to his horsemanship. 'Richard Johnson is fantastic at public relations in every way and the best even with owners in the paddock before and after the race. He would never be in a hurry with his brilliant post-race rundown,' his long-standing patron Philip Hobbs says.

'Richard Johnson rode winners for me when he was very young and is still exactly the same person now as then,' says Herefordshire trainer Matt Sheppard. David Gandolfo concurs: 'Richard Johnson is the same person he was 100 years ago.' Dicky isn't 100 – it just feels like he's been around that long.

Of course, racing being racing there were always the days when things would go wrong. There were shades of Devon Loch when, in a race at Exeter in October 2006, Johnson's mount Out The Black inexplicably decided to down tools just before the finish and catapulted its jockey over the line. And in the 2012 Champion Chase, there was a nasty looking incident when his mount, Wishfull Thinking, crashed through the inside rail, throwing him into the crowd of onlookers and photographers. Fortunately, he only suffered some bad bruising and he was back riding in the first race the following day.

When McCoy retired in 2015, Johnson grasped with both hands the opportunity to finally become champion. He established a commanding lead in the table from early on, which he never relinquished. In January 2016 at Ascot he rode his 3,000th career winner, having passed the 2,000 milestone six years earlier. It's fair to say that everyone in National Hunt racing was willing him to become champion. He was touched by what he describes as 'the tremendous support' he received from trainers and owners to help him win the title, but that only reflected the high regard in which he was held across the National Hunt community.

His long-overdue coronation came on an emotional day at Sandown Park on 23 April, after Menorah had become his 235th winner of the season. It was the highest winning total since McCoy in 2003 and the measure of Johnson's dominance can be seen by the fact that he was over 100 winners ahead of the runner-up, Aidan Coleman.

Dicky was given a guard of honour by his weighing room colleagues before being handed the champion's trophy by AP McCoy. 'It was the highlight of my career. The moment I had dreamt of for so long,' he says. The longest wait of any bridesmaid in sporting history was finally over.

For the first time in his career, Johnson started the 2016/17 season trying to retain the title, not chase it. Two top-class horses who helped him on the way to a second title – and land some valuable prizes along the way – were Defi Du Seuil and Native River. The former was a very progressive JP McManus-owned juvenile hurdler, who had joined Philip Hobbs in the autumn of 2016, having previously been trained in France.

Johnson rode Defi to an easy, odds-on win in a maiden hurdle at Ffos Las on 16 October, the first of seven consecutive victories for the horse that season. On five of those occasions McManus's retained jockey Barry Geraghty was on board, but when Geraghty was injured, Johnson was able to deputise at the

2017 Cheltenham Festival and partner the gelding to an impressive 5-length success in the Triumph Hurdle.

His association with Native River began in the Mildmay Novices' Chase at the Aintree Grand National meeting in April 2016. An out-and-out galloper who jumped brilliantly from the front and always found more under pressure, the white-faced chestnut became established as one of the stars of the National Hunt scene after a series of gutsy wins under Johnson. 'Richard Johnson was absolutely brilliant,' trainer Colin Tizzard enthused after the Aintree success. 'He had to wake him up once or twice, but he was straight back into his stride.' It was an augur of things to come.

In November 2016, Native River lined up for his first seasonal target, the Hennessy Gold Cup. Sent off a short-priced 7-2 favourite at Newbury, Johnson and his mount were either in the lead, or contesting it, for most of the 3-mile 2-furlong contest, but each time it looked like they were coming under pressure, they found more. After the last, Carole's Destrier came with a strong late run, but Johnson and his mount again dug deep, to win by half a length. It had been an absolutely pulsating race, but more was to follow. A month later, Johnson and Native River started the 11-4 favourites for the Welsh Grand National. At Newbury, the horse had carried 11st 1lb; now he was set to carry 11st 12lb and give weight all round in a competitive twenty-runner handicap on soft ground. Those at Chepstow that day or watching at home on television were about to witness one of the great Welsh National performances. Johnson tracked the leaders on the first circuit but took it up at the tenth, and he and his horse then set out to gallop their rivals into submission. They were 6 lengths clear two fences from home and although the Irish-trained outsider Raz de Maree (who went on to win the race a year later) did stay on well in the closing stages to make a race of it, Native River, with the champion jockey riding out all the way to the line, always had him held. The first two finished 15 lengths clear of the field.

The only disappointment of the season for Johnson and Native River was that such a stellar campaign didn't culminate in a Gold Cup victory in March, but a combination of the ground (too fast) and it probably being one race too many after a hard season meant the difference between a win and a gallant third place behind Sizing John and Minella Rocco. Still, as we'll see, glorious compensation awaited just twelve months later.

Johnson landed his second title with 189 winners.

Having failed to win the Gold Cup in 2017 with Native River, Colin Tizzard planned a much lighter campaign for his horse in 2017/18 with everything geared to the big day in March. In fact, due to a ligament problem, the Hennessy and Welsh National hero of 2016 only had the one run before Cheltenham, when, ridden by Johnson, he won under hands and heels in the Denman Chase at Newbury on 10 February. Despite getting his favoured ground (soft-heavy in places), Native River started the 2018 Gold Cup as only the third favourite, at 5-1, behind the RSA and King George winner Might Bite (4-1) and Irish National winner Our Duke (9-2). It was to be a race for the ages. Johnson and his mount set off in front but Might Bite and Nico de Boinville kept pressing them throughout. When Might Bite took a narrow advantage two out, there would undoubtedly have been many watching who thought 'this is where he takes over'. But Johnson and Native River were having none of it. Native River rallied, regained the lead and stayed on gamely all the way up the hill, defying Might Bite's challenge. It had been an epic duel. The *Guardian*'s Greg Wood described it as 'one of the most thrilling and compelling spectacles that anyone in the 70,000 crowd could remember'. Johnson had been superb, getting all his percentages right, and judging everything perfectly, but with characteristic modesty deflected all the praise onto his horse in post-race interviews. 'It's always down to the horse. If they get into a rhythm, riding from the front is easy as you've got nothing to get in your way.'

Eighteen years on from his first Gold Cup win, Dicky had done it again, in a race that will be talked about for years to come. The fact that he had to wait so long since his last Gold Cup success made it all the more special.

Johnson's third title was attained with 176 winners, but his fourth, in 2018/19, achieved at the age of 41, saw him top the double-century for the second time, finishing on the 201-winner mark.

The early pacesetter in the jockey's championship that year was Harry Skelton, who had finished third behind Johnson a year earlier. At one point he was twenty-seven winners ahead. However, Johnson rode a five-timer at Perth in late September (his second of the season there) to cut the deficit and then a double at Newton Abbot on 1 October put him ahead. That came just a week after he had ridden his 3,500th career winner at Warwick.

Skelton, though, kept up his pursuit over the winter and continued to give the champion a good run for his money. There was a big race win for Dicky to celebrate at Kempton on Boxing Day when La Bague Au Roi landed the Grade One Kauto Star Novices' Chase (previously known as The Feltham), and a few days later the Festive season got even better for him when it was announced he was being awarded an OBE in the New Year Honours List.

At the Cheltenham Festival of 2019, Native River couldn't match his Gold Cup heroics of a year earlier, but still finished a creditable fourth behind Al Boum Photo. Johnson finished the season twenty-three winners ahead of Skelton, who had actually bettered Johnson's 2017/18 winning tally by two.

In 2019/20, Dicky faced a strong challenge in the jockey's championship from the northern-based rider Brian Hughes. The story of this season, which ended abruptly due to the Coronavirus lockdown, is told in our next chapter. Hughes became champion, and Johnson was runner-up for the seventeenth time in his career. He was, by now, 26 years in the game. Only AP McCoy had ridden more winners: no British jockey had ridden more winners at the Cheltenham Festival.

Dicky had achieved just about everything there was to achieve, with the only two gaps in his CV being a win in the King George and, like so many great champions before him, the Grand National. He holds the record for the most appearances in the race (twenty-one) and the most rides in it without success. The closest he came was in 2002, when he was mugged by Jim Culloty and Bindaree in the shadow of the post on What's Up Boys, having been 3 lengths clear at the Elbow. In 2014, he finished second again, on another Philip Hobbs horse, Balthazar King.

When jump racing resumed again in the summer of 2020, albeit 'behind closed doors', Dicky carried on where he had left off. On Friday, 2 October 2020 he was at Fontwell on a very wet day to ride Imperial Presence, the sole runner on the card for Philip Hobbs. The 9-year-old had won last time out on good ground at Stratford, making virtually all, but was now 3lb higher in the weights and having to concede weight all round on very different going. It appeared a tough task, as reflected in the horse drifting in the betting to 5–1 in the nine-runner event. In fact, before racing began it was only fifty-fifty that the horse would run at all.

Johnson set off in front again and got some great jumps from his mount. At three out, though, it looked as if he would be passed, as Aintree My Dream and Drumcliff, both carrying much less weight in the testing conditions, loomed up beside him. But Dicky dug deep. His horse, like so many others of his 3,700–odd winners down the years, kept finding more. There was a tremendous battle on the run-in between Imperial Presence and Aintree My Dream, with Johnson straining every sinew to get his horse over the line first. He won by a neck. I was watching the race with Diana Hobbs, daughter of Philip. After punching the air, she turned to me, smiling, and said, 'He's not a bad jockey, is he!'

Not a bad jockey indeed.

UPDATE: Richard Johnson announced his retirement with immediate effect after riding at Newton Abbot on Easter Saturday, 2021. He rode a total of 3,819 winners, a number only surpassed by AP McCoy.

Big race wins
Stayers' Hurdle 1999 (Anzum)
Welsh Grand National 1999 (Edmond), 2016 (Native River)
Gold Cup 2000 (Looks Like Trouble), 2018 (Native River)
Champion Chase 2002 (Flagship Uberalles)
Champion Hurdle 2003 (Rooster Booster)
Whitbread Gold Cup (as previously known) 2006 (Lacdoudal), 2008 (Monkerhostin)
Scottish Grand National 2011 (Beshabar)
Hennessy Gold Cup 2016 (Native River)

Chapter Twenty-One

Brian Hughes

Champion 2019/20, 2021/22

Waiting Patiently

'You wouldn't believe where I was when the official call came through that I had won the title – out on a tractor rolling the fields on the farm.'
Brian Hughes

In a season unexpectedly cut short by an unprecedented national lockdown, Brian Hughes became, in 2020, the first northern-based champion jump jockey for forty years. But while Hughes bucked a trend in that respect, he maintained one in another. It's interesting to reflect that every champion since 1985 has either come from Herefordshire (Peter Scudamore and Richard Johnson) or Northern Ireland (Dunwoody, McCoy and Hughes). It's not just the retro, rural nature of Herefordshire and parts of Ulster, where horses remain an integral part of life, that accounts for this, it's also the way previous champions became 'local heroes' for later generations to follow. We've seen how Johnson was inspired by Scu. How AP looked up to Dunwoody. Hughes, born in Newtownhamilton, in southern Armagh, in 1986, looked up to McCoy. They had much in common. Both their fathers were carpenters. Both came from large Catholic families – AP has four sisters, Hughes five. Both are teetotal non-smokers. And both got to the top by being serious minded, hard-working and extremely focused.

But there were important differences too. Hughes's riding style could be described as 'quieter' than McCoy's. For his own part, Hughes, a man of great humility, is at pains not to compare himself with the twenty-time champion. 'AP was a hell of a lot better jockey than me. So is Richard Johnson. I am humbled to be mentioned in the same sentence as them but I am immensely proud to be going down in the history books as champion jockey,' he said after winning his title.

The twenty-first champion since the Second World War certainly didn't have it easy. He survived the life-threatening disease meningitis as a child. He always wanted to be a jockey and like so many other champions before him was out hunting at an early age. At the age of 14 he started riding out for trainer James Lambe. On leaving school at 16, he headed south, like McCoy, to the Irish Republic, to begin his apprenticeship as a Flat jockey with the veteran Curragh-based trainer Kevin Prendergast. He was good jockey on the level, winning twenty-two times, with his first success coming at Downpatrick in October 2002. But his increasing weight became a problem and on James Lambe's advice he came to England to pursue a National Hunt career. He got a job at the yard of County Durham handler Howard Johnson, then a major force in the jumping ranks. He got on very well for the first six months, riding eleven winners. Stable jockey to Johnson at the time was Graham Lee, who became a great source of support and influenced Hughes's own riding style. 'I loved the way he rode,' he tells me. 'Very smooth, and very quiet,' he says. Like Lee, Hughes learnt to use the whip sparingly. But when Lee left, he struggled to get rides.

His father urged him to keep at it, and fortunately he listened to his advice. Thirty-nine winners in 2007/08, after he had moved to the yard of Richmond trainer Alan Swinbank, provided the steps for Hughes to become champion conditional that season. The trainer providing the highest number of his winners that year was actually the County Durham permit-holder John Wade, one of the handlers regularly using the young Irishman.

For the next five seasons Hughes rode from 44 to 65 winners. Steadily, in his own low-key, no-fuss way, he was building up a reputation in the North as a skilful and very reliable rider, with great tactical awareness. He was also extremely conscientious. Cornelius Lysaght, the BBC's former racing correspondent, recalled meeting Hughes walking the course before racing at Ayr. 'He was busy reeling off form and analysis of every runner.'

In addition to his work ethic, Hughes also had faith. His family ties are strong: attached to his body protector is a St Padre Pio medal, which his mother believes saved him from dying from meningitis as a child.

In 2010 he pulled off a notable double over the Grand National fences by winning both the Topham and the Sefton Chase at Aintree on Always Waining and Frankie Figg. Yet, like so many champions before him, he has been out of luck up to now in the Grand National itself.[1] He says it's the race he most wants to win, even more than the Gold Cup. If he does he will

---

[1] In the 2021 Grand National, Hughes fell at the first fence on Lake View Lad.

be emulating not just two great Northern Irish champions, Dunwoody and McCoy, but also fellow Ulsterman Tony Dobbin, who won the 1997 race on Lord Gyllene and who was another rider he looked up to.

The season of 2013/14 saw Hughes's winners' total almost double from forty-four to eighty-six. It was a season that saw him record his first Cheltenham Festival success, on Hawk High for Tim Easterby in the Fred Winter, a win that was all the more satisfying since it came just a day after a narrow defeat on Attaglance in the Novices' Handicap Chase. You could say his path towards the champion jockey's title began in earnest around 2015, when he posted his first century and won the BoyleSports Hurdle at Leopardstown on Katie T for his old boss Prendergast.

A year later, when his winners total jumped to 144, he rode an 899-1 five-timer at Musselburgh in November and finished second in the other two races. Again, he downplayed the achievement, saying that any other jockey would have won on the quintet. The five-timer came during an amazing 'hot' streak, when Hughes rode forty-three winners from the start of November to mid-December.

Of course, being jump racing, there were plenty of 'down' moments too. In the spring of 2016, two falls left him with a broken collarbone, shoulder blade and four vertebrae.

Hughes added to his Cheltenham Festival success with a victory in 2016 on Ballyalton in the Close Brothers Handicap Chase; he won the same race again in 2018 on the Mick Channon-trained Mister Whitaker, who he coolly produced with a great late run to beat Rather Be literally right on the line. 'The margins can be very small,' he says. 'If you time it just right, it's a great ride, but if you don't, then it's a different story.' By now he was firmly established as the North's top jump jockey. In fact, since the start of the decade, he had been in increasing demand with a wide number of trainers. One of these was Malcolm Jefferson, a lovely 'old-school' North Country handler who enjoyed a real renaissance in the 2010s from his base near Malton in Yorkshire. Again, Jefferson was impressed not just by Hughes's riding, but his diligence. 'I think he lives in the form book. He'll come in the morning to ride out and say there's a race for such and such. It all helps,' he told the *Yorkshire Post*.

Hughes rode Jefferson's highly promising chaser Waiting Patiently – aptly named given his trainer's patient approach and the horse's come-from-behind style of running – to six consecutive victories from November 2016 to February 2018. On 13 January 2018 he piloted the 7-year-old to a facile 8-length success in a listed chase at Kempton, but sadly, by the time the horse next lined up, for the Grade 1 Ascot Chase in February, Malcolm Jefferson had died of cancer.

At Ascot, Hughes and Waiting Patiently were up against the hugely popular former King George winner Cue Card. Colin Tizzard's chaser was now 12 and retirement was looming. But having fallen in two of his last four starts, and been thrashed out of sight in the Betfair by Bristol De Mai on his previous run, Cue Card rolled back the years at Ascot, putting in a gallant performance from the front. Hughes, as always, kept Waiting Patiently off the pace towards the back and began to make his move with about half a mile to go. He overtook Cue Card two out, but the veteran rallied again, to a loud roar from the crowd. In the end, though, the younger horse prevailed by just over 2 lengths in a classic inter-generational encounter. There was relief that Cue Card was back safe and sound (he was retired after his next race when pulled up at the Cheltenham Festival), but there was also great emotion surrounding the winner, now trained by Jefferson's daughter Ruth. How her father, who had been laid to rest just a day earlier, would have loved to have seen his horse's first Grade 1 win, which was also Hughes's first win at the very highest level. For good measure, he rode a treble on the card.

Hughes finished the campaign as runner-up to Richard Johnson in the jockey's championship for the second year running, with 142 winners.

In May, his chances of winning the title were boosted when he became Grand National-winning trainer Donald McCain's first choice jockey. At Christmas that year (2018), he was very unlucky when Waiting Patiently, backed in to 4-1 for the King George, unseated him having been badly hampered at the ninth fence by the falling Bristol De Mai. The horse would surely have brought Hughes further top grade success, but has had a frustrating time of things with injuries after his Ascot win.[2]

Four days into 2019, Hughes rode his 1,000th winner at Wetherby on Friday on My Old Gold, becoming only the twenty-fifth jockey in Britain and Ireland to achieve the feat. But there was no resting on his laurels: one day later, he rode a 35-1 treble at Newcastle.

A sign of Hughes's dedication to his job – and the way he balances it with his commitment to his family – came in Grand National week of 2019 when his wife Lucy was due to give birth. Rather than accept a ride in the National, he committed himself to six rides at Newcastle to be nearer home. Lucy gave birth to the couple's second child on Grand National morning, and having made sure everything was fine with his wife and baby in hospital, Hughes then set off to Gosforth Park to fulfil his riding commitments. Unfortunately

---

[2] Hughes and Waiting Patiently finished a close second in the 2020 King George, on the horse's first run for over a year.

it wasn't a good day at the office. He broke his jaw after being kicked in the face by Bingo D'Olivate following a fall when disputing the lead. So that night, while his wife was in hospital in Middlesbrough, he was in another hospital in Newcastle. 'It broke my jaw in three places and knocked all my teeth out. It wasn't too bad,' he later remarked, proving once again that National Hunt jockeys are a breed apart.

Hughes finished the 2018/19 season on the 146-winner mark, his highest score yet, but would have easily surpassed his ambition of riding 150 winners without that Newcastle accident, which put him out of action for the rest of the season. At the time, he was lying third in the jockey's standings, behind Johnson and Harry Skelton.

Having finished in the top three in the three previous seasons, in 2019/20 the championship door finally opened for the man who had been 'waiting patiently'.

In an interview in the *Racing Post* on 1 November 2019, Julian Muscat raised with Hughes the prospects of him becoming champion that season. Muscat noted that from the start of November through to the season's close in April, Hughes had ridden more winners than Richard Johnson in two of the previous three campaigns – by eighteen winners in 2016/17 and thirteen the following year. Johnson had got a great start by winning lots of races over the summer and autumn, but his lead at the end of October 2019 was just four. 'Let's see where we are at Christmas,' replied Hughes. 'If you're in contention you'd put it to the forefront of your mind. Part of not thinking about it is to avoid putting myself under pressure. When you start to force the situation, you start making mistakes. You try too hard and overthink things.'

A feature race double at Doncaster on the Saturday before Christmas, followed by a fabulous four-timer at Carlisle a day later, put him level with Johnson on ninety-five winners. 'Jockeys Richard Johnson and Brian Hughes set for titanic battle in 2020' was the headline of the *Cumbria News & Star*, but neither the paper nor the two protagonists could possibly have predicted how the 2019/20 season would eventually pan out.

Hughes led Johnson by three when Johnson broke his right arm in a fall at Exeter on 21 January. That appeared to shift things decisively in the challenger's favour but, as we've seen, the reigning champion made a speedy return to action in late February and won on four of his first seven rides back. The pair clashed head-to-head for the first time since Johnson's return at Sedgefield on Sunday, 1 March. Johnson's mount, Strong Glance, was the 1-5 favourite, but it was Hughes who made all to win by 32 lengths on the 4-1 shot Baron de Midleton.

'Regarding the championship, I'm not getting carried away yet,' Hughes said prior to the 2020 Cheltenham Festival. Just over a week later, though, the season was all over. There was a strange atmosphere at Prestbury Park on Friday, 13 March, when the excitement of another great day's racing, topped off by Al Boum Photo's second consecutive Gold Cup win, was mixed with a feeling of dread about what lay ahead with new Covid-19 restrictions predicted to soon come into force.

On Monday, 16 March – the last day that racing took place in front of a crowd before lockdown intervened – the score was 1-1 between Hughes and Johnson. Hughes rode a winner at Kelso (the 5-2 favourite Proper Ticket in the Novices' Handicap Hurdle), Johnson, one at Hereford. Appropriately enough, the last winner of a race in Britain held in the presence of paying spectators, the 4.50 pm at Hereford, was a horse called The Edgar Wallace, named after the prolific thriller writer and racing journalist. What was happening in Britain in the last two weeks of March 2020 was truly 'stranger than fiction' – the title of my 2014 biography of Wallace.

Racing stopped altogether following 'behind-closed-doors' meetings at Wetherby and Taunton on 17 March, and on 6 April it was confirmed that the season – and the championship – was over, all of six weeks early. Hughes had done it, beating Johnson by nineteen (141-122), but not in the circumstances he would have liked. 'I felt really sorry for him because there was no coronation at Sandown. He deserved that,' Johnson, ever the sportsman, told me. Not only was there no 'coronation' or 'guard of honour' at the end of April, the news that we had a new champion jump jockey – only the fifth in thirty-five years – was submerged in the 24/7 media coverage of Covid-19.

Hughes finally got his hand on the championship trophy when jump racing resumed after a four-month break in July. Generous tributes were paid to the new champion by those Brian rode for.

Nicky Richards, son of Gordon, drew parallels with previous northern-based champions Ron Barry and Jonjo O'Neill, who had also ridden Greystoke horses: 'There are definitely similarities between the three of them in that they work very, very hard and have a lot of self-belief. Brian always has time and advice for the lads and lasses at the yard and that shows you how much of a decent human being he is.'

In the 2020/21 season, Hughes fought hard to retain his title but in the end lost out to Harry Skelton, whose story is told in our final chapter.

Big race wins
Ascot Chase 2018 (Waiting Patiently)

Chapter Twenty-Two

Harry Skelton

Champion 2020/21

A Family Affair

'A very determined jockey from a great, achieving family.'
Sir Rupert Mackeson Bt.

And so, to the final fence. As this book was going into production, a new champion was crowned. In an enthralling three-way title race which only swung decisively in his favour in the final two weeks of the season, Harry Skelton became the twenty-second post-war champion jump jockey, landing the title with 152 winners in a season that started two months late due to the national lockdown.

If the name 'Skelton' sounds familiar, it's no surprise. Harry comes from a family that has excelled in equestrianism. His father Nick was a top showjumper for over thirty years, winning gold as a member of the UK team at the 2012 London Olympics, and then, at the age of 58, an individual gold at Rio four years later on his horse Big Star. What made those accomplishments all the more remarkable was that he was coming back to the sport after a serious neck injury in 2000, which looked to have ended his career and did indeed lead to temporary retirement.

Nick Skelton's two sons certainly had a hard act to follow, but they have both done their famous father proud. Dan Skelton is a highly successful, upwardly mobile National Hunt trainer, whose horses – often super-fit front-runners – have helped propel younger brother Harry to the jockey's title.

As a youngster Harry looked as if he was on a path to becoming a showjumper like his illustrious dad. But a summer holiday working for the veteran Staffordshire trainer Reg Hollinshead in the early 2000s whetted an appetite for riding racehorses. With his light weight, a career on the Flat appeared the logical route, and he did spend time with the Classic-winning Richard Hannon yard. But when brother Dan became assistant trainer to multiple champion National Hunt trainer Paul Nicholls in Ditcheat, Harry moved to Somerset as the stable amateur.

His first winner came on 1 October 2007 on a horse called Temper Lad, trained by Jimmy Frost, in a conditional jockey's selling handicap hurdle at Exeter. Skelton was just 17 at the time. In 2009 he became the youngest jockey to win the Irish Grand National when, still a teenager, he partnered Bob Buckler's 33-1 shot Niche Market to victory in the Easter Monday showpiece. The *Irish Independent* newspaper reported:

> HARRY SKELTON, a 19-year-old from Warwickshire, in England, would have walked into Fairyhouse racecourse for the first time yesterday, unknown to the majority of the 15,076 paying customers in attendance, and hopeful more than confident about the business to which he was attending.

> But by 4.10 pm he had joined an elite crew from his chosen profession and was posing for more photographers than an average Page 3 model.

In 2009/10 he rode thirty-one winners as a conditional, but then, after such a flying start, his career began to stall. Opportunities – and winners – for Nicholls became thinner on the ground after he lost his claim, so when brother Dan branched out on his own and set up as a trainer in his own right at his father's farm at Alcester in Warwickshire in 2013, Harry went with him. 'Team Skelton' was officially born.

Having ridden just eight winners in the 2012/13 season, Skelton's tally increased to fifty-five in 2014/15 – and a year later he posted his first century.

Each year was a case of 'onwards and upwards' for Warwickshire's 'brothers in arms'. In 2016 there was a first Cheltenham Festival winner, Superb Story, who landed the County Hurdle. Nick Skelton said in a 2017 Jockey Club podcast: 'Harry said when I won the gold medal was the proudest day of his life but for me when they won there [Cheltenham] that was the proudest day of my life.'

At a time when English trainers were finding it increasingly hard to land a blow at Cheltenham against top-class Irish opposition, Team Skelton were responsible for three more Festival winners over hurdles in 2018 and 2019, including their first Grade 1 success, Roksana, in the 2019 Mares' Hurdle. While Harry rode Roksana and Ch'tibello (the 2019 County Hurdle winner), the other Skelton Festival winner, Mohaayed, who won the County Hurdle in 2018, was ridden by his girlfriend, Bridget Andrews, who a year later became his wife.

All the time he was enjoying more big race success, Harry was getting closer and closer to the jockey's title. He was third in 2017/18. In 2018/19, brother Dan went into overdrive, saddling 205 winners – the highest total since the days of Martin Pipe. One hundred and eighty-three of them were ridden by Harry – a grand enough tally that would have been enough to land him the championship in three of the previous ten years, but not in the year when Dicky Johnson, enjoying his best-ever campaign, rode 210.

In 2019/20, Skelton, having ridden Politologue to victory in the Champion Chase at the Cheltenham Festival, finished third behind Brian Hughes and Johnson in a season that, as we've seen, ended prematurely in late March due to the Covid lockdown.

Jump racing did not resume until July, and when it did it was in very different circumstances. A ban on jockeys riding at more than one meeting a day had been imposed and remained in force for the whole season. Continued restrictions meant that, save for a brief period at some 'lower tier' venues in December, the action took place 'behind closed doors', with no paying spectators in attendance. Furthermore, jockeys were also required to wear face masks, adding to the air of abnormality. Strange times, but the sport itself, even if most could only watch it on television, remained as thrilling as ever.

For much of the campaign, Brian Hughes, as consistent as ever on the northern circuit, looked likely to follow up his 2019/20 championship success. If Hughes was to be toppled, then Paul Nicholls's stable jockey Harry Cobden, who cut the champions' lead to nine in early November, appeared the best-placed challenger.

But Skelton was enjoying some nice pay days. At Sandown on Saturday, 5 December, he landed two Grade 1s within the space of forty-five minutes. What made the feat even more noteworthy is that he was never headed in either race. First, he piloted his brother's Allmankind to victory in the Henry VIII Novices' Chase. Then he rode Paul Nicholls's Politologue – the horse on which he had won the Champion Chase nine months earlier – to win the Tingle Creek.

More big race success for Team Skelton followed at Kempton Park over Christmas. In the Grade 2 Desert Orchid Chase, Altior, the dual Champion Chase winner, was the even money favourite, but Skelton, having held up the 20-1 shot Nube Negra in rear in the early stages, forged clear two out and Altior had no answer. A day earlier, the Skeltons had landed the Grade 1 Kauto Star Novices' Chase, as hat-trick-seeking Shan Blue justified 7-4 favouritism.

Going into the third week of January, Skelton was still third in the title race, behind Hughes and Cobden, but in the last three months of the season he delivered a title challenge so strong that it proved to be unstoppable. On 20 February, another big race Saturday win came on Captain Chaos, who raced at or near the head of affairs for every yard of the 3-mile Listed Swinley Chase at Ascot, and who just held off a very late challenge from the veteran course specialist Regal Encore. Again, it was a classic 'take no prisoners' Harry Skelton ride. There were two more winners on the Ascot card for him that day, adding up to a 320.75-1 treble. Skelton later said his victory on Shannon Bridge, the third-leg of his treble, was the turning point of his title challenge. 'I knew then that it could be on and once I had a sniff of something I was willing to give it my all,' he told the *Racing Post*.

On 24 March he rode a 67-1 four-timer at Hereford to cut Hughes's lead to five. He still trailed Hughes by three on Grand National day, but an impressive Grade 1 win at Aintree on My Drogo in the Grade 1 Betway Novices' Hurdle, and three winners at Southwell three days later, tilted the balance very much in his favour.

At the meeting at Bangor on 17 April, which started earlier than scheduled to avoid a clash with the funeral of HRH The Duke of Edinburgh, Skelton rode another double to extend his lead to six.

When he moved ten clear of Hughes with just three days to go, the bookies suspended betting on the title race. On the last day of the season at Sandown, Harry received his trophy, and looked to have sealed a great campaign with victory in the final big race of the year, the Bet365 Gold Cup, formerly known as the 'Whitbread'. He was first past the post on Enrilo but was demoted to third in the stewards' room due to interference with the third-place finisher Kitty's Light. Enrilo was trained by Paul Nicholls, who had just been crowned champion trainer for the twelfth time.

If ever an afternoon summed up the jump racing game it was Sandown on 24 April 2021. Or, as Skelton himself put it, 'the ups and downs'. But while losing the Whitbread would have been disappointing, 2020/21 certainly had a lot more ups than downs.

The final score in the title race was: Skelton, 152 winners from 683 rides (strike rate of 22 per cent); Hughes, 142 winners from 890 rides (16 per cent); and Cobden, 123 winners from 582 rides (21 per cent).

Harry Skelton might have become a champion showjumper, perhaps representing the UK in the Olympics like his father, but now – thirteen and a half years on from riding his first winner – he had become a champion jump jockey.

From Rimell in the 1940s to Skelton in the 2020s, we have told the story of twenty-two champions. Some won multiple titles, others 'just' one or two, but all showed tremendous skill, determination and bravery to come out top in one of the toughest sporting contests of them all. As we reflect on the thrills and spills of the last seventy-five years, let's raise our glasses to the champion jump jockeys' achievements and the great sport of National Hunt racing that they, and others, have enriched. No more heroes anymore? There are still plenty in what the late Queen Mother described as one of the last real sports that's left to us.

Big Race wins
Champion Chase 2020 (Politologue)

Champion Jump Jockeys 1945 to Present Day

Season	Champion	Number of winners
1945/46	T.F. Rimell	54
1946/47	J. Dowdeswell	58
1947/48	B. Marshall	66
1948/49	T. Molony	60
1949/50	T. Molony	95
1950/51	T. Molony	83
1951/52	T. Molony	99
1952/53	F. Winter	121
1953/54	R. Francis	76
1954/55	T. Molony	67
1955/56	F. Winter	74
1956/57	F. Winter	80
1957/58	F. Winter	82
1958/59	T. Brookshaw	83
1959/60	S. Mellor	68
1960/61	S. Mellor	118
1961/62	S. Mellor	80
1962/63	J. Gifford	70
1963/64	J. Gifford	94
1964/65	T. Biddlecombe	114
1965/66	T. Biddlecombe	102
1966/67	J. Gifford	122
1967/68	J. Gifford	82
1968/69*	T. Biddlecombe	77
	B.R. Davies	77
1969/70	B.R. Davies	91

Season	Champion	Number of winners
1970/71	G. Thorner	74
1971/72	B.R. Davies	89
1972/73	R. Barry	125
1973/74	R. Barry	94
1974/75	T. Stack	82
1975/76	J. Francome	96
1976/77	T. Stack	97
1977/78	J.J. O'Neill	149
1978/79	J. Francome	95
1979/80	J.J. O'Neill	115
1980/81	J. Francome	105
1981/82*	J. Francome	120
	P. Scudamore	120
1982/83	J. Francome	106
1983/84	J. Francome	131
1984/85	J. Francome	101
1985/86	P. Scudamore	91
1986/87	P. Scudamore	124
1987/88	P. Scudamore	132
1988/89	P. Scudamore	221
1989/90	P. Scudamore	170
1990/91	P. Scudamore	141
1991/92	P. Scudamore	175
1992/93	R. Dunwoody	173
1993/94	R. Dunwoody	197
1994/95	R. Dunwoody	160
1995/96	AP McCoy	175
1996/97	AP McCoy	190
1997/98	AP McCoy	253
1998/99	AP McCoy	186
1999/2000	AP McCoy	245
2000/01	AP McCoy	191

Season	Champion	Number of winners
2001/02	AP McCoy	289
2002/03	AP McCoy	258
2003/04	AP McCoy	209
2004/05	AP McCoy	200
2005/06	AP McCoy	178
2006/07	AP McCoy	184
2007/08	AP McCoy	140
2008/09	AP McCoy	186
2009/10	AP McCoy	195
2010/11	AP McCoy	218
2011/12	AP McCoy	199
2012/13	AP McCoy	185
2013/14	AP McCoy	218
2014/15	AP McCoy	231
2015/16	R. Johnson	235
2016/17	R. Johnson	180
2017/18	R. Johnson	176
2018/19	R. Johnson	200
2019/20	B. Hughes	141
2020/21	Harry Skelton	152
2021/22	B. Hughes	204

* indicates title was tied

Bibliography and Further Reading

Books

ARMYTAGE, Marcus, *Hot Cherry: The Best of Marcus Armytage*, Highdown, 2005.

AUSTEN, Richard, *At the Festival: Racing to Glory at Cheltenham in March*, Sportsbooks, 2015.

BEAVIS, Jim, *The History of Fontwell Park*, self-published, 2008.

BEAVIS, Jim, *The History of Uttoxeter Racecourse*, self-published, 2015.

BEAVIS, Jim, *The History of Royal Windsor Racecourse*, self-published, 2016.

BETTISON, Clive, *The Riding Career of Jack Dowdeswell*, self-published, 2007.

BIDDLECOMBE, Terry (with Pat Lucas), *Winner's Disclosure*, Hutchinson, 1982.

BUDDEN, John, *The Boss: The Life and Times of Horseracing Legend Gordon Richards*, Mainstream Publishing, 2000.

BUGLASS, Dan, *Ken Oliver: The Benign Bishop*, Marlborough Books, 1994.

CARTER, John, *Warriors on Horseback: The Inside Story of the Professional Jockey*, Bloomsbury Sport, 2016.

COLLENS, Rupert, *50 Cheltenham Gold Cups 1945–1994*, Sporting Garland, 1995.

COOK, Chris, *The Scudamores: Three of a Kind*, Racing Post, 2018.

CRANHAM, Gerry & PITMAN, Richard, *The Guinness Book of Steeplechasing*, Guinness World Records, 1988.

DAVIES, Jennifer, *Tales of the Old Horsemen*, David & Charles, 1997.

DUNWOODY, Richard, *Obsessed: The Autobiography*, Headline, 2000.

DUNWOODY, Richard, *Method in My Madness: 10 Years out of the Saddle*, Thomas Brightman, 2009.

FITZGEORGE-PARKER, Tim, *Steeplechase Jockeys: The Great Ones*, Pelham Books, 1971.

FITZGEORGE-PARKER, Tim, *The Ditch on the Hill: 80 Years of the Cheltenham Festival*, Simon & Schuster, 1991.

FRANCOME, John, *Born Lucky: An Autobiography*, Pelham Books, 1985.

FRANCIS, Dick, *The Sport of Queens*, Michael Joseph, 1957.

FULLER, Bryony, *Vincent O'Brien: The National Hunt Years*, Punchestown Books, 1992.

GRAHAM, Clive & CURLING, Bill, *The Grand National*, Barrie & Jenkins, 1972.

GREEN, Reg, *The History of the Grand National: A Race Apart*, Hodder & Stoughton, 1992.

HEDGES, David, *Mr Grand National: A biography of Fred Winter*, Pelham Books, 1969.

HERBERT, Ivor, *Red Rum 1965–1995: The extraordinary story of a horse of courage*, Century, 1995.

HERBERT, Ivor, *Winter's Tale: Study of a Stable*, Pelham Books, 1974.

HERBERT, Ivor & SMYLY, Patricia, *The Winter Kings*, Pelham Books, 1968.

JOHNSON, Richard, *Out of the Shadows*, Greenwater Publishing, 2002.

KNIGHT, Henrietta, *Not Enough Time: My Life with Terry Biddlecombe*, Head of Zeus, 2015.

KNIGHT, Henrietta, *Starting from Scratch: Inspired to be a Jump Jockey*, Racing Post, 2019.

LEE, Alan (with KING, Jeff), *Jump Jockeys*, Ward Lock, 1980.

MASSINGBERD, Hugh, *Daydream Believer*, Pan, 2001.

MATTHEWS, Mart, *The Racing Post Quiz Book*, Racing Post, 2019.

McCOY, A.P., *My Autobiography*, Orion, 2011.

MELLOR, Elain et al, *Stan Mellor: 1000 Winners* (private limited edition), Haymarket, 1992.

MORSHEAD, Sam, *Racing Through Life: A Jump Jockey's Tale*, Racing Post, 2016.

OAKLEY, Robin & GILLESPIE, Edward, *Sixty Years of Jump Racing: From Arkle to McCoy*, Bloomsbury Sport, 2017.

O'NEILL, Jonjo (with RICHARDS, Tim), *Jonjo: An Autobiography*, Hutchinson, 1985.

ONSLOW, Richard et al, *Great Racing Gambles & Frauds*, Vol 2, Marlborough Books, 1992.

O'SULLEVAN, Peter, *Calling the Horses: A Racing Autobiography*, Stanley Paul & Co., 1989.

O'SULLEVAN, Sir Peter, *Horse Racing Heroes*, Highdown, 2004.

PINFOLD, John, *An Aintree Dynasty, The Tophams and Their Grand National*, Trafford Publishing, 2006.

PIPE, Martin (with PITMAN, Richard), *The Champion Trainer's Story*, Headline Books, 1992.

PITT, Chris, *A Long Time Gone*, Halifax Portway Press, 1996.

PITT, Chris, *Fearless: The Tim Brookshaw Story*, Racing Post, 2020.
RIMELL, Fred & RIMELL, Mercy, *Aintree Iron, The Autobiography of Fred & Mercy Rimell*, W.H. Allen, 1977.
ROBINSON, Nick & LLEWELLYN, David, *The Book of Racing Quotations*, Hutchinson, 1988.
SCUDAMORE, Peter, *Scu: The Autobiography of a Champion*, Headline, 1993.
SHARPE, Graham, *Racing Dates: Classic Moments in the Sport of Kings*, Virgin Books, 1993.
SHARPE, Graham, *Racing's Greatest Characters: Fabulous Stories of Winners and Losers, Runners and Riders*, JR Books, 2009.
SHARPE, Graham, *500 Strangest Racing Stories*, Highdown, 2007.
SHERWOOD, Simon, *Nine Out of Ten*, Lambourn Press, 1989.
TYRREL, John, *Chasing Around Britain*, Crowood Press, 1990.

Newspapers, magazines, annuals and websites

British Newspaper Archive, https://www.britishnewspaperarchive.co.uk/
Jockeypedia, https://sites.google.com/view/testjockey/home
The Sporting Life
Racing Post, https://www.racingpost.com/
Racing & Football Outlook
RFO Jumping Annuals (various years)
The Horseman's Year 1948–1955 (edited by W.E. Lyon)
The Sporting Life Grand National Souvenir Magazine (1988 & 1989)

Film

150 Years of the Grand National, written and narrated by Richard Pitman, VHS BBC video, 1988.
YouTube (for old races)

Book dust jacket photographs

Top left: Stan Mellor
Top right: John Francome with HM The Queen Mother (Lord Oaksey in centre) *(Photo: David Hastings)*
Bottom left: Dick Francis
Bottom centre: AP McCoy after winning the 2010 Grand National on Don't Push It *(Photo: Steve Davies)*
Bottom right and inside cover: Tim Molony on Sir Ken

Index

Names of horses are denoted in italics

Abergavenny, Lord, 54
Adelphi Hotel, Liverpool, 24, 26
Aintree/Liverpool, 17, 27, 31, 37, 58,
    60, 64, 70, 72–3, 75, 80, 82, 90,
    94, 97, 104, 108–109, 117–18,
    133, 137, 150, 153, 158, 189–90,
    196–7, 210, 215, 223
  Grand National, 4, 5, 10, 11, 18, 21,
    25–8, 32, 34, 37–8, 41, 43, 47–9,
    55, 57–62, 64, 74–5, 77, 82, 85–6,
    92, 94–5, 97, 99, 103–105, 108,
    110, 111, 117–21, 123–4, 129,
    132–4, 136–7, 139, 145, 149–50,
    153, 156, 158, 161, 174, 176, 178–9,
    183, 186, 188–90, 194, 199, 201–
    202, 204–205, 212, 215, 217, 224
Aintree My Dream, 212
Al Boum Photo, 212, 219
Al Trui, 75
Aldaniti, 75, 77, 87
Alers-Hankey, Dominic, 115
Alexandra Parade, 153
Alfaraiso, 43
Alger, 14
Allaho, 191
Allmankind, 222
Altior, 222
Alverton, 75, 118, 154–5, 158–9, 162
Always Waining, 215
Ancil Derek, 70–2
Andrews, Bridget, 221
Andrews, Eamonn, 101
Andy Pandy, 133

Anglo, 46, 94
Another Dolly, 158
Anti-Matter, 169
Anzum, 206, 213
Approaching, 87
Archer, Fred, 4, 171
Archstone, 33
Arcot, 186
Arctic Gold, 34
Arctic Life, 195
Arkle, 52, 71, 73, 86, 95, 126
Armstrong, Sam, 78–9
Armytage, Gee, 192
Armytage, Marcus, 27, 113, 115,
    197, 200
Ascot, 73–4, 105–106, 164, 170, 174,
    189, 201, 216–17, 224
Assad, 86
Attaglance, 216
Attaturk, 128
Austen, Archie, 13
Auteuil, 39–40, 158
Authorised, 120
Average, 34
Avionne, 169
Ayr, 72, 81, 94, 123, 125, 132, 173, 215

Badanloch, 69
Bader, Douglas, 65
Bailey, Peter, 131, 138
Balding, Clare, 194
Balding, Gerald, 22, 194
Balding, Ian, 22, 194

Balding, Toby, 22, 161, 194–5
Balkan Flower, 89
Ballyalton, 216
Balthazar King, 212
Bambino II, 41
Bangor-on-Dee, 51, 61, 65, 68, 91,
    109, 156, 163, 186–7, 223
Banks, John, 144
Barclay, John, 91
Baron Blakeney, 163
Barons, David, 104, 106–107
Barrott, Doug, 128
Barry, Ron, 121–32, 137, 152–4, 167, 219
Barton Bank, 184, 196
Battleship, 5, 26
Beasley, Bobby, 73, 80, 90, 100, 130, 189
Beaumont, Peter, 186
Beau Ranger, 168
Beaver II, 40, 80
Beeby, George, 49, 52
Beechener, Cliff, 78
Belmont King, 202
Ben Nevis, 119, 150
Bengough, Colonel Piers, 170
Beshabar, 213
Best Mate, 52, 102, 199, 202
Bicester, Lord, 49, 52–4
Biddle, Ann, 123
Biddlecombe, Terry, 2, 9, 68, 73–4,
    77–81, 83–4, 88–102, 104–106,
    111, 114–17, 121–2, 126, 150
Biddlecombe, Tony, 83, 89
Biddlecombe, Walter, 89
Big Buck's, 36
Bigsun, 181
Billykin, 31
Bindaree, 174, 212
Bingo D'Olivate, 217
Binocular, 201–202
Birmingham, 15, 23, 34–5, 79–80
Birshell, 162
Birthlaw, 8

Bisgood, Commander, 19
Black Apalachi, 201
Black Hawk, 5–7
Black Humour, 171, 182
Black Secret, 117
Blandford, Roy, 94
Blissett, Luther, 168
Blitz Boy, 51
Blond Warrior, 89
Bloom, Jack, 124
Bloom, Michael, 124
Blowing Wind, 199
Bob, 13
Boccaccio, 8
Bogside, 70
Bolger, Jim, 161, 193–4, 203
Bonanza Boy, 168–71, 175
Bonnie Highlander, 114
Bonus Boy, 195
Bosley, John, 178
Bough, Frank, 137
Bounce Back, 202
Bountiful Charles, 125
Bowen, Peter, 205
Bower, John, 105
Bowgeeno, 115, 117
Box Office, 202
Brabazon, Aubrey, 34, 52
Bradbury Star, 87
Bradley, Milton, 205
Brantridge Farmer, 100
Brave Inca, 202
Brewis, Bobby, 156
Bribery, 79
Bricett, 32
Bridge Ash, 204
Bridgwater, David, 195
Brighter Sandy, 31–2
Bristol De Mai, 217
Broadsword, 163
Brogan, Barry, 100, 113, 115–16, 122,
    125, 131, 134, 138

Brooke, Lorna, 2
Brooks, Charlie, 167
Brookshaw, Peter, 103, 58
Brookshaw, Steve, 57
Brookshaw, Tim, 45, 49, 57–66, 68, 70, 80, 88, 103
Brookshaw, Tony, 57, 104
Brown Chamberlin, 146, 148, 150
Brown Jack III, 34
Brown Windsor, 205
Buckfastleigh, 14, 18
Buckingham, John, 85
Buckler, Bob, 221
Buckmaster, 147
Bula, 47, 125, 142, 145
Burlington II, 84
Burnella, 89
Burrough Hill Lad, 148, 150, 168
Butchers, Don, 45
Butler's Cabin, 201
Butters, Joe, 3

Cache Fleur, 187, 190
Cadamstown, 17, 23
Cairo III, 17
Call It A Day, 188
Callaghan, James, 145
Camacho, Maurice, 136
Cantab, 45
Captain Chaos, 222
Captain Christy, 100, 130
Captain Dibble, 173, 175
Carbon, 137
Cardinal Hill, 197
Carlisle, 22, 75, 218
Carlisle Utd, 136
Carmody, 32
Carnival Boy, 8
Carole's Destrier, 210
Carraroe, 45
Cartmel, 67, 174
Carton, 41

Carvill's Hill, 172–5
Castle, Roy, 1
Catapult II, 80
Catterick, 75, 135, 153
Cauthen, Steve, 109
Cavaliero, 33
Caviar, 32
Caulfield, Michael, 189
Cazalet, Edward (Sir), 53
Cazalet, Peter, 24, 27, 53–5, 112
Celtic Rambler, 163
Celtic Ryde, 148
Celtic Shot, 47, 167, 175
Cenkos, 208
Cent Francs, 42
Centaur, 74
Challenger Du Luc, 188
Chamberlain, Neville, 5
Champ, 191
Champion, Bob, 77
Chance, Noel, 196, 206–207
Channon, Mick, 216
Charlie Potheen, 126–9, 132
Charlie Worcester, 86
Charter Party, 165, 180–1, 190
Chatam, 171–2, 175, 199
Chatham, 96
Chauffeur, 61, 69
Chavara, 70
Chela Jau, 70
Chelsea, Lord, 94
Cheltenham, 8, 14, 17, 21–2, 24, 28, 34–8, 45–7, 51–2, 55, 59–63, 69–70, 72–3, 81–3, 90, 93, 95, 98, 100, 104, 109, 125–6, 134, 137, 142–6, 149, 154, 157–8, 163, 165–71, 173–5, 178–80, 183, 185–6, 188–9, 190–1, 195–9, 201–202, 204, 206, 210–12, 216–19, 221–2
Champion Chase, 72, 87, 125, 166, 185, 189, 196–7, 202, 204, 208–209, 213, 222

Champion Hurdle, 3, 6, 9, 10, 34–8, 45, 47, 60, 72, 99, 123, 125, 129, 135, 139, 145, 149–50, 156–8, 165, 167, 173–6, 181, 189–90, 194, 196–7, 201–202, 204, 213

Gold Cup, 3, 6, 8, 10, 17, 25, 32, 36, 38–9, 45–7, 52–4, 62, 94–6, 100, 102, 118, 123, 125–6, 130, 132, 144–5, 150, 155, 157–8, 161–2, 173–4, 176, 180–1, 185, 189–90, 194, 196–8, 202, 204–208, 210–11, 213, 215

Mackeson Gold Cup, 10, 69, 96, 98–9, 132, 136, 153, 168, 180, 188

Chepstow, 4, 45, 91, 99–100, 126, 149, 151, 156, 164, 168–9, 171, 210

Welsh Grand National, 10, 52–3, 52–3, 55, 80, 87, 91, 98, 148, 150, 168–70, 172–3, 175, 178, 184, 190, 202, 204, 206, 210–11, 213

Cherimoya, 40

Chester, 78

Cheviotdale, 22

Chickabiddy, 195

Chirol, Michael, 158

Chorus, 74

Ch'tibello, 221

Church Warden, 149

Churchill, Winston, 67

Churchtown Boy, 133

Cima, 165

Clair Soleil, 42–3, 47

Clan Royal, 158, 199–200

Clear Cut, 74, 136, 153

Clear Wood, 113

Clever Scot, 106

Cobden, Harry, 222–3

Colledge Master, 109

College Don, 80

Colling, Bob, 4

Colonial Cup, 118, 131, 189

Colonius, 100

Coloured Schoolboy, 9, 15

Comedy of Errors, 4, 99

Comique, 8

Connolly, Michael, 152

Cook, John, 97, 103

Cool Alibi, 105

Coolmore, 138

Coral Cluster, 91

Coral Diver, 96, 99, 106

Corbiere, 119, 174

Cottage Rake, 52

Cotton Coon, 65

Coventry, 23

Crawford, Wilf, 124

Crisp, 125–6, 142

Cromwell, 27

Crudwell, 52, 55

Crump, Captain Neville, 81

Cruyff, Johan, 136

Cue Card, 217

Culloty, Jim, 212

Cundell, Frank, 52–3, 71, 75

Cundell, Ken, 52, 73, 141–2

Cundell, Peter, 148

Curran, Dick, 42

Curtain Time, 70

Cyborgo, 185, 196

Dad's Army (TV series), 26

Dagmar Gittell, 80

Dainty, Frank, 13

Dale, Syd, 45, 62

Daly, Henry, 206

Daring Run, 145–6

Dark Stranger, 199

Dark Vulcan, 126

D'Artagnan, 35

Davies, Bob, 57, 67, 73–4, 96–9, 102–10, 114, 121–2, 124–5, 138, 143

Davies, Colin, 104

Davies, Hywel, 179

Davies, Roy, 105

Davis, Richard, 192
Dawn Run, 155, 157–9, 165
Dawson, Matt, 3
De Boinville, Nico, 211
De Bromhead, Henry, 10
Deacon, Raymond 'Darkie', 126
Deaconsbrooke, 104
Deal Park, 54
Deep Bramble, 199
Deep Sensation, 87
Defi Du Seuil, 209
Deigo Rubio, 53
Delachance, 5
Delaney, Brian, 141
Denman, 211
Denys Adventure, 118
Derby, 7
Derring Rose, 146
Desert Orchid, 181–2, 188, 190
Devon & Exeter (Exeter), 14, 59, 97,
        104–105, 170–2, 195, 207, 209,
        218, 221
Devon Loch, 4, 18, 25, 48–9, 55,
        161, 209
Dick, Dave, 1, 24, 42, 55
Dickinson, Michael, 97, 123, 138
Dixon, Fred, 99
Dixon, Oliver, 50
Dobbin, Tony, 216
Docklands Express, 185
Domacorn, 96
Dominick's Bar, 37
Doncaster, 33, 36, 60, 70, 90, 96, 120,
        124, 135, 168, 219
Donegal Prince, 146
Donoghue, Steve, 4
Don't Push It, 158, 201–202
Don't Touch, 148
Dorsal, 79
Double Bridge, 24
Dowdeswell, Betty, 13, 19
Dowdeswell, Jack, 2, 12–20, 22, 23, 24

Downpatrick, 215
Dr Leunt, 188
Dreaper, Jim, 172
Dreaper, Tom, 70
Drishaune, 71
Druid's Lodge, 50
Drumcliff, 212
Drumroan, 108
Dublin Flyer, 196
Dufton Pike, 65
Dundalk, 91
Dunwoody, George, 177, 178
Dunwoody, Gillian (née Thrale),
        177
Dunwoody, Richard, 1, 2, 148, 160,
        171, 173–93, 195, 197, 203–204,
        214, 216
Dwyer, Mark, 1, 166

Eagle Don, 81
Early Mist, 25, 27, 28
Earth Summit, 174
Easby Abbey, 125
Easterby, Mick, 125, 136, 166
Easterby, Peter, 123, 152, 154–6
Easterby, Tim, 216
Eastern Harvest, 72, 81
Ebony Jane, 185
Eborneezer, 45, 47
Edmond, 206, 213
Edredon Bleu, 197
Edwards, Gordon, 195
Edwards, John, 166
Edwards, Roy, 81, 90
Ekbalco, 156
Ellen's Pleasure, 103
Elsworth, David, 86–7, 181
Emery, Rene, 55
Enrilo, 223
Epsom Derby, 32
E.S.B., 4, 18, 37
Eudipe, 199

Evans, Gwynne, 50
Even Keel, 105
Ever Smile, 172
Exeter *see* Devon and Exeter
Eyecatcher, 178

Fairgreave, Jim, 54
Fairyhouse, 98, 221
Fakenham, 168
Family Business, 198
Fangbolt, 129
Fare Time, 45, 47, 60
Farrell, Paddy, 54, 88
Fearless Fred, 97
Fenwick, Charlie, 119
Ferguson, Sir Alex, 172, 199
Ffos Las, 209
Fighting Line, 52
Final Approach, 123
Final Argument, 132
Finnure, 52
Fisher, Roger, 156
Fitzgeorge-Parker, Tim, 3, 6, 12, 16,
    18, 21, 28, 34–5, 39, 46, 55, 78–9,
    88, 94, 98, 101, 106, 125, 130,
    145, 157
Fitzgerald, Jimmy, 166
Fitzgerald, Mick, 195
Flagship Uberalles, 208, 213
Flaked Oats, 196
Flakey Dove, 184
Fletcher, Brian, 25, 84, 96, 113,
    123, 136
Florida Pearl, 207
Foinavon, 85, 95
Folkestone, 2, 24, 59, 86, 93
Fontwell, 8, 28, 34, 42, 83, 91, 98,
    148, 178, 188, 208, 212
Foot-and-mouth disease, 96
Forbra, 5
Forest King, 132
Forgive N'Forget, 157

Forster, Capt. Tim, 111–20, 122, 168,
    178–80, 206
Fortria, 70
Forty Secrets, 80, 87
Fox, Freddie, 13
Foxtor, 107
Francis, Dick, 29, 36, 48–56, 68, 118
Francis, Doug, 91
Francis, Felix, 55
Francis, Mary (wife of Dick), 54–5
Francis, Vincent, 50
Francis, Willie, 50
Francome, John, 19, 67, 107, 114, 118,
    121, 123, 131, 136, 138, 141–50,
    151, 155, 157, 160, 163–4, 167,
    169–70, 174, 191
Frankie Figg, 215
Freddie, 46
Freebooter, 25, 32, 68, 70, 134
Freeman, Arthur, 91
French Colonist, 128
French Excuse, 98, 102
Frenchman's Cove, 71–3, 76
Friendly Alliance, 146
Frisky Scot, 70
Frost, Jimmy, 221

Galatian, 26, 35
Gallup, 'Britt', 83
Game Purston, 74
Game Spirit, 100
Game Trust, 178
Gandolfo, David, 1, 47, 84, 87, 91, 93,
    102, 114–15, 147, 189, 208
Gatwick (Grand Nationals), 7
Gay Trip, 4, 86, 98–100, 117
Gaye Brief, 10
Gaye Chance, 10
George VI, King, 35
Geraghty, Barry, 191, 209
Gibus, 17
Gifford, Althea (née Roger-Smith), 86

Gifford, Josh, 2, 72–3, 77–87, 90–1, 94–6, 100, 104, 106, 121, 123, 128, 149–50, 167, 196
Gifford, Macer, 78, 87
Gifford, Nick, 87
Gifford, Tina, 87
Gillam, Tony, 135
Glengyle, 17
Gloria Victis, 206–207
Gold Branch, 17
Gold Service, 171
Golden Berry, 97, 105
Golden Freeze, 173
Golden Miller, 5, 24, 117
Goldsmith, Major John, 69
Good Date, 17
Goodness Gracious, 82
Goodwood, 18, 75
Goosander, 37
Gorse Hill, 83
Gosden, John, 78
Gosden, Towser, 78
Goulding, David, 108, 132
Gowran Park, 123
Grand Canyon, 131
Grand National *see* Aintree/Liverpool
Grant, Chris, 167
Grantham, Tony, 53
Granville Again, 173–5
Great Developer, 151
Greek Scholar, 95
Greek Warrior, 131
Greenogue, 34
Greystoke, 123, 129, 153, 219
Griffin, Joe ('Mincemeat Joe'), 25–7
Grittar, 150
Guest, Richard, 195
Gwilt, Ted, 12

Haine, Johnny, 1, 107, 121
Hall, Charlie, 136, 153

Hall, Sonny, 31
Hallo Dandy, 156
Halloween, 36–7, 42, 46–7
Hamey, Tim, 4
Hanmer, John, 109
Hannon, Richard, 220
Happy Arthur, 63
Happy Mullet, 44
Harries, Robert, 50
Harrison, David, 50
Hartigan, Frank, 40
Hartigan, Hubert, 22
Harty, Eddie, 121
Hatton's Grace, 34, 36
Harvey, Luke, 187
Haslam, Patrick, 143
Hawk High, 216
Hawke, Nigel, 120
Hawkins, Colin, 132
Haydock Park, 10, 33, 59, 75, 90, 137, 154, 156, 162, 164, 186–7
Hazy Sunset, 169
Head, Captain Richard, 141–3
Hedgehunter, 199
Hedgelands, 80
Henderson, Nicky, 109, 177, 182–3
Hennessy, 202
Hennessy Gold Cup (*see* Newbury)
Hereford, 41, 89, 91, 109, 165, 179, 186, 204–205, 208, 219, 223
Hexham, 135, 137, 154, 186, 199
Hidden Value, 137
Hieronymous, 164
High Ken, 130
Highland Bud, 189
Highland Dandy, 70
Highland Wedding, 194
Hill, Benny, 67
Hill, Charmian, 158
Hill House, 84–5
Hills, Barry, 19
HM The Queen, 42, 53, 138

HM The Queen Mother, 24, 42, 53,
    82, 100, 129, 224
Hobbs, Bruce, 5, 10
Hobbs, Diana, 212
Hobbs, Philip, 188, 196, 206,
    208–209, 212
Hogg, Ken, 132
Hoiles, Richard, 198
Holland-Martin, 'Ruby', 93
Hollinshead, Reg, 221
Holt, Simon, 207
Honey End, 85, 94
Hors La Loi III, 197
HRH, The Duke of Edinburgh, 224
Hughes, Brian, 212, 214–19, 223–4
Huntingdon, 36, 119, 148–9, 186
Hurst Park, 32, 33, 37, 42, 45, 60, 62,
    78, 80
Hypernod, 32

Ike II, 58
Ilico II, 207
Impney, 35
Imperial Presence, 212
Injured Jockeys' Fund, 19, 64, 88, 102
Intelligent Outlook, 22
Irish Duke, 14
Irish Grand National, 32, 181, 183,
    201, 211, 221
Irish Painter, 152
Isle of Man, 100
Istabraq, 197

Jack Tatters, 23, 24
Java, 84
Jay Trump, 46
Jefferson, Malcolm, 216
Jefferson, Ruth, 217
Jenkins, Denzil, 91
Jenkins, John, 147, 149, 164, 195
Jenks, Bryan, 96–7
Jet Ski Lady, 194

Jimaru, 59
Jockey Club, The, 170
Jodami, 123
Joe's Girl, 91
Johnson, Howard, 215
Johnson, Ivor, 204
Johnson, Keith, 204
Johnson, Richard, 192, 199, 203–14,
    217–19, 222
Johnson, Sue, 204
Jones, Dr Arthur, 178
Jones, Earl, 80
Jones, Tom, 71, 74–5, 122, 135
Joss Merlin, 80
Jules Verne, 69
Jupiter Boy, 93
Just So, 185

Kaliking, 106
Katie T, 216
Kauto Star, 211, 222
Kelek, 33
Kelleway, Paul, 96, 106, 122, 178
Kellsboro' Jack, 43
Kelly, Barry, 187
Kelso, 75, 126, 130, 219
Kempton Park, 2, 13, 17, 22, 23, 43, 52,
    54, 71, 84, 95–6, 98–100, 106, 148,
    165, 169, 174, 181, 183, 211, 216–17
King George VI (race), 17, 21, 23, 24,
    28, 31, 37, 39, 42–3, 46–7, 49, 52,
    54–5, 72–3, 76, 86, 95–6, 118, 121,
    125, 139, 148, 150, 161, 176, 181–2,
    184, 188, 196, 199, 202, 211–12
Kennard, Les, 103–104
Keogh, Harry and Mary, 36
Key Royal, 37
Khamsin, Sheikh Ali Abu, 47, 146
Kibreet, 196
Killiney, 142
Kilmore, 45–6, 85, 193
Kilpatrick, Alec, 81

Kilpatrick, 97
King, Jeff, 1, 103, 121
King, Willie, 63
King Flame, 143
King Weasel, 156
King's Dream, 98
King's Nephew, 71
Kingsley, Maurice, 38
Kingston, Robert, 183
Kinnersley, 4, 11, 90, 98–9, 142, 162–3
Kipling, Rudyard, 155
Kitty's Light, 224
Knight, Henrietta, 102, 112, 176
Knock Hard, 17, 36
Kribensis, 181, 190

La Bague Au Roi, 211
Lady Rebecca, 206
Lady Rowley, 13
Lake View Lad, 215
Lamb, Ridley, 108
Lambe, James, 215
Lambourn, 9, 12, 19, 22, 27, 46, 75,
    129, 142, 143
Lanveoc Pulmic, 24, 42
Lanzarote, 47, 142, 145
Larbawn, 78, 87
Las Meninas, 138
Last Suspect, 174, 179
Latalomne, 208
Le Coudray, 206
Le Jacobin, 33
Le Mare, Noel, 135, 137
Leach, Paul, 166
Lean Ar Aghaidh, 75
Leap Man, 21
Lee, Graham, 215
Legal Prince, 54
Legal Steps, 194
Lehane, Johnny, 80–1, 92
Leicester, 23, 32–3, 45, 61, 70, 74, 82,
    90, 124

Leigh, Lord, 59
Lendl, Ivan, 203
Leopardstown, 216
L'Escargot, 131, 136
Letcombe Bassett, 112, 178
Letcombe Regis, 18
Leverhulme, Lord, 69
Limb of the Law, 18
Limerick, 38
Lincoln Place, 207
Lingfield, 32, 54, 82, 144–5, 171
Linwell, 161
Little Polveir, 166, 175
Llewellyn, Carl, 200
Longway, 113
Looks Like Trouble, 206–207, 213
Lord Gylenne, 57, 205, 216
Lothian Princess, 70
Loyal Monarch, 24
Loyal Tan, 77, 92
Lucius, 108, 110, 118, 132
Lucky Dora, 63–4
Lucky Time, 15
Lucky Verdict, 170
Ludlow, 24, 33, 44, 58, 60, 68, 109, 208
Lumino, 39

Mackeson, Sir Rupert, 21, 24, 27, 32,
    55, 203, 220
Maggots Green, 205
Magic Orb, 81
Magnier, John, 138
Maguire, Adrian, 1, 183–7, 195,
    205–206
Majetta Crescent, 154
Major Rose, 86
Make A Stand, 196, 202
Maljimar, 198
Mallard Song, 178
Man Alive, 132
Manchester, 17, 59, 68–70, 78
Mandarin, 39, 45, 47

Manicou, 24
Marally, 44
Marcianus, 54
Mariner's Log, 54
Market Rasen, 89, 94, 113, 116, 121,
    129, 154, 171, 182, 202
Markham, Ivor, 57
Marshall, Bryan, 16, 17, 21–9, 33, 35,
    67, 117, 169
Marshall, Caroline (Binty), 21, 25
Massingberd, Hugh, 100
M'As Tu Vu, 54
McCain, Donald, 217
McCain, Ginger, 4, 135–7, 156
McCourt, Graham, 182
McCoy, AP, 1, 2, 31, 175, 177, 183,
    191–207, 209, 212–16
McCoy, Peader, 183, 193
McCririck, John, 141
McGhie, Jimmy, 153
McManus JP, 2, 158, 191, 198–201, 209
McMurrow, Leo, 33
Meerkat, 153
Mellor, Elain, 64, 71–2, 81, 83
Mellor, Stan, 40, 45, 61–2, 67–76, 80–1,
    83–4, 90–1, 93, 95, 99, 105–107,
    109, 119, 121–2, 148, 169, 175, 202
Menorah, 209
Merry Fox, 125
Merryman II, 69
Midnight Court, 47, 144, 150
Might Bite, 211
Mighty Montefalco, 198
Miinnehoma, 173, 185–6
Mildmay, Lord, 9, 16, 27
Mill Boy, 23
Mill House, 62, 71, 95
Mill Reef, 194
Milord II, 23
Minella Indo, 191
Minella Rocco, 210
Mister Whitaker, 216

Mitchell, Cyril, 80
Mohaayed, 221
Moloney, Jack, 41
Molony, Danny, 30, 36, 38
Molony, Martin, 31–5, 37–8, 49, 52, 67
Molony, Stella, 38
Molony, Tim, 30–8, 43, 49, 68–9, 123,
    134, 153, 160, 191
Molony, Will, 30, 32, 38
Mon Mome, 201
Monksfield, 156
Mont Tremblant, 25, 42
Montcalm, 14–15
Moonsun, 45
Moorcroft Boy, 185
Morecambe, Eric, 149
Morgan, Laurie, 109
Morley, David, 107
Morrissey, Jimmy, 93
Morshead, Sam, 10, 146, 163–4
Mospey, 14
Mould, David, 1, 79, 83, 90, 92–3,
    104, 112, 121, 150
Mould, Jenny, 180
Mr Frisk, 27
Mr Geneaology, 184
Mr Mulligan, 196, 202, 205
Mr Snugfit, 174
Mrs Muck, 165
Mrs Wentworth, 106
Multigrey, 113, 141
Mungret College, 31
Murless, Noel, 22
Murphy, Declan, 186
Murphy, Timmy, 200
Musselburgh, 216
My Drogo, 224
My Old Gold, 217
My Tent Or Yours, 201

Naas, 152
Narvik, 148, 150

Nash, Colin, 178
National Spirit, 9, 34
Native River, 209–11, 213
New Money, 134
Newbon, Gary, 102
Newbury, 5, 12, 19, 36, 40, 45, 54–5, 82, 84–5, 100, 107, 115, 131, 163, 171, 183–4
  Hennessy Gold Cup, 71, 86, 100, 107, 118, 121, 129, 131, 150, 158, 164, 168, 175, 183, 210–11, 213
Newcastle, 123, 125, 127, 154, 156–7, 165, 217–18 (*see also* Whitbread Gold Cup)
Newmarket, 3, 40, 78, 135, 178
Newport, 5
Newton Abbot, 14, 42–4, 53, 59, 61, 65, 97, 103–104, 113, 165, 168–9, 171, 186, 195–6, 207, 211, 213
Niche Market, 221
Nicholls, Paul, 36, 196, 220, 222–4
Nicholson, Clifford, 31, 64
Nicholson, David ('The Duke'), 6, 83, 161–6, 177, 180–5, 196, 204–206
Nicholson, Fernie, 50
Nicholson, Frenchie, 6, 7, 8, 23
Nicolaus Silver, 4, 69
Night Nurse, 118, 123, 154, 156
Niven, Peter, 171
Nohalmdun, 166
Nordic Touch, 194
Normandy, 96–8
Norther, 91, 102
Norton's Coin, 181–2
Nottingham, 44, 54, 63, 74, 83, 90–1, 117, 163, 184
Nube Negra, 222
Nugent, David, 19

Oakprime, 162
Oasis, 59
O'Brien, Dermot, 26, 31

O'Brien, Vincent, 17, 25–6, 28, 31, 36, 52
Odysseus, 82
O'Grady, Eddie, 32
O'Grady, Willie, 32
Oliver, Ken, 60, 63, 81, 123, 125, 131–2, 137, 152
Oliver, Michael, 179
Oliver, Rhona, 60, 63, 81
Olympian, 174
Omerta, 183
One for Arthur, 174
One Man, 188, 190, 196
O'Neill, Bobby, 51
O'Neill, Jonjo, 121, 123, 125–8, 132, 143–6, 148, 151–9, 163, 167, 169, 198–200, 219
Or Royal, 196
Ordnance, 25
Orient War, 98
Osbaldeston, 142
Osceola, 142
O'Sullevan, (Sir) Peter, 46, 68, 85, 100, 133
Our Bara Boy, 151
Our Duke, 211
Out and About, 77
Out the Black, 209
Ouzo, 74
Owen, George, 32, 49, 51–2, 57–8, 68–70, 75
Owen, Jane, 57, 68
Oxo, 37, 60–2, 161

Paddington Bear, 124
Paget, The Hon. Dorothy, 8, 23, 24–5, 42
Pappageno's Cottage, 63, 90
Parker, Solly, 58
Parthenon, 49
Payne, Herbie, 113
Peacetown, 70, 80

Pearlyman, 166
Pegwell Bay, 168
Pendil, 47, 100, 106, 125–6, 130, 142
Persian War, 86, 98, 104
Persse, Atty, 22, 27, 40
Perth, 58, 94, 128, 154, 188, 211
Phantom Brig, 14
Phillips, Zara, 204
Phoenix Park, 194
Piggott, Lester, 19, 54, 78
Pinch, Nicky, 7
Pipe, Martin, 1, 10, 135, 163–4,
      166–72, 174, 182–4, 187–8, 192,
      194–7, 199–200, 202, 206, 222
Piper, 89
Pippykin, 59
Pitman, Jenny, 119, 120, 173
Pitman, Richard, 101, 114, 120–2, 126,
      130, 141–3, 148
Pitt, Chris, 7, 57, 60, 62, 64–5, 69, 79
Playlord, 124, 132
Pleasure Seeker, 154
Plumpton, 19, 35, 81, 113–14, 186
Pneuma, 127
Poet Prince, 8
Politologue, 222–4
Pollardstown, 75, 145–6
Poor Flame, 7, 8
Popham Down, 85
Possible, 49
Potentate, 106
Potter, Lawrence, 113
Pounding, 44
Powell, Captain/Major John Bay, 13,
      14, 15, 16, 17, 19, 23
Prairie Dog, 74
Prendergast, Kevin, 215–16
Prescott, Sir Mark, 57, 65–6, 167
Pretentious, 94
Price, Captain Ryan, 40–5, 47, 78–82,
      84–6, 106
Pridwell, 197

Prince Carl, 138
Prince Hindou, 34
Prince of Denmark, 33
Prince Regent, 8
Proper Ticket, 219
Proud Stone, 153
Pukka Major, 169
Punchestown, 186–7
Pyrrhus III, 34

Quare Times, 86
Queen of the Dandies, 33
Quick Approach, 90
Quick Polish, 97

Rag Trade, 4, 11, 137, 149, 158
Raggerty, 184
Rahiib, 168
Rank, J.V., 25, 50
Ransom, Philip, 156
Rathconrath, 146
Rather Be, 216
Raz de Maree, 210
Reaghstown, 138
Realt Na Nona, 156
Red Alley, 79
Red Alligator, 86, 123
Red Hugh, 116
Red Marauder, 199
Red Rum, 25, 38, 108, 123, 133, 135–9
Red Thorn, 90, 102
Red Trump, 35
Rees, Billy, 34
Rees, Fred, 6, 30, 34, 42, 167
Regal Ambition, 171
Regal Encore, 223
Regal Flame, 71
Reid, Don, 152
Reid, John, 189
Reid, Roddy, 105
Relevance, 156
Remittance Man, 182

Renfree, Jim, 81
Renton, Bobby, 80, 97, 134–5
Resurgent, 52
Reverando, 83
Richards, Sir Gordon, 6, 13, 16, 55,
    197, 202
Richards, Gordon W., 74, 108, 118,
    123–4, 127, 129, 131–2, 153–4,
    156, 188
Richards, Nicky, 129, 219
Rigg, (Dame) Diana, 85
Rightun, 7
Rimell, Fred, 4–11, 12, 23, 58–60, 69, 81,
    88, 90–1, 94–9, 117, 142, 162, 223
Rimell, Mercy, 8, 9, 81, 94, 117,
    146, 163
Rimell, Scarlett (Knipe), 10, 81
Rimell, Tom, 8
Riverside Boy, 184, 190
Roberts, Dave, 195, 205
Robinson, Willie, 1, 71, 93, 189
Rock, Billy, 193
Roi d'Egypte, 24
Roimond, 49
Roksana, 221
Rolling Ball, 171
Roman Fire, 18
Rooster Booster, 208, 213
Roquefort, 25
Rose Park, 161
Rosyth, 45, 81–2, 84
Rough and Tumble, 150
Rowland Roy, 23, 24
Rowlie, 4
Royal Danieli, 26
Royal Derbi, 174
Royal Feathers, 116
Royal Frolic, 3
Royal Mail, 75, 109
Royal Marshal II, 118, 120–1
Royal Stuart, 51
Royal Tan, 25–7

Roylat, 161
Run and Skip, 157, 164–5, 175
Russell, Lucinda, 174
Russian Hero, 32–3, 49, 58
Rusty Bridge, 205

Saffron Tartan, 45, 47
Salisbury, 40
Sandown Park, 17, 23–4, 27, 32, 42,
    44–5, 54, 70, 82, 84, 106, 127, 144,
    174, 199–200, 202, 209, 219, 222–3
    Whitbread Gold Cup, 10, 71–2, 75,
    78, 87, 124, 127–8 (at Newcastle),
    130, 132, 138–9, 187, 199, 205,
    208, 213, 223
Sandy Abbot, 69–70, 72, 76
Sandy Saddler, 113
Sandy Sprite, 124, 132
Saxon Warrior, 75
Scott, Brough, 68, 72–3, 75, 104
Scott, Gerry, 69
Scottish Grand National, 10, 13, 23,
    63, 97, 105, 124, 132, 166, 175,
    189, 202, 208, 213
Scottish Memories, 72
Scrunch, 156
Scudamore, Geoffrey, 161
Scudamore, Michael (jockey &
    trainer, Peter's father), 20, 37, 43,
    60–1, 83, 89, 94, 161
Scudamore, Michael (Peter's son,
    current trainer), 175
Scudamore, Peter, 1, 146–9, 151,
    160–77, 180–3, 188, 191–3, 197,
    203–204, 206, 214
Scudamore, Tom, 175
Sea Lane, 162
Sea Pigeon, 123, 145–6, 150, 154, 156, 159
Sebastian V, 108
Sedgefield, 91, 138, 147, 218
See More Business, 196
See You Then, 149

September Air, 31
Sewell, Anna, 141
Shan Blue, 22
Shannon Bridge, 223
Sharpe, Graham, 115, 143
Shaw, Tommy, 123
Sheila's Cottage, 24
Sheppard, Matt, 10, 208
Sherwood, Simon, 164–6, 181
Shoemark, Bill, 84
Shrewsbury, Lord (Charles
       Chetwynd-Talbot), 64–5
Silent Valley, 165
Silver Fame, 25, 32, 34
Simon, 11
Simpson, Rod, 168
Sir Gosland, 70
Sir Ken, 34–5, 38
Sizing John, 210
Skelton, Dan, 220–2
Skelton, Harry, 211, 218, 220–4
Skelton, Nick, 220–1
Smarty, 199
Smith, Bill, 99, 142
Smith, Denys, 86, 91, 94, 123
Smith-Eccles, Steve, 149–50, 164
Smyth, Ron, 16
Solar Cloud, 165, 206
Solomon II, 106, 110
Soothsayer, 101
Southwell, 70, 124, 146–7, 163, 171,
       186, 192, 198, 223
Spartan General, 90–1
Spearing, John, 131, 148, 164, 175, 195
Specify, 104
Sputnik One, 60
Spy Legend, 34
Stack, Tommy, 118, 122, 124–5,
       129–31, 133–9, 142–4
Stainsby, 82
Stan Royal, 152
Statecraft, 53

Stately Home, 205
Straight Border, 68
Stalbridge Colonist, 71, 73, 95
Stephenson, Arthur, 123, 129, 135, 138
Stephenson, Willie, 31, 33, 37, 161
Stevens, Ray, 130
Stewart, Sir Jackie, 75
Stopped, 144
Storm Tiger, 76
Strands of Gold, 168, 175
Stranger, 54
Stratford, 67, 74, 91–2, 99, 106–107,
       116, 131, 152, 180, 186, 195, 212
Stroller, 43
Strombolus, 138–9
Strong Glance, 218
Sundew, 43–4, 47, 117, 137
Super Chant, 138
Superb Story, 221
Supreme Master, 184
Suzerain II, 8
Swainson, Bill, 137
Swan, Charlie, 33
Sweet Duke, 174
Sweet Millie, 154
Swinbank, Alan, 215
Swing Along, 97
Swordsman, 178
Synchronised, 155, 198, 202

Taafe, Pat, 86, 99
Table Mountain, 97
Tam Kiss, 116
Tam o'Shanter, 40
Tamalin, 118
Tangognat, 168
Tarascon, 138
Tate, Martin, 94
Taunton, 2, 8, 15, 61, 146–7, 163, 171, 219
Taxidermist, 44
Taylor, Graham, 168
Teddy Tudor, 124